The Generation
X Librarian

THE GENERATION X LIBRARIAN

Essays on Leadership, Technology, Pop Culture, Social Responsibility and Professional Identity

Edited by Martin K. Wallace,
Rebecca Tolley-Stokes
and Erik Sean Estep

McFarland & Company, Inc., Publishers
Jefferson, North Carolina, and London

LIBRARY OF CONGRESS CATALOGUING-IN-PUBLICATION DATA

The generation X librarian : essays on leadership, technology, pop
culture, social responsibility and professional identity / edited by
Martin K. Wallace, Rebecca Tolley-Stokes, and Erik Sean Estep.
p.   cm.
Includes bibliographical references and index.

ISBN 978-0-7864-6309-1
softcover : 50# alkaline paper ∞

1. Librarians — United States.   2. Librarians — Psychology.
3. Librarians — Attitudes.   4. Librarians — Effect of technological
innovations on.   5. Librarians — Professional ethics.   6. Librarians —
Public opinion.   7. Library administration — Social aspects.
8. Library science — Social aspects.   9. Generation X.
I. Wallace, Martin, 1973–   II. Tolley-Stokes, Rebecca, 1971–
III. Estep, Erik Sean.
Z682.2.U5.G46   2011   020.92 — dc22   2011006979

BRITISH LIBRARY CATALOGUING DATA ARE AVAILABLE

Cover images © 2011 Shutterstock
Front cover by Bernadette Skok (bskok@ptd.net)

Manufactured in the United States of America

*McFarland & Company, Inc., Publishers
Box 611, Jefferson, North Carolina 28640
www.mcfarlandpub.com*

Table of Contents

Preface

This collection of essays discusses Generation X perspectives on librarianship. For the most part, each essay is contributed by a professional librarian belonging to the Generation X cohort, but we, the editors, have also included some contributions from non–Gen Xers and non-librarians whose essays provide substantive accounting of Gen X librarians from other perspectives. Acknowledging that a variety of definitions of the term "Generation X" exist, we have chosen the broadest definition, considering Generation X to be comprised of those individuals born in or between 1961 and 1981. This is not an attempt to be definitive, but to be inclusive, as the reader will discover that some of the essays present differing criteria.

The editors of this book, all three of us Gen X librarians, began formally discussing this book in 2008, when a mutual friend of ours, Rory Litwin, suggested the topic as a project for Library Juice Press, and we ran with it. Many thanks to Rory for the idea for the book and for bringing the three of us together to work on it. Individually we had been interested in generational dynamics, feeling that Generation X dwells in a unique period of history. Unprecedented advances in technology, an exploding postmodern popular culture, and economic globalization, along with ever-widening economic injustice, ceaselessly expanding U.S. hegemony, and environmental degradation at a critical scale — all of these things Generation X has borne witness to as no generation before ours has. For the most part, the motivation for compiling this book was to learn firsthand the effect that these things have had on libraries and librarianship.

Major themes identified within the contributions to this book include generational differences and stereotypes, technology, library management and leadership, social justice and the responsibilities of librarians, and the portrayal of librarians in popular culture. As Generation X is largely a "transitional" generation, many of the papers focus on change in the library. While certainly not exhaustive, the essays found in this book help to fill many gaps left open in the professional literature about Generation X librarians. The editors would consider the majority of the essays herein to be of scholarly quality and we encouraged our contributors to maintain a scholarly approach; however, a few of the essays seemed to embody a very "Gen X voice" that would have been lost if kept to the strictest scholarly standards, so we left them mostly intact. Finally, we were very pleased to have one contribution (and one of our favorites) submitted from non–U.S. librarians in Bosnia and Herzegovina.

Acknowledgments

I would like to acknowledge all of the Boomer librarians who have encouraged me and mentored me along the way. Particularly Patricia Stinson-Switzer, who rescued me from retail by helping me land my first library job as a clerk in 1998; Gay Woods, who later hired me for a library specialist position that I was hardly qualified for — thank you for seeing my potential and for the great challenge! And Jim Bird, who currently tolerates my Gen X attitude toward work and who remains patiently flexible with my work-life imbalance.

Martin K. Wallace • Orono, Maine • Spring 2011

My co-editors Martin K. Wallace and Erik Sean Estep were persistent and patient, and demonstrated fortitude in working together to bring this project from its earliest seed as an idea, to the proposal level, and finally to the manuscript stage; and I thank them for their dedication and wisdom. Many thanks to our contributors, whose diligence in writing revisions and responding to moving deadlines made our task easier. I would be remiss without thanking several teachers — one Gen X, two Boomers, and one silent generation — who encouraged my writing, editing, and creative activities over the years: Tayari Jones, Judy Odom, Callie Redd, and Carol Transou. And finally, the greatest thanks to my husband Ian, daughter Elsa, and the rest of my family for their support, encouragement, and love as I worked on this book.

Rebecca Tolley-Stokes • Johnson City, Tennessee • Spring 2011

I'd like to thank my co-editors Martin K. Wallace and Rebecca Tolley-Stokes for all of their hard work in seeing this process through. We did it! My life friends Chris Meyer and Theodore Randall provided a sympathetic ear throughout the process. And my sister Britton, mother Lani, and my late father David Andis Estep provided indispensable support. Even though my father didn't live to see this book published, I would not have gotten here without him.

Erik Sean Estep • Greeneville, North Carolina • Spring 2011

Introduction

Martin K. Wallace,
Rebecca Tolley-Stokes, and Erik Sean Estep

The phrase "Generation X" comes from the title of Douglas Coupland's famous novel *Generation X: Tales for an Accelerated Culture*. In that book, we get our first glimpse of the Generation X template: young burnouts, made cynical by the consumerism of Boomers, hiding away and making cynical comments about kitschy pop culture.

Several years later the narrative extends with Ben Stiller's *Reality Bites,* featuring Generation X icons Stiller, Winona Ryder, Janeane Garofalo, and Ethan Hawke. Again, we see the fascination with pop culture (a Dr. Zaius statue serves as a comic prop and generational signifier). Ryder plays the frightened, newly minted graduate, Hawke her slacker love interest, and Garofalo, the best friend who, significantly, videotapes their every move (being self referential is another part of the Generation X received wisdom). Stiller is an executive for MTV — another Generation X touchstone — and, true to Hollywood convention, Ryder ends up with the brooding Hawke rather than the conventional but boring Stiller.

But like all generations must, Generation X grew up; and while doing so it left a record of successes throughout the 80s, 90s and 00s. Members of Generation X operate at the forefront of their field in many areas such as business, sports, the arts, and technology. Across the board, two of the most innovative entrepreneurs in U.S. business are Tony Hsieh and Jeff Bezos who established Zappos and Amazon, respectively. Athletes like Tony Hawk, Michael Jordan, Sammy Sosa, Brett Favre, Steffi Graf, Lance Armstrong, David Beckham, Tiger Woods, Venus Williams, and Serena Williams changed the sports they played and then commanded their brand empires, complete with merchandising, endorsements, and video games.

As for their part in creating our contemporary culture, Generation X has Peter Jackson, Jodie Foster, Steven Soderbergh, Quentin Tarantino, Spike Jonze, M. Night Shyamalan, and Sofia Coppola to thank for their vision and direction in cinema. Musicians such as Henry Rollins, Eddie Vedder, Dr. Dre, Trent Reznor, Liz Phair, Marilyn Manson, Gwen Stefani, P. Diddy, Tupac Shakur, Eminem, Lauryn Hill, Beyonce Knowles, and Britney Spears write music, sing songs, and produce performances whose effects are felt by several generations. Television talk shows are headed by the likes of Rosie O'Donnell, Jon Stewart, Conan O'Brien and Tucker Carlson.

For all those Muggles and wizards out there, J.K. Rowling, the author of the most successful series of children's books, *ever*, is of the Generation X cohort. Her international success is astonishing. Rowling's vision influences children and adults in nearly every country. In fact, *Harry Potter and the Half-Blood Prince*, the sixth of J.K. Rowling's fantasy series, sold about 9 million copies in Britain and the United States in its first 24 hours. The only book in publishing history to open nearly as well was Rowling's previous book in the series, *Harry Potter and the Order of the Phoenix* ("New Potter"). And certainly, there are countless other sage Generation Xers who have awed the world with their poetry, essays, plays, and prose.

In academia, Generation X preferences for collaboration, openness, community, flexibility, diversity, interdisciplinarity, and work-life balance are challenging the tenure system that does not readily accommodate their values. The Collaborative on Academic Careers in Higher Education administered by Harvard's Graduate School of Education interviewed twelve professors born between 1964 and 1980. The results were published in *New Challenges, New Priorities: The Experience of Generation X Faculty*, and covered generational clashes as well as work-life balance. The biggest differences described were in the older generations' relative formality with students and their relative lack of comfort with technology (Helms 4).

As a group, Generation X feels overlooked at times, especially in light of all the media attention given to a loudly aging Boomer population and the hyper-savvy, "Xtreme," Generation Y. But despite all the press, there remain many more commonalities across the generations than differences. In fact, it has been argued that the proliferation of new technology — created by Generation X to help cobble their lives together and integrate work and family into a manageable lifestyle, like the internet, SMS texting, and social networking — have brought all generations closer together.

It has also been argued that, given their identity as latchkey kids, Generation Xers crave community and connection. With formal communities of neighborhood and workplace diminishing, the quest for new types of affiliation and making connections is at the heart of the Gen X identity.

Once Generation X begins leading libraries and implementing cultural and institutional changes that reflect these priorities, they will form policies that undergird their sense of fairness and shape the organizational culture. But is librarianship ready for Gen Xers to become leaders of the field? We often hear contradictory messages: on the one hand, there is allegedly a shortage of librarians to fill leadership roles, due to the impending era of Baby Boomer retirements; alternately, we hear horror stories about the old guard in libraries who resist the new ideas of Gen Xers, or fail to understand them at all. Demographically speaking, it will be impossible to miss the surge of Generation X librarians moving into leadership positions; but without Boomer cooperation to mediate the transition, librarianship may be headed for cataclysmic shift in values and attitudes.

Seminal works on the topic of Generation X have referred to this generation as the "ignored," the "lost," and the "forgotten" generation. Considering how Gen X seems to have fallen within the cracks of the generational divide, it is no surprise that until only recently has there been a serious attempt made to analyze and understand this generation. B. Jane Scales suggests in her 1999 literature review that Gen Xers have been all but ignored in the education and library science literature. She notes a handful of articles written for the librarian who must serve Gen Xers, but very few substantive articles for the up-and-coming Gen X professional librarian (26).

Have Gen Xers truly been forgotten? Are Gen Xers still being ignored in the education and library science literature — not only as library users, but as viable professionals? *The Generation X Librarian* reveals that the scholarly and professional literature on Generation X librarians has progressed significantly since the 1990s; additionally, the contributors to this book have added substantive and critical weight to this growing body of literature, filling in many of the remaining gaps previously left unarticulated.

This collection also draws a comparison of intra-generational attitudes, values and characteristics of Generation X that shows the shift in qualities between the early and core Gen Xers and the tail-end Gen Xers who share many of their qualities with the Y Generation. By exploring these differences, the book identifies some important dynamics behind these shifts: as the profession has become increasingly comprised of Gen Xers and as the body of literature has become more inclusive of Gen X attitudes, values and other characteristics, Gen Xers have responded, adapted and "matured" contrarily to previous assumptions and expectations much held in the 1990s.

This book demonstrates how far Gen Xers have come on the path from extreme loafers to librarians extraordinaire; glimpses of Gen X librarians, as viewed both from within and from without the profession, are assessed. Drawing from such sources as existing library literature, original research, surveys, pop culture and the personal experiences of practicing Gen X library professionals, a picture of Gen X librarians is painted up, stripped away, reevaluated and remodeled — much the way the larger cohort of Gen X across the professional spectrum has been since the early 90s.

WORKS CITED

Helms, Robin Matross. *New Challenges, New Priorities: The Experience of Generation X Faculty.* The Collaborative on Academic Careers in Higher Education. Harvard Graduate School of Education, Cambridge, MA. 2010. Web. 28 Sept. 2010.

"New Potter Book Topples U.S. Sales Records." *MSNBC.com. MSNBC* 18 July 2005. 28 Sept. 2010. Web. 29 Sept. 2010.

Scales, B. Jane. "A Neo-Modern Summary of the Futcha: An Exploration of the Generation X in Our Midst." *Reference Librarian* 30.64 (1999): 21.

SECTION ONE

GETTING TO KNOW US

From Paper to Pixels:
Generation X as Digital Librarian

Emily Symonds

To declare that Generation X has unique characteristics that suit us to the field of digital librarianship would be a bold statement to make. Librarians before my generation had skills such as computer programming, database design, and metadata creation; some of them even had "digital," "metadata," or "electronic" in their job titles; however, there is certainly a unique relationship between Generation X and digital librarian positions. An issue with focusing on a single generation is the implication that the definitive qualities exclude all other generations, an implication those us of not from the Greatest Generation may feel acutely. Just look at a title like *The Dumbest Generation*, a 2008 book about Generation Y, to see how stark that comparison can be. Even the span of Generation X isn't definitive; this volume uses 1961–1981 as the range. Bernard Rosen uses the years 1965–1984 (61). William Strauss and Neil Howe, who call it the 13th Generation, use 1961–1981 (8). Jeff Gordinier in *X Saves the World* writes, "Ask [the experts] when all the Gen-X people were born, and you will still get a variety of dates" including 1965–1978, 1960–1980, 1961–1981, 1963–1981, and 1960–1977 (21). A 1997 *Time* cover story defined it as 1965–1977 (Hornblower 58). These last two options would push me into the Y years, completely eliminating me from this discussion.

Most Generation X librarians probably did not consciously seek out digital positions. We started as catalogers or worked in IT. We wanted to be writers or editors and found our way to librarianship. We learned about digital resources through an interest in moving and visual images. We liked history but did not want to be teachers or professors. We wanted collaboration between people and a convergence of ideas. We followed a meandering path through different jobs and fell into roles that needed filling. While we were introduced to personal computers at a young age and used a regular card catalog less than previous generations, we were not quite the digital natives that Generation Y is considered to be. We did, however, discover more and new forms of access as we got older and adapted from DOS and Apple IIE to CSS and XML. We were "the first generation to have grown up with the computer, the first to have color television in their homes and VCRs in their schools, the first to send email, the first to surf the Internet" (Rosen 57). Skills bled from one area to another; when my parents commented on my nimbleness in changing the cruise control features on my car's steering wheel with my thumbs, I attributed it to childhood video games and remote controls.

What this contributed to was a complicated relationship with technology — we are used to changes in hardware and software systems and moved quickly from floppy disks to flash drives to cloud computing. We knew rotary phones and now smart phones, have seen version after of version of software packages, watched personal computers get smaller and smaller, and have moved from using a specific computer system to emulating it on a different system. We know that technological advances can make tasks easier, but we also recognize that specific advances can't always be trusted. Smith and Clurman write, "That's why Xers are not only the most enthusiastic embracers of tech, they are also the most incredulous" (106). Technology for me is a tool. I want to work with systems that make my job easier and make it easier for others to find the information I'm providing, but I do not want to be so dependent on one system that my data, my metadata, can't be accessed anywhere else.

Two people born at either end of any of those spans of years that are supposed to encompass Generation X will have had very different experiences within that cohort. Those in the earlier years may be more directly compared to the Baby Boomers, while those at the tail end are compared to Millennials. There are common trends in Generation X, however, that helped inform our professional attitudes and decisions. One is the idea of a generation without a cause or a generation from a lost time. Gordinier declares, "We come from a lost world, it's true, and much of what defines us is our ambivalent stuckness between a hunger for the new and an attachment to the old" (125). In his analysis, Rosen writes that the "ideology that sustained their predecessors, the dream of endless progress, has been abandoned" (8). This lostness may be a direct reaction to the causes of previous generations, notably Baby Boomers, but also a result of X's place, or lack of place, in the world. Gen Xers came of age with more fathers and mothers working outside of the home, more professional parents whose jobs required moves, and with a high rate of divorce, a rate that nearly tripled between 1960 and 1979 and that was the highest in the Western world by 1986 (Rosen 43).

While it may seem romantic or noble to campaign for a cause, it is also difficult to do so when finding a decent job is so pressing. In 1988, males in their early twenties earned 54 percent as much as older males, a decrease from 74 percent in 1967; at the same time the rate of homeowners between 18 and 24 fell by one-third between the 1960s and 1980s (Strauss and Howe 327). A *Time* article stated that Generation X had "come of age after the U.S. took what some economists call the great U-turn. Energy prices first soared in 1973, and workers' wages stagnated. Between 1979 and 1995, some 43 million jobs were lost through corporate downsizing" (Hornblower 60). This was followed by the dot com bubble surge and burst, and these are only the economic issues that followed the youngest Xers into our twenties.

These patterns may have contributed to a larger sense of isolation but also greater self-reliance and independence. Pragmatism, though some may call it cynicism, is another key characteristic — having an alternate plan and being able to live in a changing world. "You don't get a job right out of school and work there until you retire. You don't major in one thing and never master any other field over the course of your life. You stay flexible, continually adaptable" (Smith 101). In the early and mid–1990s Gen Xers were termed "slackers," but that casual attitude really meant adaptability, flexibility, and fluidity. Jeff Gordinier observes that "fair number of slackers were hypersmart.... Even when it looked like the slackers were wasting their time, they weren't. They were learning; they were sponging up information" (26). Smith and Clurman advised marketers targeting Gen Xers to "learn to surf" the web, referring to a 1996 Internet Explorer advertisement, and defining the depiction of web surfing as "things linked together almost serendipitously by theme, by alphabet, by visual puns. Choices instantly made, without risk and always reversible if they begin to bore or lead down a dead end" (93). Many of those supposed slackers were just gathering information, formulating future plans, evaluating their environment, making random connections seem obvious, and still looking for their place.

Like many in my generation, when I started college in 1996, I had been playing on the Internet for at least a year, mainly through my family's dial-up connection and a nearly unending supply of AOL disks. I shared an email account with my mom, who had received one through her graduate program, but I only knew a few other people with email access. I used microfilm, microfiche, and photocopies from bound journals to collect articles for school papers but never the Internet, which I used purely for recreation and only through a Yahoo! gateway. As a college freshman, I received my own university email account and lessons in PINE. My high school friends, now at their own colleges, also had their own email accounts, and we began to exchange fewer letters and phone calls in favor of online communication. During four years of registering for classes, I registered by phone; there wasn't online registration yet, but using an automated telephone system was still better than having to register in person. My peers and I were using the Internet to connect with our interests — chat rooms, writing groups, audio clips, music sharing, and the like. I did not know anyone relying on the Internet for research. The university's library catalog was accessible by computer, but we still visited the library to check out books and make photocopies of journal articles. When I was a sophomore, a doctoral student who had been my instructor the previous year paid me to take her list of references, find the bound journals in the library, and make photocopies for her. The highest-tech part of the job was using a machine to add money to the copier card.

By the end of college, the Internet had become more of a general information resource for me. I visited the websites of graduate programs I was interested in, looked up driving directions for car trips, emailed with program directors and graduate students, subscribed to relevant mailing lists, and visited chat rooms. I was comfortable with a computer as a word processor and as a web portal, but I did not consider myself to be technologically savvy. For one thing, I did not know any programming languages and was not creating my own websites. However, I did have basic HTML knowledge through a freshman-year class, and an understanding of querying databases, even though we just called it running reports, through my job in the university development office.

While I was in college reading books and writing about those books, metadata or digital librarianship was already a recognized field. A 1997 editorial discussed the seven responsibilities of digital librarians including search engine and browser development, metadata creation, remote or virtual reference, and archiving ("Digital Librarian" 79–80). Two years later Roy Tennant's column discussed required skills for the new millennium such as markup languages, metadata, indexing and databases, user interface design, computer programming, and web technology (39). When Tennant's editorial was published, I was a junior in college and had already decided to pursue a graduate degree in creative writing, but my colleagues from the early years of Generation X were in their 30s and working as systems librarians, catalogers, and web librarians; some of them were even in jobs that were defined primarily as digital positions.

In a content analysis of electronic resources jobs, Karen Croneis and Pat Henderson examined job postings in *College & Research Libraries* from the years 1990–2000 that contained the words "electronic" or "digital" in their titles. With this study the authors were expanding on earlier studies by other researchers who had analyzed job postings for trends in automation, technology, and electronic services. For the defined period, over 200 postings were found with 50 of them being selected for an analysis. The findings showed an increase over the years of librarian jobs with either "electronic" or "digital" in the title, with the first "digital" announcement appearing in 1996 and then increasing by five between 1998 and 2000 (223). This type of analysis continued into the 2000s with a study of announcements for head of cataloging positions that looked at, among other trends, new required or desirable skills, such as knowledge of non–MARC metadata and digital projects or project management (Zhu 56–57). A 2009 study by Choi and Rasmussen examined advertisements in *College & Research Libraries* from 1999 to 2007 and found 363 advertisements, with 111 of those classified as "digital librarian positions" (459).

In his book about Generation X, Rosen states, "Having grown up with the new information technology, elite Xers ... are adept at identifying and solving problems and at formulating and merchandising ideas. By organizing and manipulating information, they create ideas and images, they rearrange words, sound bits, and pictures, all of which inform, influence, and amuse audiences" (4). This analysis corresponds to the findings of job advertisement trends in the 1990s and early 2000s. In their study of digital librarian job advertisements from 1999 to 2007, Choi and Rasmussen verified the theory that "digital libraries and technology have brought a new dimension to librarianship.... New challenges and opportunities led by technological change motivate the development of new library positions and evolving qualifications" (466).

This is the type of job that works across departments and institutions and that requires collaboration through the sharing of resources, information, and standards but also leadership in developing programs and projects and in creating those standards in the first place. John Chapman looked at the roles collaboration, research, education, and development of projects and procedures in metadata librarian positions, stating that "while none of these individual roles is unique to the metadata librarian compared to other librarian positions, the combination is unusual and especially distinctive within the technical services or cataloging environment" (280). Choi and Rasmussen also noted the emerging trend of "increased demand for interpersonal and communication skills, and adaptive skills to keep up with changes and challenges within library and information environments" (468). Croneis and Henderson found that responsibilities such as partnerships were common in digital librarian descriptions, with digital projects and initiatives and leadership being two characteristics unique to the digital position announcements (234). Digital librarians are found in multiple departments across libraries. We work in special collections, technical services, reference, or systems departments. We work with manuscripts, books, realia and ephemera, videos, oral histories, and photographs; we work with graduate schools on electronic theses and dissertations or with faculty on institutional repositories; we work with research data and publications.

The adaptability and flexibility that characterizes Generation X in the workplace enabled me to get both of my librarian positions in a competitive market. I was willing to move almost anywhere and apply for jobs that were a little different from what I had been doing. Additionally, I had a strong background in other fields and could discuss their relevance. I worked in museums and knew how to handle artifacts. I interned in a university archives and a museum's art library and saw materials that few people outside of those departments knew about. I also knew how to work with the people in the museums and small cultural organizations that partnered with my first employer. In my current position, the two full-time digital positions work with colleagues in technical services, special collections, archives, and other campus libraries. Digital librarians and others in the field continue to face the concern of silos of digital collections, and because of that we continue to look for ways to work with similar organizations and to share our metadata, our knowledge, and our best practices. As a poet, I learned how to capture the essence of an idea with the most appropriate words; now I capture the essence of a digital image with detailed but concise descriptions to lead people to that photographic collection and its thousands of images.

I did not grow up wanting to be a librarian, and even when I chose the field as an adult, I did not do so because I had been an English major who loved the written word, even though I was, but because I wanted to organize information and materials. Like many Gen Xers entering the workforce full-time, I quickly acknowledged that I would not be working for a single employer my entire life. My first full-time position was entry-level with little room for advancement and with very little sense of security. When

I found library science in my mid–20s I had already completed a graduate program in creative writing and was in the middle of a certificate program in museum studies. I had worked in college development offices, academic departments, at a newspaper, and for a packing-and-shipping store. When I fell upon librarianship, making a transition from language to objects to information, I did not recognize at the time how my work experience led me to that decision. Eventually I was able to connect what I had done with what I could do in my professional life. As an editorial assistant for a monthly publication, I kept track of our magazine's back issues and tried to determine what article was needed when readers emailed about articles they had read but remembered only the barest details. I expanded on the spreadsheet of issue dates, article titles, and authors by adding keywords that could provide more details. Even though I worked on a computer and maintained multiple versions of the same article, I was more interested in organizing file cabinets of correspondence, contracts, and tear sheets. As a student in a museum studies program, I wanted to be a registrar and catalog artifacts. Only later did I think more about being able to find those artifacts in a database, especially after working on a project where I knew the museum had a pulpit and could see it on display but could not find its record in the database through category searches, only with the exact identification number.

When I entered the School of Library and Information Science at Indiana University, I was prepared to become an archivist and did not consider the school's burgeoning Digital Libraries specialization or its course in metadata. It was August 2005 when I moved from North Carolina to Indiana for another degree program, and I already knew what classes appealed to me: archives yes, rare books maybe, metadata no. I wanted to work with papers and objects, not computer files and pixels. My track changed in just my second semester when I completed classes in electronic records management and electronic description of archival materials. The first taught me I did not want to be a records manager, electronic or otherwise, while the latter introduced me to TEI and EAD through projects encoding correspondence and print finding aids. Based on that course, I was able to get a temporary job the following year converting a finding aid into EAD, and that along with my museum studies experience, including a few internships and volunteer positions, led to a job offer as a metadata and digital initiatives librarian before I even completed my MLS. Now I'm at a different university with the title of metadata librarian. I never took the metadata class in my library science program, but I work with it every day. The folders I use are only on the computer, and I sometimes don't even see the original items I'm cataloging in a digital form.

As Generation X librarians take on positions of greater authority and continue to develop digital librarianship as an essential contributor to libraries and information, no one will think we are slacking off. Good metadata is not the hallmark of a slacker; we don't take anything for granted, including the information we have and the resources we use. Like many, our job descriptions will develop, our reporting lines will change, and our go-to software and tools will be switched or updated. Our purpose will remain the same, however, to make information searchable, findable, and usable. In a generation when we went from card catalogs to faceted searches through customized web interfaces, why shouldn't we be able to do even more with cataloging, displaying, harvesting, and aggregating data to make information and resources available in more formats and with greater ease?

WORKS CITED

Chapman, John W. "The Roles of the Metadata Librarian in a Research Library." *Library Resources & Technical Services* 51.4 (2008): 279–285.

Choi, Youngok, and Edie Rasmussen. "What Qualifications and Skills Are Important for Digital Librarian Positions in Academic Libraries? A Job Advertisement Analysis." *The Journal of Academic Librarianship* 35.5 (2009): 457–467.

Croneis, Karen, and Pat Henderson. "Electronic and Digital Librarian Positions: A Content Analysis of Announcements from 1990 through 2000." *The Journal of Academic Librarianship* 28.4 (2002): 232–237.

"The Digital Librarian." Editorial. *The Journal of Academic Librarianship* 23.2 (1997): 79–80.

Gordinier, Jeff. *X Saves the World: How Generation X Got the Shaft but Can Still Keep Everything from Sucking.* New York: Viking, 2008.

Hornblower, Margot. "Great Xpectations." *Time* 9 June 1997: 58–64.

Rosen, Bernard Carl. *Masks and Mirrors: Generation X and the Chameleon Personality.* Westport, CT: Praeger, 2001.

Smith, J. Walker, and Ann Clurman. *Rocking the Ages: The Yankelovich Report on Generational Marketing.* New York: HarperBusiness, 1997.

Strauss, William, and Neil Howe. *Generations: The History of America's Future, 1584 to 2069.* New York: William Morrow, 1991.

Tennant, Roy. "Skills for the New Millennium." *Library Journal* Jan. 1999: 99.

Zhu, Lihong. "Head of Cataloging Positions in Academic Libraries: An Analysis of Job Advertisements." *Technical Services Quarterly* 25.4: 49–70.

Understanding Gen X at Work: Securing the Library's Future

Christy Groves and William Black

Generation X employees are, to a great degree, the ones who have driven a redefinition of the library's role and can best help maximize its relevance. The individuals we hire today understand the evolving information needs and learning styles of our diverse users. Gen Xers have grown up in an information-dense society and are comfortable with an ever-present internet and active social network culture. Broad connectivity is an integral part of their lives, building an expectation for finding information on any possible topic, anytime, anywhere.

Gen X employees are key to the library's sustainability. Because Xers are closely connected to many of our users and can understand, interpret, and respond to their needs, it is vital that we provide Gen X employees with an environment that is conducive to their success. This chapter will describe the work styles of Gen Xers, ways to support their employment expectations, and how to keep them engaged by providing the control they need and the challenges they seek. The authors will detail strategies for retaining Gen X employees and offer suggestions for mentoring them into becoming the leaders who will shape the future of the profession and ensure the relevance of libraries.

Literature Review

Most of the generational research focuses on marketing and providing library services to Generation X as patrons, not on interacting with them as colleagues or leaders. The literature describing Gen Xers at work and the impact they have on organizational relevance and sustainability emphasizes Generation X in entry level positions, possessing little managerial experience (Mosley 185). Generation X is frequently referred to as the "slacker generation," painted in a light of rebellion against the established, practical, and career driven generations of "Traditionalists" (born between 1922 and 1943) and "Baby Boomers" (born between 1943 and 1960). Jason Martin notes that Generation X has been accused of having a poor work ethic, a short attention span, and poor people skills (3–5).

Just as often, however, the literature highlights positive aspects of Generation X — creativity, entrepreneurial spirit, flexibility, and comfort with changing technology. Marshall Lager states that more than any generation before them, Gen Xers are comfortable with technologies that provide convenient access to the products and services they desire and need (31). Online services such as Amazon and iTunes have developed and maintained excellent relationships with Generation X because they present a level of personalization and interactivity with each customer (Lager 30). Further, these services offer instant gratification through quick software downloads, fast shipping, and online package tracking services. Gen Xers easily transfer this customization and expectation of immediacy to the work place. Lager contends that Gen Xers demand relevance, whether it is through their work or the products and services they consume (31).

With members of the Baby Boomer and Traditionalist generations delaying retirement, and as the latest generation, the Millennials, joins the work force, more is being written on generational diversity in libraries. This has included suggestions for how to best understand employees of different generations as well as suggestions for creating harmony among them. In the end, people want similar things at work no matter what generation they are from (Deal 212). Research in the fields of business and advertising can help expand our understanding of Gen Xers' workplace characteristics, collegiality, and managerial techniques and their applicability to the library profession.

As Elizabeth Yates points out, while it is important to recognize generational differences, it is ultimately more important to attend to them by dealing with the issues when they arise and focus on the library's relevance to its users (27). Generation X employees will eventually be assuming management roles and leading our libraries (Mathews 52). It will be important for these employees to be prepared for this vital role through mentoring and the fostering of partnerships within and outside organizations. Mathews states that the creativity and vision possessed by Generation X librarians can provide for a boundless future (52).

Growing Up X

To understand Generation X employees, it is important to recognize the societal forces that shaped their outlook. Robert Wendover notes that "every new generation of workers is a product of the influences they absorbed as they came of age" (36). Generation X employees experienced a revolution in communication technology at a young age. Most Gen X employees are comfortable with using this technology since PCs, Apples, and cellular phones became popular during their adolescence. They are well versed in using PDAs, iPhones, computers, the Internet, and an array of software and social networking applications.

At the same time, Gen Xers watched as their family and friends struggled with economic recession, increased levels of divorce, inflation, exploding transportation costs, jobs being shipped overseas, and corporate scandals. As inflation drove everyday living expenses higher, many of their families needed two incomes to survive. With both parents working, Xers found themselves latch-key kids — unsupervised for several hours each day and fending for themselves. Because they had to learn to deal with life on their own without the structure that parental presence would provide, they are now often self-directed and highly independent.

Many of those same Gen X employees who experienced their parents getting downsized out of work entered the work force themselves in the late 1980s when another economic boom and subsequent crash hit (Armstrong 41). Yet another boom and crash hit in the mid 1990s, when almost all of Generation X was in the work force. These two economic catastrophes "only reinforced the cynicism and skepticism of this generation" (Martin 4). These events so negatively influenced Generation Xers that many are now wary of organizational and institutional culture. This wariness has affected their life priorities.

Portrait of the Gen Xer

The events and societal forces that shaped Generation X are directly responsible for their work style characteristics. In contrast to past generations, economic factors, personal satisfaction, and a desire for professional advancement often outweigh the Xer's loyalty to the organization. Many X employees are not only very independent, they also possess a desire to make a difference in the work they perform. They have a strong need to balance work and home life and are frequently perceived as having very little loyalty (as we used to know it) to the organization that employs them.

Generation X is even "seemingly defined by the fact that it has no true defining experience" (Martin 3). Regardless, there are many popular misconceptions about Gen Xers. They have even been disparaged by older generations as the "lost generation," workers who are happiest sponging off their parents while drifting from one low paying job to another (Tulgan 38). While it is not entirely fair to apply sweeping generalizations to generations, in order to best describe Generation X employees, the authors have taken the liberty of summarizing some typical Gen X characteristics.

Immediacy — Raised in a culture of instant results, Gen Xers crave a quick response. Easily bored, they thrive on change and want to know that their suggestions for improvement have been heard by their supervisors and what directions might be taken as a result. This expectation of immediacy applies to their need for supervisory feedback, as well. Generation X employees want validation of their efforts through regular confirmation that their hard work is paying off. This validation can take the form of recognition, training and development opportunities, money, or an elevation in status.

Independence — Because Generation X employees typically have had to be self-sufficient from a young age, they are very comfortable working on their own. They desire little supervision and prefer the flexibility to execute responsibilities as they see fit. This is actually in contrast to their need for regular validation of their performance.

Gen Xers want to be recognized for their competencies and trusted to carry out their responsibilities.

Creativity — Generation X employees know no other environment than one that is fast-paced, flashy, colorful, and unpredictable. Thus, it is in such an environment that they thrive. Generation X employees are not afraid to learn new technologies, tools, and strategies to make their jobs more interesting, relevant, and efficient. Further, due to having to be self-sufficient, Generation X employees are confident in their abilities to learn and their power to create. They will use this to their advantage, and their organizations will benefit.

Innovation — Gen Xers want to make an impact. They have fresh ways of viewing situations and want to use their creative thinking to improve work processes and outcomes. Gen X employees frequently view problem situations as ways to resolve a challenge and learn new skills.

Opportunity — Gen Xers want to seize opportunities when they encounter them. To Generation X, delay is harmful. Generation X employees also seek opportunities to showcase their talents and abilities because they recognize that the future is uncertain. They build up their skills through learning new technologies and are entrepreneurs, creating for themselves portable assets for the future.

Experiential — Generation X was the first generation to grow up with video games. As such, they are accustomed to a multi-faceted learning environment. Gen Xers are quickly bored with rote lectures and respond better to instruction that incorporates a variety of interactive learning techniques. While in school, their activities were focused less on individual performance and more on team-based learning (Wiethoff 53). They want to take learning into the workplace and apply their education in a real life situation.

Community Focus — Gen Xers are quite accustomed to great diversity, both in their personal and professional lives. Generation X is the first generation to have a clearly global perspective. Many Xers have had opportunities to study and work overseas that were not available to previous generations. These experiences and the relationships formed with people from other countries have broadened their focus and vision. Comfort with technology coupled with the continual rise of the Internet has fueled Xers' involvement in the new possibilities of connecting with others from diverse backgrounds via social networks. Xers are utilizing these connections to share and distribute information faster and more widely than ever before. For example, a simple post by blogger Jeff Jarvis regarding poor customer service from Dell single-handedly spurred a rebellion from millions of Dell owners (Jarvis 13). Gen Xers are not afraid to share their opinions, and they have friends everywhere.

Finding the Right Balance

Balance between work and family life is very important to Generation X. Xers do not want to feel that they are owned by their employer or that they are tied to an inflexible work schedule. Rather, they believe that work and personal time enhance each other and the result is a well-rounded individual. Unlike the generations before them, while Generation X employees need a sense of achievement from their jobs, they do not want their work to negatively impact their quality of life (Yu 36). Gen X employees are determined to spend more time with their children and spouses than their parents did. To them, work is what you do so you can have a life (O'Brien 7; Armstrong 41). If this balance is threatened, Xers are not afraid to seek employment at an organization that provides them with the flexibility they need.

Additionally, we can no longer rely on the old sense of dedication to keep Gen Xers in one place for a long period of time. Xers display less job devotion than Baby Boomers and Traditionalists and do not share the same "live to work" mantra. Rather, Xers "typically want, and will require of employers, greater give-and-take between their professional and personal lives" (Sayers 476). This means Gen X employees actively seek flexible work schedules. They frequently display significant involvement with the activities of their family, some even operating as helicopter parents and juggling multiple family commitments. Attendance at children's sporting events, school programs, and medical appointments is much more common for Xers than in previous generations. Gen X employees may also be pursuing an education, via distance or by taking classes in the evenings or on weekends. Employees may be caring for aging parents. These outside obligations are all an important part of Gen Xers' lives. Xers have no problem with the concept of working, but they want to be able to work on a schedule that allows them to be heavily involved with their family, too. Library managers are challenged to provide the flexibility Gen Xers need while meeting the ever-changing demands of users for longer hours and faster service.

Managing Generation X

According to Bruce Tulgan, managers who fail to understand the needs and expectations of Gen Xers diminish one of their most valuable resources (25). Buckingham and Coffman state that "every great manager has the same goal: to turn each employee's talent into performance" (213). However, Generation Xers are complex individuals. Because Generation X employees have grown up with such a sense of independence (again, due to their upbringing) they are uncomfortable with managers who hover because it makes them feel crowded and unable to express their creativity while completing projects and solving problems. They may actually blame their hovering supervisor if a project does not turn out as planned. Tulgan states that managers who honor Xers' independence foster their innovation by granting them day-to-day autonomy and enough creative responsibility to deliver original solutions (79).

Tulgan reiterates that Gen X functions best when managed as a responsible, independent, and creative force—free to take risks, to make mistakes, and to thrive on challenges (234). Xers' creativity can be valuable to library managers who are embarking on new trends in library and information science, such as developing new ways of providing access to information and connecting with users. Because Generation X employees are adaptable and comfortable with evolving technologies and information resources, they have an innate understanding of library users. Gen Xers' adaptability can, however, present obstacles because they frequently view work challenges as interchangeable Legos and generally have weak skills in understanding institutional hierarchies. These are deficiencies that managers must address. As life-long learners, however, Generation X employees look to their managers as teachers — challenging them and seeking opportunities to gain new skills (that could possibly be taken elsewhere).

While Generation X employees demonstrate characteristics of independence, Tulgan states that Xers also crave tangible validation so that it can be shown to someone else when they "inevitably are in search of a new job" (142). Tulgan also states that Xers' desires for short-term rewards can have a beneficial impact on the organization if managers recognize their contributions (141). Wiethoff suggests that providing timely feedback is the most important action managers can take in working with Xers (54). Because Generation X employees lost faith in organizations and institutions in their adolescence, it is important for managers to understand that Xers have an intense ambition due to their "quest for security in this unstable world" (Wiethoff 53; Tulgan 143). For Gen Xers, mastering new technological skills is tied to success and security in unstable times. Employee loyalty and productivity from Generation X workers comes when they believe they are working for a manager willing to invest in their career. Thus, relevant training, challenge, and opportunity are crucial. Tulgan states that "managers enjoy mutually beneficial relationships with Xers who are highly motivated, whose skills are improving routinely, and who are less likely to move along in search of a new manager" (69).

Challenging and Retaining Generation X

Retention is closely tied to keeping employees challenged and vital to the longevity and sustained relevance of libraries. It is important for managers to provide challenges and opportunities that take into account the generational characteristics of their Gen X employees. Aparna Nancherla contends that thirty percent of employees seek new challenges at other organizations because they were not provided such opportunities by their current employer (18). According to Sayers, the Gen X work style is typically motivated by a desire to enhance professional skills and thus marketability to future employers (480). Unlike the generations before them, Xers are not afraid to leave a job if it is not rewarding them and building marketable skills. While this will be tempered somewhat in economic downturns, Xers will be driven to seek an amenable match between their job and their needs. Still, it would be a mistake for employers to assume that Xers are job hoppers, jumping from one challenge to another, growing bored quickly. In fact, Deal has found that younger generations are not more likely to job-hop than older generations were at the same age (43). Gen Xers just need to be on a path that is going somewhere they want to go (Lancaster 244).

A number of factors are important in challenging and retaining the X Generation. Gen Xers expect to like and share fundamental values with their co-workers. Developing a true team environment in which Xers have an opportunity to gain and show respect is important. Generation X employees thrive in a team setting and are frequently thinking ahead for how challenges and opportunities can strategically position them for a career move upward.

Because recognition is very important to Xers, if an employer is in any way able to influence monetary and non-monetary rewards, these can be very useful motivating factors impacting employee retention. According to Hays, Generation X employees have job expectations somewhat different from generations before them (46). Security of potential long term employment is not something they expect. Since they are the first generation of workers who became employed after years of corporate downsizing, Gen X employees are looking for daily proof that work matters (Hays 46). In fact, because Xers seek frequent and immediate feedback from their supervisors and are frustrated by delays, the best way to retain a Gen X employee is to reward that individual directly on the basis of performance and to do so quickly (Hays 48). Xers aren't just seeking a "pat on the back." They are seeking an honest evaluation of how they are doing on a given project. If the evaluation is less than positive, Gen Xers are not afraid to improve skills, make adjustments, or seek other job opportunities.

Flexibility is key to retaining Gen X employees. Since they view their job as being a blended part of their lives, the Xer's definition of work is "getting the job done," whether it be on a flexible schedule or remotely rather than logging in 8 hours a day, 40 hours a week. As such, Gen X employees may jump at the opportunity for benefits such as on-site child care and extra vacation days ("Rewards" 30). Lancaster states that the top three reasons Gen Xers stay with an organization are autonomy, a good work schedule, and sufficient time-off (247).

Supporting Xers' desires for life-long learning is another key to retention. Xers continually seek training on new skills to keep them fresh, relevant, and marketable. Training is obviously an important management tool for supervising Xers but it has become a very valuable tool in retention as well (Lancaster 295).

Gen X employees are very interactive, demanding from their employers the opportunity to participate in the organization's decision making process and provide feedback to their supervisors as well. Unfortunately, communication up the organizational ladder is frequently an obstacle for Xers. Managers of Xers may actually be "shocked by how willing they are to give feedback, whether or not it was sought" (Lancaster 269). This sort of feedback should actually be nurtured, particularly as Baby Boomer and Traditionalist managers retire, because Xers have excellent ideas and insights for growth and relevance. After all, Xers will be leading the libraries of the future.

Sandwiched Generation

Gen X librarians are a "sandwiched generation." This phrase is typically used to describe people who are caring for young children and suddenly find themselves responsible for an elder at the same time. It is used here to describe those Gen X librarians who are no longer the new kids on the block, but who also have not been in the profession quite as long as many of their supervisors. Gordon suggests that Gen X librarians are "nestled between long-term librarians and their younger customers and between traditional librarianship and technology" (46). Many Traditionalists and Baby Boomers haven't retired yet, but Gen Xers are looking for these positions to become vacant (Gordon 46). No longer new, but unable to move upward into higher and more encompassing levels of responsibility, Generation X is still straddling a middle ground in libraries. However, this inertia does not mean that Generation X librarians should coast along with no thought to preparing for the future. Rather, in preparation for the inevitable time when older generations leave the work force, Generation X librarians "need to ask their administration if they have set up succession planning and ways to transfer" their knowledge when they do retire (Gordon 46). Generation X needs to be prepared to pursue mentoring opportunities and seek out current library leaders who are eager to pass along institutional memories. Gen Xers have been around long enough to remember libraries that operated without much technology. Many Gen X librarians have used card catalogs as well as Twitter, and therefore have a broad understanding of the history of libraries that shape how they operate today. While comfortable with rapidly changing library trends, according to Gordon, many Gen X librarians "also said they shared professional values with their Baby Boomer colleagues" (46). This level of comfort and understanding provides Gen X librarians with a unique perspective that simply cannot be held by the generations before or after them.

Generation X as Leaders

Gen Xers' unique perspectives position them to lead libraries into the future when Traditionalists and Baby Boomers retire. The pursuit of a balanced life and the ability to work independently and creatively is actually an asset Gen X librarians bring to the library profession. As stated previously, Generation X employees are self-sufficient, concerned about their future, and appreciative of good mentorship. "Gen Xers always have built careers with an eye on establishing enough experiences to make them supremely employable no matter what cataclysmic event occurs next" (Lancaster 191). Gen Xers eagerly seek new skills that move them toward positions of leadership and must look to their supervisors as mentors in this process. In turn, effective supervisors can help expand the Xer's knowledge and skills, and provide valuable insights into his or her organization. Due to Xers' ongoing quest to gain new skills, current library leaders seeking to pass along institutional memory must demonstrate commitment to Xers' learning and growth and help them foster strong working relationships to ensure ongoing organizational success (Gordon 46).

Today, there are four generations in the work force: Traditionalists, Baby Boomers, Generation Xers, and Millennials. While Generation X employees must foster relationships with Traditionalists and Boomers, they must also form new partnerships with the incoming Millennials. It will not be long before Generation X will be solely responsible for mentoring and managing the next generation of employees. How Generation X will balance this responsibility with the characteristics that shape them as managers is crucial for the relevance and sustainability of libraries.

TABLE 1
INFORMATION SEEKING BEHAVIOR AND THE GENERATIONS

	Traditionals (Silents, Veterans)	Boomers	Xers	Millennials (Nexters)
Approximate dates of birth	1922–1943 (Pre–World War II)	1943–1960	1961–1980	1981–1999
Characteristics that influence information seeking	• Accustomed to top-down flow of information • Formal • Learning environment that is stable	• Formal feedback • Interactive and non-authoritarian	• Highly independent • Entrepreneur • Comfortable with change • Raised with instant access • Want frequent, immediate feedback • Self-directed • Sample and learn by doing • Not attracted to classroom	• Globally concerned • Diverse • Cyberliterate • Media savvy • Collaborative • Multitaskers • Teamwork • Technology • Multi-media
Information Seeking	• Like materials that are organized and summarized • Example: *Reader's Digest* • Dewey Decimal	• Easy to scan format • Example: *Business Week*; *USA Today*; *People*	• Prefer fewer words • Don't read as much • Visual stimulation — headlines, subheads, quotes, graphics, lists • Example: *Spin, Fast Company, Wired*, chat-room dialogue	• Readers • Lively and varied materials • Chat (instant messaging) • Search engine (Google)

Source: Zemke, R., C. Raines, and B. Filipczak. "Generation Markers." *Across the Board* 39.4 (2001): 20. Print.; Zemke, R., C. Raines, and B. Filipczak. "Generation Gaps in the Classroom." *Training* 36.11 (1999): 48–54. Print.; Lancaster, L.C. "The Click and Clash of Generations." *Library Journal* 15 Oct. 2003: 36–39. Print. Summary provided by Eileen Abels.

Millennials & Beyond

It is critical that our organizations provide the dynamic work environment necessary for supporting rapidly evolving technologies and the needs of our users. The future will bring new organizational challenges, many of which are already being seen in our latest group of employees — the Millennials. These digital natives, already coming into our organizations, view life as a social network and the library as a platform. They establish and communicate their identities simultaneously in the physical and digital worlds (Palfrey 20). They see their work life through connections and are used to dealing on a quite personal level with friends and strangers. They are owners of a social identity that is far broader than what other generations have experienced and one with far less control.

To these individuals, the library helps build value. It is not a centralized entity but part of a distributed system. It is a means to an end. Its value can be enhanced by the wisdom of its users. Millennials' philosophy is, "let's try it." They think operations should be transparent and simple. Their focus is on collaboration and rapid response. They are conditioned from years of playing online games where "the player who contributes most gets to lead the team" (Fisher 49). Games are a large part of how humans learn, cope, tell stories, and socialize. Through games, we learn about teamwork, individual achievement, and other cultures ("Super Bowl, Olympics, Super Mario").

Managing such individuals will present interesting scenarios. We will need to build adaptable organizations that support the Millennial ethos and beyond, focusing on relationships and understanding the library as part of a system rather than as an end in itself. We will need to give these employees the control they need to succeed and provide them with an environment that promotes operational creativity.

The reliance on media that is inherent in Millennials will continue to expand into the next generation, which could be called Generation G (for Google). A recent Kaiser Family Foundation report found that this group devotes an average of seven hours and thirty-eight minutes in a typical day to using entertainment media, much of which involves media multitasking (Rideout). These future employees view entertainment, information, and research as part of one accessible database. This pattern of connecting with the world will surely impact how we design our library services and reach our users in the future.

WORKS CITED

Armstrong, Tabitha. "Gen X Family Values." *The Lane Report* 1 Jan. 2005: 41.
Buckingham, Marcus, and Curt Coffman. *First, Break All the Rules: What the World's Greatest Managers Do Differently*. New York: Simon & Schuster, 1999.
Deal, Jennifer J. *Retiring the Generation Gap*. San Francisco: Jossey-Bass, 2007.
Fisher, Anne. "When Gen X Runs the Show." *Time* 25 May 2009: 48–49.

Gordon, Rachel Singer. "NextGen: The 'Bridge' Generation." *Library Journal* 15 Nov. 2005: 46.

Hays, Scott. "Generation X and the Art of the Reward." *Workforce* 78.11 (1999): 45–48.

Jarvis, Jeff. *What Would Google Do?* New York: Harper Collins, 2009.

Lager, Marshall, et al. "Generation Nation: Generation X." *Customer Relationship Management* 10.11 (2006): 30–31.

Lancaster, Lynne, and David Stillman. *When Generations Collide.* New York: Harper Business, 2002.

Martin, Jason. "I Have Shoes Older Than You: Generational Diversity in the Library." *Southeastern Librarian* 54.3 (2006): 4 –11.

Mathews, Brian S. "NextGen: The Inevitable Gen X Coup." *Library Journal* 15 Mar. 2006: 52.

Mosley, Pixey Anne. "Mentoring Gen X Managers: Tomorrow's Library Leadership Is Already Here." *Library Administration and Management* 19.4 (2005): 185–192.

Nancherla, Aparna. "Retention Tension: Keeping High-Potential Employees." *T&D* 62.3 (2008): 18.

_____. "Wandering Eyes." *T&D* 62.7 (2008): 22.

O'Brien, Keith. "The Culture War with Millennials Is Overhyped and Wrongheaded." *PR Week* 18 Aug. 2008: 7.

Palfrey, John, and Urs Gasser. *Born Digital: Understanding the First Generation of Digital Natives.* New York: Basic Books, 2008.

"Rewards for the Ages." *Workforce Management* 85.24 (2006): 30.

Rideout, Victoria, Ulla G. Foehr, and Donald F. Roberts. *Generation M2: Media in the Lives of 8- to 18-Year-Olds: A Kaiser Family Foundation Study.* Menlo Park: Henry J. Kaiser Family Foundation, 2010.

Sayers, R. "The Right Staff from X to Y: Generational Change and Professional Development in Future Academic Libraries." *Library Management* 28.8–9 (2007): 474–487.

"Super Bowl, Olympics, Super Mario: How Games Help Teach." *Christian Science Monitor* 5 Feb. 2010. Web. 30 Sept. 2010.

Tulgan, Bruce. *Managing Generation X: How to Bring Out the Best in Young Talent.* New York: W.W. Norton, 2000.

Wendover, Robert W. "From Ricky and Lucy to Beavis and Butthead: Understanding the New Generations." *Agency Sales* 35.8 (2005): 37–39.

Wiethoff, Carolyn. "Management Basics: Managing Generation X." *Indiana Libraries* 23.2 (2004): 53–55.

Yates, Elizabeth. "Millennials: Invite Us to the Party." *AALL Spectrum* 12.7 (2008): 25–27.

Yu, Hiu-Chun, and Peter Miller. "Leadership Style: The X Generation and Baby Boomers Compared in Different Cultural Contexts." *Leadership and Organizational Development Journal* 26.1–2 (2005): 35–50.

Generation X Librarians, Faculty and the Rise of Information Literacy

Leslie Porter Mathews and Sergio Rizzo

The relationship between academic librarians and faculty has long been a topic of serious scholarship for librarians. However, as librarians know all too well, the same cannot be said of the faculty. Indeed, the persistence of what librarians have dubbed the "faculty problem" has led some to conclude that it is an unavoidable fact of academic life. Approaching this longstanding division of academic labor from a historical perspective, specifically that of Generation X, provides a unique contribution to the discussion. Furthermore, highlighting the generational values and interests that have shaped the debate so far, we can better assess what, if anything, has or will change in how academic librarians and faculty relate to one another and work together.

Generation X's contribution to this critique can be seen in the evolution from "bibliographic instruction" to "information literacy." The dean of bibliographic instruction, Evan Farber, was the first to fundamentally question the hierarchy and assumptions of the research university when he described the "university-library syndrome" (Farber 62). Building on Farber's work, Larry Hardesty further diagnosed "faculty culture" as an obstacle to the undergraduate library's mission (339–367). While clearly indebted to this earlier scholarship, Generation X's move towards information literacy signals an important shift in thinking reflected by Bell and Shank's "blended librarian" model (Bell and Shank 373). Contrary to the essentialism in Farber's retrospective essay, "Plus ca Change ... (The More Things Change)," we assert that Generation X librarians see the new technologies that are defining their generation as offering fundamental changes to the role of academic librarians and their relationship to faculty.

Generation X: Background

Although there has always been some dispute about the exact dates, for our purposes, members of Generation X were born between 1961 and 1981. Gen Xers have been called everything from slackers to the MTV generation to the Latchkey Generation.

29

Now members of Generation Y are entering the workforce, with digital natives not far behind them. It should be noted that we consider the small Generation X, about 48 million strong (in comparison with 72 million Baby Boomers), to be quite distinct from Generation Y, even if together they make up what has been referred to in the literature as "NextGen" librarians. Following the generational categories propounded by Howe and Strauss in their books *Millennials Rising* and *Millennials and Pop Culture*, Susan Gibbons in *The Academic Library and the Net Gen Student* makes a significant contribution to understanding how recent generational changes have and will impact the academic library. However, for her, the future of academic libraries has little to do with Generation X and everything to do with Generation Y, or using the term she prefers, "the Net Generation" (Gibbons xv).

In talking about any generation, there is a danger of stereotyping; however, many researchers suggest that there are common characteristics shared by members of the group that can be helpful for our analysis. Generation X kids were the first kids who grew up with two working parents or divorced parents, an unstable economy, a hole in the ozone layer, homelessness, AIDS, national debt, crack, video games, and the advent of MTV. This generation saw their parents lose their jobs to downsizing and, as a result, formed a suspicious or skeptical view of hierarchy and corporations. As they witnessed the phenomenon of downward mobility, Gen Xers learned that they don't want to fall victim to it themselves.

There was a flurry of research about Gen X in the early and mid–90s that characterized the generation as apathetic slackers. Gen X college students were portrayed negatively in Sacks' scathing account of what it was like to teach journalism to what he dubbed an "almost unteachable" generation: "Like McDonald's customers expecting neatly packaged $1.99 Big Macs, these postmodernists harbored a strong sense of being entitled to easy success and good grades, even though they were often unwilling to work to achieve them" (Sacks xiii). In a 1990 *Time* magazine article, the authors critiqued the generation as antithetical to Baby Boomers:

> The twentysomething generation is balking at work, marriage and baby-boomers values. Why are today's young adults so skeptical? They have trouble making decisions. They would rather hike in the Himalayas than climb a corporate ladder.... They possess only a hazy sense of their own identity but a monumental preoccupation with all the problems the preceding generation will leave for them to fix.... They reject 70-hour workweeks as yuppie lunacy, just as they shirk from starting another social revolution [Gross and Scott].

This same *Time* article also polled members of Gen X about various things, including jobs. In response to the question "There is no point in staying in a job unless you are completely satisfied," 58 percent agreed. The generation was accused of being whiners or crybabies, and yet they faced the toughest economic climate of any generation before them since the Great Depression. "Between 1983 and 1992, the median weekly earnings of young men aged 16 to 24 who were full-time workers fell 9 percent, from $314 per week to $285 per week in constant 1992 dollars" (Zill and Robinson 26). In addition, over 40 percent of this group also faced the reality of growing up with divorce (Zill and Robinson 29). Because of economic conditions, many Gen Xers spent a large portion of their twenties living at home and delaying marriage. In this climate, Gen Xers could not be sure of much — their jobs, relationships, or moving up in the world.

Now, the generation has come of age, and while most of the literature on generations seems to be about Generation Y and digital natives, Gen X is now seen in a different light. By 1997, *Time* offered another profile; but this time, it was almost celebrating the generation for its desire for success, integrity, entrepreneurial spirit and grit: "Indeed, adversity, far from discouraging youths, has given them a harder, even ruthless edge. Most believe 'I have to take what I can get in this world because no one is going to give me anything'" (Hornblower).

As the web began to emerg, Gen Xers were among its early leaders: "High-tech wunderkinder, such as Yahoo! Web-search founders Jerry Yang, 28, and David Filo, 31, are role models because of their affinity for risk and their entrepreneurial spirit ... today's twentysomethings have learned to cope. They may be cynical about institutions, but they remain remarkably optimistic as individuals" (Hornblower). Over ten years after the second *Time* article was published, Xers remain at the forefront of some of the world's most popular and profitable technology companies, particularly Sergey Brin and Larry Page, the founders of Google.

While *The Chronicle of Higher Education* was already pinning its hopes for the future on Millennials (Gen Y) in 2000, calling them "the next great generation" (Brownstein A71) after apparently giving up on Gen X, others saw it differently. In the same year, *Brandweek* reconsidered Xers "long-time media whipping posts, once decried as surfboarding grungers and overeducated yet disenfranchised slackers, Xers emerge in our research with a considerably different reputation: self-reliant, entrepreneurial, techno-focused, media-savvy, socially tolerant and, slowly but surely, parents" (Kraus 28).

Generation X Librarians

Generation X librarians entered the profession with an unprecedented knowledge of technology. While they experienced the rise of desktop computers in their youth — think TRS80, Apple IIE, Commodore 64 — they are also well versed in the world of new technology. Rachel Singer Gordon has dubbed this group the "bridge" generation because they remember the way things used to be, but are fully immersed in the new (Gordon 46). This separates them from Generation Y and Digital Natives, who have been steeped in technology from childhood and who don't remember the card catalog being carted away.

Gen Xers entered the profession at a time when technology and the Web began playing a central part in the library's daily functions, resulting in an environment where "finding the balance between technology and traditional service will be especially difficult" ("Shedding the Stereotypes" 168). Gen Xers, with their flexibility, adaptability, and entrepreneurial skills, seemed like a perfect fit for this climate of uncertainty. Mosley called for a new type of librarian who is "clear-sighted, responsive, flexible, and proactive with user interactions and the services being provided" ("Shedding the Stereotypes" 170). This new librarian "may need retraining in traditional reference sources or cataloging procedures but ... offers in return a high technology literacy level, individual flexibility, and multi-tasking expertise ... the librarian may bring a knowledge-base or skill set that includes marketing techniques, customer service philosophy, innovative thinking, and positive teamwork expectations" ("Shedding the Stereotypes" 170). Mosley warns that the introduction of these new librarians into the traditional hierarchical library may be a rocky one.

> Generation X librarians are likely to have behavior patterns, personality quirks, and expectations that are misunderstood by senior staff and could be badly mishandled in the traditional hierarchical library setting. They have grown up in and gone through the educational area when teamwork and quality assurance are the buzzwords, asking "why" was encouraged, and the basic slogan is "just do it." Often they perceive department or individual boundaries as something to be swept away or a roadblock to accomplishing a successful change ["Shedding the Stereotypes" 172].

These librarians, who typically fill the entry-level positions of reference and instruction librarians and newer, technology-oriented positions such as e-resources librarian or web services librarian, have been known to move around more frequently than their Boomer predecessors. Instead of using the pejorative term "job hopping," we would argue that this phenomenon is more of a survival technique as well as a manifestation of the Gen Xer's desire to have fulfilling, challenging jobs — jobs that hold their interest, allow their opinions to be heard, and allow them to become agents of change. They will leave a job and find a new one if it is not the right fit. "Loyalty to oneself has been part of the socialization of Generation X and, for many, technology served as the focal point of library school training. If managers do not offer the younger generation the opportunity to further these skills, some Xers will leave and join other library and non-library organizations that will" (Cooper and Cooper 19).

Gen Xers have a new mobility that previous generations never dreamed of—both in terms of their ability to move from one job to another, but also in terms of the Internet and social networking. Many Gen X librarians have been drawn to the Web 2.0 movement, which espouses the use of new technologies in libraries in order to increase productivity, sharing, and marketing. Gen X librarians have been using technologies such as blogs, wikis, Facebook, Twitter, RSS, social software, cloud computing, etc., and have been blogging about it now for years, even though some of the technologies they have been talking about have yet to be widely adopted in libraries. While Gen X librarians do publish in academic journals, blogging is one of the primary ways they communicate with each other and the library community to share their successes, failures, or to solicit ideas from others. This can give these librarians a virtual community if they lack a community of receptive colleagues or coworkers or if they lack the feedback they seek on the job.

Some new and Gen X librarians have gotten together and created group blogs such as "In the Library with the Lead Pipe." The blog's tagline is particularly telling, "The murder victim? Your library assumptions. Suspects? It could have been any of us." Interestingly, and quite typically for newer and Gen X librarians, these librarians are subverting the traditional hierarchy by introducing their own kind of peer review system. In the *About* section, they explain, "Our goal is to explore new ideas and start conversations; to document our concerns and argue for solutions. Each article is peer-reviewed by at least one external and one internal reviewer" (Badman et al.).

Gen Xers are known for their willingness and aptitude for experimentation and use of trial and error and risk taking. "Along with their technical orientation, Xers have an ability to bring together seemingly unrelated elements from diverse information resources. This talent results in creative solutions to problems and a comfort with competition, a reality that many traditional librarians are not prepared to face" (Cooper and Cooper 19). Rather than hash an idea out in a committee, Gen Xers are likely to strike out on their own and try a project, sometimes without consulting the "right" people. We would posit that instead of lack of respect for hierarchy, this is a reflection of Gen X librarians' frustration with the traditional, relatively slow way things have worked in libraries. At conferences, advocates of web 2.0 often encourage each other to try something out and then ask for forgiveness later. Many times the only way these librarians can prove the value of a new technology is by showing it in action and demonstrating how it can benefit their colleagues. At the ALA Preconference "Reinvented Reference III" in 2007, Michael Stephens, the keynote speaker and author of the well-known blog *Tame the Web*, noted how the traditional hierarchical structure of libraries could quash a great idea.

In the coming decades, Gen X librarians will be taking charge of libraries. In his article, "The Inevitable Gen X Coup," Brian Mathews, author of the blog *The Ubiquitous Librarian*, states, "I think our elders are a bit nervous about leaving the library legacy in our hands, questioning our values and commitment. Yet the profession needs us, perhaps more than is imagined, to ensure that libraries remain relevant in contemporary society" (52). Mathews is one of many Gen X voices that emphasizes the idea of marketing libraries. The concept of marketing is a newer one in libraries — not necessarily introduced by Gen Xers — but definitely part of their identities as twenty-first-century librarians. Mathews authored a book entitled *Marketing Today's Academic Library: A Bold New Approach to Communicating with Students* in which he asks the question: "Do libraries need to advertise?" (1). His resounding answer is "yes," and that librarians can incorporate the marketing methods of the business world to do it. This trend of looking to other industries, especially business, is one that librarians are beginning to realize is crucial to their success. These ideas can be seen in Bell and Shank's concept of the "blended librarian," which incorporates technology, teaching, collaboration and marketing as key roles for the academic librarian (Bell and Shank 372–5).

Bell and Shank coined the term "blended librarian" in 2004 and invited others to participate in the *Blended Librarian* online forum at LearningTimes, which has since evolved into a vibrant community where librarians present and share ideas in the form of free webinars and discussions. Bell and Shank stated, "We define the 'blended librarian' as an academic librarian who combines the traditional skill set of librarianship with the information technologist's hardware/software skills, and the instructional or educational designer's ability to apply technology appropriately in the teaching-learning process" (374). Bell, who is a Boomer, and Shank, who is a Gen Xer, are leading with ideas about technology that have much appeal for tech-savvy Gen Xers. This is an example that illustrates how librarians of different generations are working together to forge new ideas and a good reminder that age and generation are not necessarily factors that define who people are and what they do.

Working with Faculty

One area in which librarians tend to have a lot of freedom is their faculty liaison responsibility. This is a very traditional area of librarianship, and one that Gen Xers can take advantage of by using their independent streak to create new and unconventional partnerships with faculty. Many librarians are expected to work with a certain number of faculty, teach a certain number of classes, or to publish, that is, if they have faculty status. According to Murray-Rust, about 40 percent of librarians have some version of faculty status (B10) and as a result of this, they can experience a certain amount of pressure from their supervisors and the library administration to produce. In this case, each librarian is in effect working for him or herself to get ahead. There is no team here, because each person will be evaluated on individual effort and individual results. This structure encourages a certain amount of independence and creativity and discourages teamwork at the same time. It also plays into the Gen Xer's natural self-reliance; they are "loyal to their own skills, and they change jobs to augment and hone their skills. They seek achievement of their own goals and value individuals over the chain of command" (Ruch 42).

In 2005, Given and Julien published their analysis of the BI-L/ILI-L mailing lists postings from 1995 to 2002. This study illustrated librarians' feelings of frustration and negativity in dealing with faculty and the fact that "librarians' professional goals (i.e., aiding and teaching students in the effective use of information resources) were at odds with faculty members' research, teaching, and service work" (27). On the mailing lists, Given and Julien documented that librarians complained that faculty were "possessive, inflexible, rude, touchy" (32), and the list goes on. In addition librarians who posted to the mailing lists felt faculty members "do not understand librarians' work, do not see the intellectual content association with library instruction, and do not respect librarians" (34). If Gen Xers enter into a climate where these views are expressed by their colleagues, they face a conundrum — how to proceed?

While working with faculty can provide librarians with a degree of freedom, it can also be a source of frustration as the study of the mailing lists attests. Bell notes, "At some institutions, faculty-librarian relationships may be a source of professional frustration. Faculty may be unreceptive to gestures for collaboration. But passionate academic librarians achieve success with two important qualities: risk taking and persistence. A personal vision shaped by these two is a third ingredient for success" (Bell 636). Sarah Faye Cohen echoes this sentiment and illustrates persistence with her energetic outreach efforts in which technology plays a central role. She has this advice for others: "Perhaps you've been shut down by faculty members or whole departments. Try again. Faculty are vital members of our patron group: if you would try again with students, try again with faculty" (Cohen 474).

The ACRL Competency Standards for Information Literacy, established in 2000, have been the subject of much debate since they have been introduced. In an environment where Generation X librarians are expected to incorporate the standards into their instruction classes, the standards provide librarians a chance to justify their unique and creative approaches to instruction. The standards call for solutions tailored to specific situations at specific institutions; this kind of open-endedness is required in a climate where no national standard for implementing information literacy exists. Some have argued that these standards ask librarians to go beyond what is traditionally expected of them, but Gen X librarians are likely to welcome the chance to operate outside of traditional boundaries in the current instructional climate that tends to push information literacy. However, as Bell and Shank note, library school courses do not address pedagogy or instructional design:

> One area in which academic librarians lag is in our understanding of pedagogy and adoption of instructional design theory and practice. These skill sets have long been ignored within library education, despite academic librarians being integral to the teaching and learning process. Many members of our profession are woefully deficient in their knowledge of how learning takes place, how structures for effective learning are designed, and how learning outcomes are assessed [373].

With the push to go out and teach, librarians have a mandate to strike out on their own and push the envelope of what has been previously accepted. One thing about this free-agent type of operation is that many faculty/librarian partnerships that are forged by Gen X librarians who stay at jobs for just two or three years are likely to be associated with that librarian only. When he or she moves on, the partnership may not continue because the librarian did not share this information with others or because the person took on additional responsibilities. This would seem to have a negative effect on libraries because individually forged successes may wither and die if they are not known or acknowledged. D'Angelo and Maid, who stress that it is typically individuals rather than institutions who create partnerships, note that "a great deal of time and energy are spent on advocacy and frequently individual efforts are not sustainable beyond the work of the individual librarians or librarian-faculty team" (213).

Information Literacy Debate

Information literacy has been controversial with librarians since it was introduced in 1989. ACRL defines it as "a set of abilities requiring individuals to 'recognize when information is needed and have the ability to locate, evaluate, and use effectively the needed information'" (Association of College & Research Libraries). New librarians enter the field and are expected to teach library instruction geared towards the ACRL Information Literacy Competency Standards for Higher Education, but they enter into the profession at a time when debate among librarians persists as how to proceed; they enter a world where, according to Owusu-Ansah, "the exact delineation of the academic library's educational role still lacks clear definition" (415). This is a problem that can only be solved at a higher level, yet new librarians are supposed to come into it and begin teaching. In 2005, Stanley Wilder famously called for the end of information literacy altogether, claiming that it teaches nothing more than mechanical skills and removes librarians even further from the status they should occupy — that of professor (B13). Grassian, in a rebuttal to Wilder, defined information literacy as higher order thinking, "Information literacy goes beyond seeking for and identifying information, to higher levels of judging and applying what one learns, both effectively and responsibly. The ultimate goal of information literacy instruction is, in fact, to see this many-faceted approach integrated into instruction throughout all curricula, throughout all grade levels, and indeed, throughout one's working life and beyond."

Bell and Shank assert that information literacy has helped librarians make advancements in the world of academe. It has both allowed librarians to work more directly with students as well as served to legitimize librarians' role in the learning process. Instead of being seen as hovering on the boundaries of the learning process, Bell argues, librarians will be seen as essential to this aspect of students' lives.

> The information literacy movement is a tremendous boon to librarians whose passion focuses on students for it creates more opportunities for direct interaction with students. In a way that traditional bibliographic instruction never did, information literacy initiatives serve to legitimize academic librarians' participation in the teaching and learning process, and validate for faculty our contributions to student learning [Bell 636].

Gen X bloggers have added their voices to the debate, including Steve Lawson, Iris Jastram, and Wayne Bivens-Tatum. Steve Lawson, on his blog, *See Also: A Library Weblog by Steve Lawson*, created a post titled "Information Literacy: A Non-Definition" in response to a post by Iris Jastram on her blog *Pegasus Librarian* entitled "What is information literacy anyway?" Lawson adds his own definition to the fray: "I think the role of information literacy in higher education is to take what students already know and complicate it, extend it, deepen it, and test it" (Lawson). Jastram had begun the conversation by explaining that she had to do a ten-minute presentation to a group of faculty about information literacy in which she says, "I wish I knew what information literacy was" (Jastram). She ends up presenting information literacy as a "habit of mind" regarding finding, evaluating, and using information ethically, which is clearly founded on ideas from the Standards and is similar to how Grassian described it. She and others in a small group created a document that distills the Standards into an approachable set of questions for students.

Bivens-Tatum talks about two schools of instruction — what he refers to as the "kitchen sinkers" and the "minimalists." The kitchen sinkers, as the name implies, would throw everything at students in a one-shot library instruction session, including all the intricacies of the OPAC. He falls into the minimalist category, and tries to give students what they need to get started. His philosophy mirrors Jastram's: "I emphasize what I call the geography of information. If you want this kind of thing, you look in this kind of place." He gets at the "habit of mind" idea a bit, "research skills are learned over time with practice, even for librarians" (Bivens-Tatum). This is an example of one librarian creating an individual philosophy as it relates to teaching and information literacy. When new librarians — of any generation — are faced with the information literacy debate, what do they do? Some, like Jastram continue to question what defines information literacy, and may look to their peers by posting to their blogs, seeking input from others.

There are many articles about successful librarian-faculty partnerships and collaborations; these articles represent hard fought individual successes. A significant exception to the prevailing piecemeal approach towards collaboration is the success many libraries have found integrating their information literacy programs into freshman composition or "writing across the curriculum" programs. Currently, however, there is no nationally accepted systematic program for implementing library instruction and information literacy into the curriculum. Each success is hard won and depends on individuals or task forces who work to create partnerships with faculty and others. Because the ACRL Standards are so wide ranging and most libraries do not have an information literacy program in place, most librarians create partnerships one at a time through outreach and relationship building, and almost all begin with librarians. Many libraries have had success integrating an information literacy component into the English Department, specifically for freshman English. At the University of Alabama, librarians use the term "negotiated" to describe how they worked with the Director of Freshman Composition to get library instruction into the program (DeForest, May, and Spencer 155). Holliday and Fagerheim worked to integrate information literacy into English composition at Utah State University (169–184). These are just a few examples of successful partnerships, but it should be noted that most are being integrated into basic level composition classes, which, while they reach many students, may not be the most effective way of integrating information literacy into a curriculum. In the coming years, perhaps Gen X librarians will reevaluate this approach, seeking to make the blended approach more widespread.

We would posit that the ACRL Information Literacy Competency Standards can be a way for Gen X librarians to enter into faculty-librarian partnerships or collaborations. While the debate rages on, librarians still have to teach classes and work with faculty. Even as Owusu-Ansah claims that the Standards require librarians to do things that would typically be outside of their purview (Stevens 254), we would argue that Gen X librarians are looking for just such an opening to stretch their skills and abilities. Information literacy, as Bell and Shank contend, can be an ideal way for librarians to work on learning outcomes and get faculty buy-in. Stevens notes that the standards shift the focus away from faculty to student outcomes, allowing librarians to shift their focus as well. "The thoroughness of the Standards encourages librarians and faculty to think outside of their traditional roles and relationships to one another, blurring boundaries, extending relationships, transcending and transforming traditional purviews in an effort to enhance student learning" (Stevens 255).

Stevens notes that "new instruction librarians at institutions across the United States may be surprised to find that teaching faculty are not always eager to collaborate with librarians in integrating information literacy into their classes and departments" (255). This harsh reality can require Gen X librarians to come up with creative, untraditional, and perhaps unsustainable solutions in order to survive and reach their quota of classes. Gen X grew up in a time when the educational system was going through an experimental phase that moved away from rote learning ("Mentoring Gen X Managers" 187). Since Gen Xers "think in terms of problem solving, asking 'why' and giving anything a try" ("Mentoring Gen X Managers" 187), it shouldn't be a big surprise that Gen X librarians are trying new approaches with faculty as well as with teaching library instruction and information literacy that include marketing and technology as Bell and Shank espouse. Emily Missner, a business librarian at Drexel University, has created a "newsletteret" called LIB-BIZ-KIT that she uses to push out content to faculty and students. In an interview with the authors, she explained that she signs the faculty and administrators up for the newsletter. She noted, "When it comes down to it, isn't part of instruction also marketing?" (Missner).

As Mosley explains, "[Gen Xers] expect diversity and alternative ways of doing things, they often lose patience with dictated initiatives.... Generation Xers have an extremely low tolerance for anything resembling hypocrisy, phoniness, and unnecessary bureaucracy" ("Mentoring" 187). If an instruction program or method is not working, it's likely that Gen Xers will question it and devise an alternative plan. Meredith Farkas, who became Head of Instructional Initiatives at Norwich University after working for three years as the Distance Learning Librarian, documented all the changes she made to the instruction program in her blog, *Information Wants to Be Free*. In a few short months, she had changed the freshman orientation from a "boring tour" to an interactive experience including a funny movie and activities; she worked aggressively to improve instruction statistics by continually contacting all of her liaison faculty throughout the semester; and she changed the assessment rubric for library instruction classes ("Making Progress").

In an interview with the authors, Farkas reflected on being a Gen Xer. "I think being a member of Generation X probably makes me far less tolerant of the 'that's the way we've always done it' attitude, and immediately after becoming the head of instruction, I began working hard to change a lot of programs that had been done the same way since before I came to Norwich. I don't think anyone before had really questioned whether what we were doing for freshman orientation tours and English 101 instruction was effective, and I had a strong sense from interactions with students that it wasn't." Farkas is an example of a Gen Xer who is very proactive and has been able to makes change happen. In addition, she rose quickly to a position where she could affect the changes she thought necessary for improvement.

Sarah Faye Cohen, a librarian at Champlain College, blogs about her library experiences on her blog *The Sheck Spot*. In the *Who Am I?* section, Cohen gives an insight into the Gen X librarian mindset: "*Nouns:* Reader. Librarian. Teacher. Writer. Listener. *Adjectives:* Curious. Energetic. Open Minded." She writes about presenting on the topic of information literacy at a faculty conference in 2008, "It was really interesting to talk about information literacy at a faculty conference rather than a library one. The issues and concerns that these faculty members expressed are not far from those I've heard on library blogs or in the literature. The difference I think is that faculty are surprised to hear that the library would think about information literacy in any way other than as a ploy for using the library" ("You Never Know"). In this post, Cohen uncovers a common theme when it comes to library instruction, in that librarians often have to hook, trick, or convince faculty to have information literacy or library instruction (e.g., Wittberg et al.; DeForest, May, and Spencer; Badke; McGuinness). This type of language is commonplace in the literature of faculty-librarian partnerships.

Gen X librarians like Cohen often see technology as a way to connect with faculty. Cohen contends that faculty are subject experts, but they certainly aren't technology experts, and she takes the "blended librarian" view that the library is the place faculty should turn to learn these skills as opposed to the help desk or IT because "librarians are educators with an awareness of the pedagogical opportunities technology offers" (Cohen 473). Cohen's view on technology offers some insight on how Gen X instruction librarians think: "Libraries are known on our campuses as places where your needs are met through creativity, knowledge, and service. That service model should extend beyond finding books and articles. It should also include introducing technology to our patrons, especially our faculty members.... Our focus in introducing technology to faculty should mirror our focus in information literacy: it's not just about information, it's about the right information at the right time" (Cohen 473).

Cohen stresses showing faculty how technology can benefit them for personal and professional development purposes, not only how they can integrate it into their classes; this is an example of thinking beyond the traditional role of the liaison librarian in that Cohen acts as a technology ambassador and shows faculty how they can use technology for their own benefit. Cohen's approach reflects the ideas espoused by Bell and Shank, "The concept of the blended librarian is largely built on creating a movement that will encourage and enable academic librarians to evolve into a new role in which the skills and knowledge of instructional design are wedded to our existing library and information technology skills. It is the blended librarian who will excel as the academic professional offering the best combination of skills and services to enable faculty to apply technology for enhanced teaching and student learning" (Bell and Shank 373).

Faculty Issues

While librarians are struggling with the "faculty problem," faculty are facing their own challenges including fewer tenure track positions hand in hand with a world filled with adjuncts. This means that adjunct faculty are spread thin, often teaching several classes at various institutions to make ends meet. These adjuncts often teach entry-level courses such as composition or English 101, classes with which librarians normally work to integrate library instruction and information literacy. This presents a challenge for both faculty and librarians. Adjuncts sometimes don't even have office space or a phone on campus, making it quite difficult for librarians to reach them. Another issue to consider is that Gen X faculty are now entering the ranks as well. This brings up more questions — will Gen X faculty work with librarians differently? Will they be more open to integrating technology into their classes? Will their Gen Y counterparts have yet different expectations? Only time will tell. Bell and Shank would encourage taking the relationship to a new level with classes that go beyond the traditional; "transforming our relationship with faculty requires that we concentrate our efforts to assist them in integrating technology and library resources into (hybrid/blended) courses. We must also add to our traditional role a new capacity for collaboration to improve student learning and outcome assessment in the areas of information access, retrieval, and integration" (374).

It is well documented that librarians discuss the issue of librarian-faculty partnerships in the literature far more than faculty do, and when librarians discuss it, they do so within their own literature (Stevens 257). Stevens cites a 1998 study by Still of discipline-specific pedagogical journals that sought to determine the faculty's view of libraries and librarians. Out of 13,016 articles, only one half of one percent contained any information about libraries (Stevens 257). Stevens argues that librarians need to publish articles about information literacy outside of the library literature. We would argue that Gen X librarians are slowly beginning to publish and present outside of library-specific journals and conferences, however many of their contributions may be at conferences. This could make it difficult for information about these partnerships to be disseminated on a larger scale because many conferences do not publish proceedings.

Conclusion

As Gen X librarians continue to wrestle with the challenge of delivering effective instruction that integrates information literacy while getting faculty buy-in, managers and administrators will need to find ways to encourage and highlight their new librarians' successes. Until there is a national K–12 standard for information literacy that includes nationally mandated testing, faculty and administrators are not likely to be focused on embedding information literacy into the curriculum. Now that President Barack Obama has introduced National Information Literacy Awareness Month, there is hope for information literacy to be embraced on a national level in the future. In the meantime, without a national standard, individual efforts and free-agent tactics will continue to be the best way for librarians to promote their value and services. Library managers will have to find ways to be open minded about how Gen Xers go about doing their jobs as well as to encourage communication and sharing among instruction librarians. Instead of creating an environment where Gen Xers feel they have to subvert the hierarchy to get things done, managers should work to design incentives for creating successful instruction partnerships that embed information literacy into the curriculum beyond English Composition. The one-on-one personal relationships that librarians develop with faculty need to be acknowledged and celebrated by librarians and managers so that they can continue to exist once the individual leaves the institution. The legacy of successful partnerships must live on so that individual persistence pays off and benefits others.

WORKS CONSULTED

Association of College & Research Libraries. "Information Literacy Competency Standards for Higher Education." ACRL 18 Jan. 2000. Web. 30 Sept. 2010.

Aviles, Kitzzy, et al. "If Higher Education Listened to Me..." *Educause Review* 40.5 (2005): 17–28.

Badke, William. "Can't Get No Respect: Helping Faculty to Understand the Educational Power of Information Literacy." *The Reference Librarian* 43.89–90 (2005): 63–80.

_____. "Information Literacy and Faculty." *Online* 32.3 (2008): 47–49.

Badman et al. "About." *In the Library with the Lead Pipe.* 1 May 2009. Web. 28 Feb. 2010.

Barratt, Caroline C., et al. "Collaboration Is Key: Librarians and Composition Instructors Analyze Student Research and Writing." *Portal: Libraries and the Academy* 9.1 (2009): 37–56.

Bell, Steven J. "A Passion for Academic Librarianship: Find It, Keep It, Sustain It — A Reflective Inquiry." *Portal: Libraries and the Academy* 3.4 (2003): 633–642.

Bell, Steven J., and John Shank. "The Blended Librarian: A Blueprint for Redefining the Teaching and Learning Role of Academic Librarians." *College & Research Libraries News* 65.7 (2004): 372–5.

Bennett, Scott. "Campus Cultures Fostering Information Literacy." *Portal: Libraries and the Academy* 7.2 (2007): 147–168.

Bivens-Tatum, Wayne. "Two Schools of Instruction." *Academic Librarian: On Libraries, Rhetoric, Poetry, History, & Moral Philosophy.* 23 June 2009. Web. 28 Feb. 2010.

Boisselle, Juliet Habjan, et al. "Talking Toward Techno-Pedagogy." *Resource Sharing & Information Networks* 17.1 (2005): 123–136.

Brownstein, Andrew. "The Next Great Generation?" *The Chronicle of Higher Education* 13 October 2000: A71.

Christiansen, Lars, Mindy Stombler, and Lyn Thaxton. "A Report on Librarian-Faculty Relations from a Sociological Perspective." *The Journal of Academic Librarianship* 30.2 (2004): 116–121.

Cohen, Sarah Faye. "Talking 2.0 to the Faculty: Why, Who, and How." *College and Research Libraries News* 69.8 (2008): 472–475.

_____. "You Never Know." *The Sheck Spot.* 13 Nov. 2009. Web. 28 Feb. 2010.

Cooper, Julia F., and Eric A. Cooper. "Generational Dynamics and Librarianship: Managing Generation." *Illinois Libraries* 80.1 (1998): 18–21.

D'Angelo, Barbara J., and Barry M. Maid. "Moving Beyond Definitions: Implementing Information Literacy Across the Curriculum." *The Journal of Academic Librarianship* 30.3 (2004): 212–217.

DeForest, Janet, Rachel Fleming May, and Brett Spencer. "Getting Our Foot (Back) in the Door: Reestablishing a Freshman Instruction Program." *The Reference Librarian* 41.85 (2004): 151–167.

Diller, Karen R., and Sue F. Phelps. "Learning Outcomes, Portfolios, and Rubrics, Oh My! Authentic Assessment of an Information Literacy Program." *Portal: Libraries and the Academy* 8.1 (2008): 75–90.

Ducas, Ada M., and Nicole Michaud-Oystryk. "Toward a New Venture: Building Partnerships with Faculty." *College and Research Libraries* 65.4 (2004): 334–335.

Elrod, Susan L., and Mary M. Somerville. "Literature-Based Scientific Learning: A Collaboration Model." *The Journal of Academic Librarianship* 33.6 (2007): 684–691.

Farber, Evan. "College Libraries and the Teaching/Learning Process: A 25-Year Reflection." *Journal of Academic Librarianship* 25.3 (1999): 171–177.

Farber, Evan Ira. "College Librarians and the University-Library Syndrome." *College & Undergraduate Libraries* 7.1 (2000): 61–69.

_____. "Plus ca Change ... (The More Things Change...)." *Library Trends* 44.2 (Fall 1995): 430–38. 28.

Farkas, Meredith. "Making Progress on Library Instruction." *Information Wants to Be Free.* 7 Jan. 2009. Web. 28 Feb. 2010.

_____. Personal Interview. 6 January 2010.

Fosmire, Michael, and Alexius Macklin. "Riding the Active Learning Wave: Problem-Based Learning as a Catalyst for Creating Faculty-Librarian Instructional Partnerships." *Issues in Science and Technology Librarianship* 34 (2002): n.p. Web. 26 Feb. 2010.

Gibbons, Susan. *The Academic Library and the Net Gen Student.* Chicago: American Library Association, 2007.

Given, Lisa M., and Heidi Julien. "Finding Common Ground: An Analysis of Librarians' Expressed Attitudes Towards Faculty." *The Reference Librarian* 43.89 (2005): 25–38. 28 Feb. 2010.

Gordon, Rachel Singer. "The 'Bridge' Generation." *Library Journal* 15 Nov. 2005: 46. 28 Feb. 2010.

Grassian, Esther. Guest Opinions. "Information Literacy: Wilder Makes (Some Right, but) Many Wrong Assumptions." *LAUC.edu.* LAUC. 15 Feb. 2005. Web. 6 Jan 2010.

Gross, D.M., and S. Scott. "Living: Proceeding with Caution." *Time* 16 July 1990: n.p. Web. 28 Feb. 2010.

Hardesty, Larry. "Faculty Culture and Bibliographic Instruction: An Exploratory Analysis." *Library Trends* 44.2 (1995): 339–367.

Heiman, Rachel J. "The Ironic Contradictions in the Discourse on Generation X or How Slackers Are Saving Capitalism." *Childhood* 8.2 (2001): 274–292.

Holliday, Wendy, and Britt Fagerheim. "Integrating Information Literacy with a Sequenced English Composition Curriculum." *Portal: Libraries and the Academy* 6.2 (2006): 169–184.

Hornblower, Margot. "Great Xpectations." *Time* 9 June 1997: n.p. Web. 26 Feb. 2010.

Howe, Neil, and William Strauss. *Millennials Rising: The Next Great Generation.* New York: Vintage Books, 2000.

Ivey, Robert T. "Teaching Faculty Perceptions of Academic Librarians at Memphis State University." *College and Research Libraries* 55.1 (1994): 69–82.

Jastram, Iris. "What is Information Literacy Anyway?" *Pegasus Librarian.* 7 Dec. 2009. Web. 28 Feb. 2010.

Kotter, Wade R. "Bridging the Great Divide: Improving Relations Between Librarians and Classroom Faculty." *The Journal of Academic Librarianship* 25.4 (1999): 294–303.

Kraus, Stephen J. "Gen Xers' 'Reinvented Traditionalism.'" *Brandweek* 5 June 2000: 28. Web. 28 Feb. 2010.

Lawson, Steven. "Information Literacy: A Non-Definition." *See Also ... A Library Weblog by Steve Lawson.* 7 Dec. 2009. Web. 28 Feb. 2010.

Manuel, Kate, Susan E. Beck, and Molly Molloy. "An Ethnographic Study of Attitudes Influencing Faculty Collaboration in Library Instruction." *The Reference Librarian* 43.89–90 (2005): 139–161.

Mathews, Brian S. "The Inevitable Gen X Coup." *Library Journal* Mar. 15 2006: 52.

_____. *Marketing Today's Academic Library: A Bold New Approach to Communicating with Students.* Chicago: American Library Association, 2009.

McGuinness, Claire. "What Faculty Think — Exploring the Barriers to Information Literacy Development in Undergraduate Education." *The Journal of Academic Librarianship* 32.6 (2006): 573–582.

Missner, Emily. Personal Interview. 18 Jan. 2010.

Mosley, Pixey Anne. "Mentoring Gen X Managers: Tomorrow's Library Leadership is Already Here." *Library Administration and Management* 19.4 (2005): 185–192.

_____. "Shedding the Stereotypes: Librarians in the 21st Century." *The Reference Librarian* 37.78 (2003): 167–176.

_____, and Wendi Arant Kaspar. "Making the Good Hire: Updating Hiring Practices for the Contemporary Multigenerational Workforce, Part One." *Library Administration and Management* 22.2 (2008): 92–99.

Murray-Rust, Catherine. "Should Librarians Get Tenure? Yes, It's Crucial to Their Jobs." *The Chronicle of Higher Education* 30 Sept. 2005: B10.

Osif, Bonnie A. "Generations in the Workplace." *Library Administration and Management* 17.4 (2003): 200–204.

Owusu-Ansah, Edward K. "Beyond Collaboration: Seeking Greater Scope and Centrality for Library Instruction." *Portal: Libraries and the Academy* 7.4 (2007): 415–430.

Ruch, Will. "How to Keep Gen X Employees from Becoming X-Employees." *Training and Development* 54.4 (2000): 40–43.

Sacks, Peter. *Generation X Goes to College: An Eye-Opening Account of Teaching in Postmodern America.* Chicago: Open Court, 1996.

Stephens, Michael. "Participatory Culture & User Generated Content: Reference Services in the 2.0 Age." Reinvented Reference III. RUSA MARS/RSS Preconference, ALA National Conference. Washington, DC. 22 June 2007. Keynote address.

Stevens, Christy R. "Beyond Preaching to the Choir: Information Literacy, Faculty Outreach, and Disciplinary Journals." *The Journal of Academic Librarianship* 33.2 (2007): 254–267.

Strauss, William, Neil Howe, and Peter George Markiewicz. *Millennials and the Pop Culture: Strategies for a New Generation of Consumers in Music, Movies, Television, the Internet, and Video Games.* Great Falls, VA: LifeCourse Associates, 2006.

Wang, Rui. "The Lasting Impact of a Library Credit Course." *Portal: Libraries and the Academy* 6.1 (2006): 79–92.

Wilder, Stanley. "Information Literacy Makes All the Wrong Assumptions." *The Chronicle of Higher Education* 7 Jan. 2005: B13.

Wittberg et al. "Reeling in the Faculty: Baiting the Information Literacy Hook." ACRL 14th National Conference. Seattle, WA. 13 March 2009. Panel Discussion.

Zill, Nicholas, and John Robinson. "The Generation X Difference." *American Demographics* Apr. 1995: 24–32.

X Marks the Spot

Rebecca Feind

The very concept of Generation X is one that defies scrutiny, lest its reality disappear, much like the idea of consumer confidence. If you look too closely, its chimerical nature seems to become its most defining quality, as no one trait can possibly encompass all the individuals born between 1965 and 1982. For the sake of argument, let's consider the broader issue of Gen X librarians by using the age old problems of the generation gap, defined by the Oxford Dictionary of English (revised edition) as "a difference of attitudes between people of different generations, leading to a lack of understanding." Or as social science researchers Twenge and Campbell put it, "there are true differences in generations. Growing up in the 1990s was a fundamentally different experience from growing up in the 1970s or especially the 1950s" (863). What fundamentally different experiences shaped the library users who were born between 1965 and 1982 who are now working in libraries? For the past fifteen years, and for roughly the next thirty-five, Generation X has already or will become the provider of information to library users. For those of us who entered the library profession in the early 1990s, the library catalog was in the midst of transforming from a highly standardized print tool to an online version that itself has been reinvented from text to hypertext. We learned about print indexes in library school and even as we were learning the subject-specialized periodical indexes, those tools were migrating to CD-ROMs. In my professional lifetime of sixteen years, I have learned and used reference tools in multiple formats. Generation X librarians are conditioned to the constant change in technology in our profession because that is what we've always known. In the midst of that change, standard reference tools transformed but also became touchstones for providing effective reference service. Bibliography remains the constant in the world of changing modes of access.

Why would attitudes in librarianship be shaped by a generation gap, and why is that important? Consider these questions: How old were you the first time you used a photocopying machine? How old were you when you first saw a web browser? How old were you when you watched the Space Shuttle Challenger explode? Have you purchased the same song on a cassette tape, a compact disc, and as an mp3 file? Besides the obvious, the Internet, a.k.a. "the interweb," itself a Gen Xer if we accept that the Internet that we know as it exists today came into existence in 1969, what are the fundamental differences in how we access information, and how have those differences influenced this cohort as practitioners?

As I have developed my professional skills, I have watched and experienced library technologies grow in complexity. I think back to the not so distant days when periodical indexes were split — most recent years electronically, previous years in print, and before that, when periodical indexes were only available in print format. It was so easy to know which journals an index covered; simply flip to the front of a volume and check the list. Now librarians have to contend not only with which journals a database indexes, but exactly which years are indexed or contain full-text, and the depth of the full-text provided. Let me be clear — I am not advocating a "good old days" mentality based on a personal appreciation of paper. I remember exactly how time consuming a search in sources like *America: History and Life* or *Historical Abstracts* could be, especially when the most recent four years had not yet been collated into a five-year index. If ever an index was meant for digitization, it is an ISI citation index. However, the level of engagement with a print source required thinking about facets of a topic as a necessary time saving strategy for conducting an effective search. Deciding which sources to consult required prioritization of the search results. Even when periodical indexes became electronic, there was still a stately pace to searching the CD-ROMs, writing out search strategies, and waiting ten or fifteen minutes just for the results to display, plenty of time for the searcher to mull over keywords and anticipate the next step in the process. Now, a keyword search in a database such as *Engineering Village* can retrieve forty years worth of citations in moments, which can then by sorted in a myriad of delightful ways. Peer reviewed, type of source, specified date range? Grand improvements indeed.

So where's the clash of attitude in an environment of ever changing digital access? It is in the expectation that locating information will be inherently easier when so much more of it is available. Being a subject bibliographer is all the more challenging when there is so much more information available and one is called upon to make websites linking to it "easy." Frankly, it isn't easy, and that's not just the technology or the stereotypical Gen X attitude talking. Many of our current digital tools are built on content that was constructed using very specific sets of rules, so the access points within online catalogs and indexes don't necessarily lend themselves to becoming magically more effective simply because the data has been transferred from a print to electronic platform. In many situations, the databases are still searching representations of information, not the information itself. Knowing when a database is searching the full text of a body of information versus the representation of a body of information, and knowing how to negotiate representation of concepts through controlled vocabulary, is something a Generation X librarian should be prepared to do, as we experienced the transition of major library tools from print to electronic contexts. Our ongoing role will be to choose, create, and promote research tools that make it clear to the user exactly what is being searched.

When I began as a graduate student at University of Missouri in 1991, a blinking cursor was the face of the online catalog terminal — it was necessary to type "LUMIN" just to bring up a menu. In 2010, the conversation has turned to enhanced web based interfaces for library catalogs. However, online public access catalogs and integrated library system are new on the scene in the recording of human knowledge, and how they are used today as search tools has gone beyond the scope of their original construction. In his entry "Online Public Access Catalogs" in the *Encyclopedia of Library and Information Science*, Kevin Butterfield gives a good explanation of the emphasis on utility and the role of standards in this significant transformation from card catalog to database, pointing out that in the history of online catalog development, "the development of Integrated Library Systems (ILS) and OPACs has been primarily a response to the problems of production and maintenance within libraries. Automated authority control, inventory tracking of serials, circulation and acquisitions were among the initial reasons for their development" (2269). As with every piece of technology, there are intended uses and the unintended uses that arise once a tool is produced. It is easy, and perhaps natural, for users to assume that when they are searching an online catalog, they are searching the full text of the information it indexes, rather than the representation of information. As Butterfield explains, "Keyword searching within OPACs has become problematic. Web search engines lead users to believe that OPACs provide deeper access to content than they actually do. The OPAC keyword search is dependent upon the key words being used within the MARC record" (2271). Librarian Thomas Mann clarifies, "If someone wants books on any subject, he or she must be able to determine which books are relevant solely from the brief catalog records that represent the books within the computer catalog" (48). The conflagration of bibliographic databases jostling against each other on the World Wide Web makes the landscape of searching inherently more complex, as library users now need to know if they are searching representations of knowledge or the full-text of sources.

In her article calling for enriched use of metadata in bibliographic records, "Scope of the Library Catalog in Times of Transition," Jina Choi Wakimoto addresses the need to recognize the impact of user expectations on future design of online catalogs without abandoning the core principles of cataloging. Wakimoto agrees with Butterfield that some users of library catalog databases have been influenced by the appearance of Internet search engines, but points out that these are not the only clients of the library catalog. She states, "We have 'Net-generation users who are accustomed to the simplicity of the Google interface, are content to enter a string of keywords, and want only the results that are available online. On the other hand, we have sophisticated, experienced catalog users who understand the purpose of uniform titles and Library of Congress classifications and take full advantage of advanced search functions" (412). This distinction between the expectations of generations of library patrons contrasts with the limitations of the traditional role of the Library Catalog as a standardized tool.

Wakimoto's article articulates the role of the local library catalog as a tool that is specific to the library's user community. "What distinguishes the catalog from the Web is the quality of the resources, considered valuable to that library's users, carefully selected by subject specialists in the discipline to serve the curricular and research needs of the university's students and faculty. Providing appropriate and context-sensitive resources for the local users is what makes the catalog viable and valuable" (412). This also contrasts with the historical role of a card file catalog, which could be filled with cards distributed from a national service. It also contrasts with the idea of filling a local catalog with MARC records downloaded from a vendor. While technology offers the possibility of increased access and enhanced inventory control, technology has not solved the problem of improving subject access without the intervention of a skilled cataloger.

Even if enhanced subject access was not part of early ILS' development, and how to enhance subject access remains a crucial discussion at this time, the emergence of online catalogs coupled with the rise of the Internet allowed for previously unheard of access to the representation of remote collections. Generation X came of age in an era of enhanced access to books, with state consortiums like Illinet, Ohiolink, and Melvyl providing students and faculty with previously unheard of access to huge collections. In 1991, access to OCLC was on a dedicated terminal and required knowing how to craft search statements in strings of 4, 3, 2 characters. Library users with appropriate passwords can search WorldCAT at their convenience. Information overload was creeping into the library user experience years before the sparkly distractions of Facebook and YouTube had entered mainstream experience. The role of bibliography is paramount in an era of increased information access and needs to be applied in conjunction with other traditional tools, such as controlled vocabulary and reference sources, in order to help researchers identify relevant resources.

While online catalogs have evolved from print sources to databases, and the invention of the web browser turned searching the Internet into an explosion of graphics, reference sources have also been increasing in number, but often in their typical quiet, print based way. As scholarship has become broader and deeper in scope, and topics previously not covered by reference literature have received attention, the number of subject specific reference sources has grown. Reference sources such as the six-volume *Encyclopedia of African-American Culture and History: The Black Experience in the Americas* (2006) or the two volume *Encyclopedia of Gender and Society* (2009) reflect new areas of scholarship and publishing. ARBA Online, the database of reviews of reference sources, originally known as *American Reference Books Annual*, documents the available wealth of reference tools that reflect the growing body of knowledge. The printed *Guide to Reference Books*, affectionately known as "Sheehy," "Mudge" or "Balay" depending on your generation, has transformed into the database http://guidetoreference.org and expanded its scope to include reviews of online as well as printed sources. Generation X librarians, as a group, are first-hand witnesses to growth and accessibility of knowledge and have also experienced what might be termed the "side-effects" of seeing knowledge being alternately freed and trapped by changes in technology. The excitement and elation factor has been taken to an elaborate extreme. While we and our patrons were at one time delighted to see, on a flickering screen, the catalog record for a book held remotely; now we and our patrons sigh heavily if we can't immediately access the full text, either because the item has not been digitized, our library does not own access to it, or our wireless connection suddenly ends.

As librarians, we should pay attention to our own experiences and expectations of technology and gather information on our patrons' expectations of library technology to inform decision-making. The consumer culture values of ease and convenience are in direct conflict with the financial role of copyright and the commoditization of information. Rather than allowing the rapid pace of technological developments to punch holes in the relationships between future and practicing librarians, the opportunity to reflect on the most effective advances in library technology can be the glue to sustain and build our professional community and practices.

WORKS CITED

Butterfield, Kevin. "Online Public Access Catalogs." *Encyclopedia of Library and Information Science.* Ed. Miriam Drake. New York: Marcel Dekker, 2003. 2268–2273.

"Generation Gap." *The Oxford English Dictionary.* 2nd ed. 1989.

Mann, Thomas. *The Oxford Guide to Library Research.* 3rd ed. New York: Oxford, 2005.

Twenge, Jean, and Stacy Campbell. "Generational Differences in Psychological Traits and Their Impact on the Workplace." *Journal of Managerial Psychology* 23.8 (2008): 862–877.

Wakimoto, Jina Choi. "Scope of the Library Catalog in Times of Transition." *Cataloging & Classification Quarterly* 47.5 (2009): 409–426.

Stuck in the Middle with You: Generation X Librarians

Lisa Carlucci Thomas and Karen Sobel

There is nothing glamorous about being in the middle. Middle managers rarely occupy the spacious corner offices. The middle of the ladder just doesn't compare to the view from the top, the monkey in the middle never wins, and most people prefer not to get in the middle of something or stand on middle ground. Yet, despite these stereotypes, in the middle is an important place to be: it's a supportive, essential, transitional position where one both actively learns and actively teaches. In today's library, Generation X librarians are the middle generation of the workplace. Librarians from the Baby Boomer generation continue to have a strong presence in the profession and many hold senior administrative positions. Meanwhile, an influx of fresh new librarians from Generation Y (also known as the Millennials or the Net Generation), brings different sets of skills, experiences, and expectations to the work environment. Concurrently, the concept of "the library" — its role, place, purpose, and future — is in the middle of a great debate, fueled by the rapid advancement of technologies, changing social and communication norms, and an ever-expanding realm of digital content. These changes cross generational boundaries, affecting everyone seeking or providing access to information.

Each generation offers different perspectives about workplace culture and brings different attitudes about the tools and technologies in libraries today. These varying viewpoints develop from a combination of knowledge gained through personal experience, educational training, and zeitgeist. Baby Boomers have decades of experience working with print collections and library automation, while Generation Y newcomers have used computers and online tools since preschool. Generation X librarians were trained in the print world and experienced the shift from print-centered to electronic research during formal education. Most Gen Xers adapted to the evolving digital research environment during high school, college, or graduate school. They know firsthand what it feels like to struggle with academic research needs while simultaneously figuring out new technologies. Moreover, they understand the challenges of incorporating digital technologies into the library, and recognize the practical, often contradictory, realities of stewardship of information and modernization of related services.

This chapter provides an overview of the unique strengths of Generation X librarians and their role in bridging the different attitudes, ideals, and expectations of the multigenerational library. Three themes are addressed: 1. "Show & Tell or Show & Do?"— Generation X at Work; 2. "Duck, Duck, Google"— Adapting to New Technologies; and 3. "Building Bridges, Building Consensus"— Communication & Mediation. In summary, this chapter highlights the essential and purposeful place of Generation X librarians in libraries today and considers the influential ways this generation is leading from the middle and transforming modern libraries.

"Show & Tell or Show & Do?"— Generation X at Work

Much has been written about the interactions of Boomers, Gen Xers, Millennials, and their collective predecessors, the Traditionalists, in the library workplace. Traditionalist librarians developed the structures and systems of the twentieth century library based on the professional vision and values of the generations before their own and bequeathed this legacy to subsequent generations. With Traditionalist librarians now past retirement age, they have become a minority generation in libraries, leaving Baby Boomers, Generation X, and Millennials to take on and negotiate new intergenerational challenges.

In the work environment, Boomers are often characterized as idealistic and competitive, having grown up during a time of economic prosperity and academic opportunity. Generation X is described as independent, skeptical, and more flexible in adapting to change than Boomers. Millennials are considered to be collaborative and optimistic employees; they are experienced multitaskers from the beginning of their professional careers. Jason Martin's article on generational diversity in the library outlines these characterizations in detail and describes ways that "each generation brings its own sets of values, rules, and etiquette to the library" (9). Martin states it is "important to [Generation X] to evaluate people based on their merit rather than experience" (9). This value has allowed Gen X librarians to develop into excellent generational mediators as they have matured in the profession. Gen X librarians facilitate information sharing when communication gaps exist between Baby Boomers and Millennials, and support and advocate for intergenerational awareness and skill development in library workplaces.

Nowhere are these strengths more apparent than when examining matters related to technology. Technological innovations over the last 35 years, such as library automation, networked data sharing, electronic communication, the Internet, and the social Web, have revolutionized the concept of the library. These rapid changes have accelerated the rate at which the generational skill gap is growing in the library workplace, and Generation X librarians are playing a central role in bridging that gap. Martin identifies Gen Xers as "adaptable, independent, and creative people who are well versed in technology" (9). Lancaster's description emphasizes Generation X's eagerness to "improve processes, to automate functions, to make things run better," "to use what they learned in school to the library's best advantage," and "to keep learning" ("The Click and Clash of Generations" 38). Kipnis and Childs reported that while "each generation is unique," members of Gen X and Gen Y have "overlapping traits," such as confidence in searching online resources, preference for visual learning tools and multimedia, and a desire for collaboration and customization in information sharing environments (26–30). This similarity allows Generation X to relate to and support the styles and attitudes of the Millennials effectively, as well as facilitate communications across generations, promote peer-to-peer skill development, and otherwise foster an environment supportive of change and technological advancement.

"Duck, Duck, Google"—Adapting to New Technologies

Generation X has a particular advantage in that their technological expertise was gained over time and through necessity during their formative years. This generation of librarians gained familiarity and developed their skills at the point of need due to the introduction of computers for research and productivity during their formal education. This contrasts with both the Baby Boomers, who primarily learned computer skills after completing their degrees, and with Millennials, whose interaction with computers and other technologies often began in early childhood. While Millennials' facility with technology has received much attention and study, Thomas and McDonald disregard the idea that Millennials are "any more intuitively skilled than other groups in finding or understanding information" (96), or, by extension, any more knowledgeable about appropriate applications of information technologies in libraries. Generation X librarians have developed their knowledge and expertise in this area through their firsthand experience gained both as students and young librarians, as they were required to become fully versed in the print and the digital information environments.

Since most Generation X librarians were required to gain functional familiarity with hardware, software, email, the Internet, and other computer technologies concurrently with their academic and professional development, they have the special ability to empathize with those facing the challenges of learning to navigate print and electronic content in library collections. They've had the experience of having to write a research paper using Microsoft Word software while simultaneously learning about unfamiliar subject areas, building research skills, and figuring out the mechanics of the computer. This is a challenge that Baby Boomer librarians or Millennial librarians generally did not face as students, due to the respectively lacking or ubiquitous roles of technology during the times of their educations. Of course, personal experiences vary dramatically by a librarian's generation and his or her specific placement within their generation, as well as individual skills and interests — there is no "one-size-fits all" assessment.

Still, there is no doubt that Generation X came of age academically at a time when information technology was emerging on the educational scene. A whirlwind review of popular and professional articles from 1970 through the mid–1980s shows growing support for incorporating computers into both K–12 and higher education. Interestingly, educators proposed teaching computer skills to that whole range of students from the start. Even in the early 1970s, major publications such as *The Education Digest* were discussing the necessity of computer education, as well as proposed methodologies ("Use of Computers for Instruction" 49). A few forward-thinking publications, such as *Popular Electronics*, were discussing computer skills as a type of information literacy far before this idea reached the mainstream (Salsberg 4). By the late 1970s, the popular press, including *U.S. News and World Report*, had begun frequent discussion of the prevalence of computers on school and college campuses ("Some Lessons for the Decade Ahead; Students Learn How to Study — and Like It" 79). Within a very few years, educational publications had moved into in-depth discussions of using computers to teach a variety of subjects at many levels. (Hennings 41–34, Kiester 56–58). Meanwhile, a *Saturday Evening Post* article discussed computers as a modern "toy," drawing parallels with model train sets of the past (Kohl 34–36). It discussed programming as a modern form of teen entertainment (Kohl 34–35), and provided parents with surprisingly modern guidance on computer terminology (Kohl 36). *Science Magazine*, circa 1982, somewhat cynically lauded Apple Computer's plan to give one computer to each U.S. K–12 school (Norman 1484–1485), while *Time* was already stating that having a small number of fairly inaccessible computer labs in schools did students very little good (Van Voorst 69). This was one of the earlier popular articles to discuss computers as a necessity, even in cash-strapped schools (Van Voorst 69).

Remarkably little retrospective commentary has been written on Generation X's formative experiences with technology, as well as the societal factors that shaped these experiences. However, data from the time period reveals important financial factors that led to less home computer ownership. Much of this effect stems from the relatively higher costs of computers in the 1970s through the early 1990s — the years that Generation X filled schools and universities and received much of its education. Members of Gen X will remember that computers and computer labs were often considered a rare novelty in schools or were not available at all to due to the high cost. This expense proved challenging to institutions of all levels, from elementary schools to universities.

During the 1980s and early 1990s, different types of computers were marketed for the office and the home. Home computers were primarily designed for word processing and games. Office computers had significantly more RAM and applications. During the 1990s, home and office computers merged, but divisions arose between desktop and portable computers. A price divide also emerged between lower-priced and premium-priced computers. Representative prices are shown on opposite page.

Information professional Marisa Urgo provides interesting statistical analysis and commentary on Gen X's experience with computers. She writes, "In 1984, 15.3

Year	Mean income for all households in the U.S.	Representative sample computer price
1970	$10,001	"Kitchen Computer," the first home computer, $10,600. (http://www.islandnet.com/~kpolsson/comphist/comp1969.htm)
1975	$13,779	IBM 5100 Portable Computer, $8975–$19,975. (http://www.islandnet.com/~kpolsson/comphist/comp1975.htm)
1980	$21,063	Digital Equipment announces the DEC Datasystem 408 computer. U.S. $8,995. Features built-in monitor, keyboard, and printer. (http://www.islandnet.com/~kpolsson/comphist/comp1980.htm)
1985	$29,066	Home: At the Winter CES, Atari introduces the Atari 65XE computer, with 65xx processor and 64 kB RAM. It is to replace the Atari 800 XL. U.S. $120.Office: Apple Computer officially renames the Lisa 2/10 computer as the Macintosh XL. U.S. $3,995. (http://www.islandnet.com/~kpolsson/comphist/comp1985.htm)
1990	$37,403	Home: IBM introduces the IBM Personal System/1 computers, with 10 MHz 80286 processor, built-in VGA, and monitor. U.S. $999 to U.S. $1,999.Office: Toshiba announces the T1000XE portable computer. It features 2 MB RAM, and 20 MB hard drive. Weighs 6.2 pounds. U.S. $2,699. (http://www.islandnet.com/~kpolsson/comphist/comp1990.htm)
1995	$44,938	Home and Office: IBM unveils its new IBM PC 300 desktop systems, with 75 MHz and 90 MHz Pentium CPUs. Complete systems start at U.S. $2,000. (http://www.islandnet.com/~kpolsson/comphist/comp1995.htm)
2000	$57,135	Home and Office: Compaq Computer and Gateway unveil personal computers using the 1 GHz Athlon processor. Complete systems start at U.S. $2,500. Premium: Apple Computer introduces introduces the PowerBook G3/500 portable computer. It features 500 MHz G3 processor, 128 MB RAM, ATI Rage Mobility 128 graphics controller, 6 GB hard drive, DVD-ROM drive. U.S. $3,499. (http://www.islandnet.com/~kpolsson/comphist/comp2000.htm)

Source: Income figures from http://www.census.gov/hhes/www/income/histinc/h05.html. Computer prices from Ken Polsson's *Chronology of Personal Computers* http://pctimeline.info/

percent of all 3- to 17-year-olds had access to computers; by 1993 that number had doubled to 31.9 percent. It is not insignificant that during this ten-year period, Generation Xers aged from early teens into twenty-somethings" (Urgo 106). She furthers her discussion by noting that members of Gen X often display both an ease with learning new technologies and a positive attitude toward them (Urgo 106–108). Interestingly, she later touches on a theme that many Generation X librarians mention off-hand: that they value time away from technology. Urgo notes, "Generation Xers are not necessarily burdened by technology or the change it creates, but we are also not so enamored or awed by it that we become overwhelmed. For most Generation Xers, information and information technology is a fact of life, as much a part of our day as going to the store or calling a friend on the phone" (Urgo 158).

Gen X librarians performed research in variety of formats throughout their lives.

They have considerable respect for Baby Boomers' facility with print resources and traditions, having studied in libraries in the pre-digital age, and having apprenticed under their advisement as new professionals. Likewise, Gen X librarians and younger Baby Boomers often have an advantage with electronic formats, having adjusted to the transition of using older or now obsolete formats over time. Thus, Gen X's experience proves very useful when a patron comes in with an old CD-ROM or a 5.25-inch disk. Rachel Singer Gordon makes related commentary in her book *The NextGen Librarian's Survival Guide.* She cites a 30-something librarian who responded to a question on Gordon's survey with: "I feel as if I straddle both 'old' or traditional librarianship (I used card catalogs until college) and newer technologies and theories (I've worked on the Web for years and feel comfortable with and enjoy all the new ways of communicating). I like the idea of being a bridge between library theories and the world of technology we find ourselves in" (Gordon 5–6). A recent Facebook status update from librarian Ahniwa Ferrari echoes this sentiment. He wrote, "Ahniwa Ferrari bridges the gap between analog and digital" (Status Update, 29 Jan. 2010). Ferrari, born in 1980, is the Online Resources Consultant at the Washington State Library. When asked to elaborate on his Facebook status update, he replied, "I also bridge the gap between Gen X and Millennial (depending on whose numbers you use), though I identify more with Gen X (most of the time).... I work with a great team of pretty progressive librarians, but still have the role of keeping them informed about uses of new(ish) technologies" (Email, 28 Feb 2010).

Of related and significant interest to librarians is the accessibility of information. Gen X librarians have been locating information on the Internet since early in their careers, if not before. Those using the nascent Internet were naturally wary of information posted online because few authoritative Web sites or databases were available. Gen X librarians learned through trial and error that information may be freely available if one knows where to look, but one needs to search strategically and develop a critical eye for useful, relevant, authoritative sources.

"Building Bridges, Building Consensus"— Communication and Mediation

Here's an experiment. Find several colleagues who were born right around 1980 (or 1960, or 1945 — as long as there are several people from the same range). Serve them all coffee in your office. Ask them a research question and ask them what means they would use to answer it, and then ask them which generation they belong to. Listen to an argument break out. Finally, ask the warring parties to explain their reasoning — unless they've become too heated to discuss their generations rationally, which can happen.

Librarians who are borderline members of Gen X will often defend their generational membership in terms of technology. In an informal survey based on the experiment described above, librarians on both the 1960 and 1980 borders of Gen X argued that they belonged in Generation X because they were "comfortable with but not addicted to technology." This is not generally considered a typical definition of Gen X membership, yet both parties felt that it constituted proof. Such attitudes are striking, since librarians have such extensive contact with literature, cultural artifacts, and current events. Yet, they still refer to the idea that technology is a main indicator of the generational divide. Conversely, Thomas and McDonald cite research indicating that "few differences were perceived" between Millennials and "older others who had become accustomed to the conventions and norms of the same types of cultural, artistic, and technical environments" (97). This leads to the conclusion that despite the belief that technology differentiates the generations, generational expectations of technology may not vary as widely as one might anticipate. Generational differences are often too strongly emphasized, thus overlooking the importance of understanding generational strengths and similarities, "taking full advantage of the benefits" (Martin 4) and discarding tired and counterproductive stereotypes. For example, in Lynne C. Lancaster's article "The Click and Clash of Generations," comparing behaviors of Traditionalist, Baby Boomer, and Gen X librarians, she discusses a Generation X librarian who wore a short skirt and flip flops while presenting to the American Library Association in 2003. Lancaster identifies this librarian's attire as a symbol of Generation X (36). Perhaps this is accurate, or perhaps not; the librarian's choice of attire may have simply been an attribute of youth or personal preference.

Cultural historian Siva Vaidhyanathan has discussed the problems of the very concept of generations in great detail. One of his major arguments is that it takes a lot of money to buy the technologies commonly associated with Generation X and the Millennials. In his article "The Generational Myth," he takes the discussion even further by linking income, college education, and individual preferences. He asks, "Is it just college-educated Americans who are eligible for generational status?" (B7). If a person is not wealthy enough to own the technologies by which we define American generations, does he or she simply fall through the cracks? Librarians of all ages with a fluency in understanding different levels of exposure, familiarity, and engagement with technology are those best able to serve the diverse needs of their institutions and communities. As Lancaster argues, "only by supporting one another will librarians bridge the generational divide and lead their libraries successfully into the future" ("The Click and Clash of Generations" 39).

Conclusion

Generation X librarians serve a critical, positive role as the middle generation of today's library workplace. Their seasoned perspectives and broad understanding of both traditional media and modern technologies are essential to fostering communication and collaboration in the contemporary multigenerational library. Even though generational generalizations are imperfect, cultivating awareness of the cultural and behavioral traits of each group allows libraries to exist and grow productively as diverse workplaces. Despite the infinite potential combinations of income, culture, upbringing, and individual preferences, generations are "joined to one another through the shared experiences of their formative years" (Martin 5). These experiences define each generation's awareness, social patterns, value systems, workplace ethics, expectations, and more.

Only time will tell what legacies Generation X will leave to the field of librarianship. Changing societal values related to library and information science, including immediacy of access, convenience, privacy, and mobility will define the next developments in the field. These changes require librarians to be flexible, adaptable, and sensitive to the static and the evolving norms and expectations of multiple generations. Generation X's strengths in demonstrating a positive yet evaluative attitude toward technology, along with their ability to keenly communicate and teach the generations that precede and succeed them, will facilitate this change and create the foundation for the library of the future. Generation X librarians, leading from the middle, know that it's truly the most exciting place to be.

WORKS CONSULTED

Bridges, Karl, ed. *Expectations of Librarians in the 21st Century.* Westport, CT: Greenwood Press, 2003.

Costello, Barbara, Robert Lenholt, and Judson Stryker. "Using Blackboard in Library Instruction: Addressing the Learning Styles of Generations X and Y." *The Journal of Academic Librarianship* 30.6 (2004): 452–460.

Ferrari, Ahniwa. Email. 28 Feb. 2010.

_____. Status Update. *Facebook.com.* 29 Jan. 2010. Web. 28 Feb. 2010.

Geck, Caroline. "The Generation Z Connection: Teaching Information Literacy to the Newest Net Generation." *Alki* 20.1 (2004): 5–6, 8.

Gordon, Rachel Singer. *The NextGen Librarian's Survival Guide.* Medford, NJ: Information Today, 2006.

Hennings, D. G. "Using Computer Technology to Teach English Composition." *The Education Digest* 46 (April 1981): 41–43.

Hill, Angel, and Jim Johnson. "Stephen Abram on the New Generation of Librarians." *Texas Library Journal* 84.3 (2008): 118–120.

Income Surveys Branch, Housing & Household Economic Statistics Division. Historical Income Tables — Households: Table H-5: Race and Hispanic Origin of Householder: Households by Median and Mean Income: 1967 to 2007. U.S. Census Bureau, 21 Sep. 2009. Web. 23 Dec. 2009.

Kiester, S. V. "It's Student and Computer, One on One [Teaching of Physics at the University of California at Irvine]." *Change* 10 (January 1978): 56–58.

Kipnis, Daniel G., and Gary M. Childs. "Educating Generation X and Generation Y: Teaching Tips for Librarians." *Medical Reference Services Quarterly* 23.4 (2004): 25–33.

Kohl, Herbert. "Should You Buy Your Child a Computer?" *The Saturday Evening Post* 254 (December 1982): 34+.

Lancaster, Lynne C. "The Click and Clash of Generations." *Library Journal* 128.17 (2003): 36–39.

_____. *When Generations Collide: How to Solve the Generational Puzzle at Work.* Synopsis by Rod Cox. 1 March 2004. Web. 30 Sept. 2010.

Libutti, Patricia O'Brien. *Librarians as Learners, Librarians as Teachers: The Diffusion of Internet Expertise in the Academic Library.* Chicago: American Library Association, 1999.

Martin, Jason. "I Have Shoes Older Than You: Generational Diversity in the Library." *The Southeastern Librarian* 54.3 (2006): 4–11.

Norman, Colin. "A Plan to Give an Apple to Every U.S. School." *Science* 215 (19 March 1982): 1484–1485.

Pankl, Robert R. "Baby Boom Generation Librarians." *Library Management* 25.4–5 (2004): 215–222.

Pew Research Center. "Millennials: Confident. Connected. Open to Change." PewResearch.org. 24 Feb. 2010. Web. 30 Sept. 2010.

Polsson, Ken. *Chronology of Personal Computers*. 1 Nov. 2009. Web. 23 Dec. 2009.

Salsberg, A. "Computer Literacy." *Popular Electronics* 19 (1972): 4.

"Some Lessons for the Decade Ahead; Students Learn How to Study—and Like It." *U.S. News and World Report* 31 Dec. 1979: 75.

Stealers Wheel. "Stuck in the Middle." Stealers Wheel. A&M. 1972.

Sweeney, Richard T. "Reinventing Library Buildings and Services for the Millennial Generation." *Library Administration & Management* 19.4 (2005): 165–175.

Thomas, Charles F., and Robert H. McDonald. "Millennial Net Value(s): Disconnects Between Libraries and the Information Age Mindset." *Free Culture and the Digital Library Symposium Proceedings*. Ed. M. Halbert. Atlanta: MetaScholar Initiative at Emory University, 2005.

Urgo, Marisa. *Developing Information Leaders: Harnessing the Talents of Generation X*. New Providence, NJ: Bowker Saur, 2000.

"Use of Computers for Instruction." *The Education Digest* 36 (May 1971): 49.

Vaidhyanathan, Siva. "The Generational Myth." *Chronicle of Higher Education* 55.4 (2008): B7.

Van Voorst, Bruce, Philip Faflick, and Roger Witherspoon. "Peering into the Poverty Gap [Disparity in Distribution of Computers Between Rich and Poor Schools]." *Time* 15 Nov. 1982: 69.

SECTION TWO

LEADERSHIP

Managing Millennials: Advantages of Generation X Librarian Approaches

Breanne Kirsch and Jonathan Kirsch

As management guru Peter Drucker once noted, although "management must have considerable authority, its job in the modern organization is not to command. It is to inspire." (151). Generation X librarians, whether purposely or unconsciously, have embodied this idea while emerging in positions of oversight and increased responsibility in libraries. The uniqueness of Generation X librarians cannot be fully defined without illustrating their relationship to the next generation of librarians. The Millennial librarians who come after them are increasingly looking to Generation X librarians for important precedents and organizational norms. It has been our experience, through working in a variety of academic libraries and knowing Generation X librarian supervisors, that the management approach of our forebears has a tremendous potential to form a meeting of the minds with Generation Y librarian perspectives. Generation X librarians are successfully achieving this through styles of management that include establishing positive relationships, creating flexible work environments, using technology effectively, and resolving conflict.

A thorough literature review of Generation X and Generation Y librarians must begin with the fundamental generational identities constructed during two formative eras.[1] They involve stereotypes with which some librarians are probably familiar. Generation Xers are known as pragmatic but individualistic (McGrath 191). They like to create boundaries between their professional and private lives (Becker 345; Patterson 17). Generation Xers are known for their independence, cynicism, and adaptability, traits which proliferated in an environment of chaotic job markets, hands-off parenting, and technology in flux (Frandsen 34). Generation Y is often portrayed in contrast to Generation X. Where Generation X librarians dislike micromanagement their emerging Millennial colleagues crave structure, supervision, and feedback (Arnold and Williams 18). Current literature juxtaposes the skeptical outlook of Generation Xers and the more trusting, optimistic tolerance of Millennials (Martin 7–8). While such comparisons occur frequently in the literature to differentiate these generations, important implications and caveats are often unexpressed. Differences between two generations do not necessarily signal incompatibility; to the contrary, differences often involve symbiotic or complementary relationships. Discussing the generational dynamics in our own experiences is relevant as libraries increasingly represent generational diversity in the workplace, from the Silent Generation to Millennials. The way that libraries broach and examine generational differences will have an enduring impact on their capacity to operate effectively and serve users professionally (Lancaster 36).

Positive Relationships Through Open Communication

Generation X librarians tend to use management approaches that encourage the development of positive relationships with Millennial librarians because they adopt an open atmosphere in the library workplace. This openness manifests in the willingness of Generation X librarians to explain their decisions. In the past, a lack of readiness on the part of supervisors to explain their decisions has been one of the biggest complaints from younger librarians trying to relate to some library leaders ("Conference Call" 45). A study of ARL directors found that of sixteen ranked individual leadership traits, the one directors valued least, and the one which Generation X librarians wanted to see valued more, was "being committed to explaining decisions" ("Conference Call" 45). Generation X librarians' open, communicative approach creates a positive relationship with Millennials because they know what is being asked of them and why.

For example, as a reference librarian at an academic library, Jonathan was asked to substitute at the last minute to instruct an ESL class in the library. Jonathan's supervisor, a Generation X librarian, had originally been scheduled to teach the class. She explained the detailed scheduling conflicts that required the change. As his superior, she was not obligated to explain herself, but she chose to keep Jonathan fully informed. Although Jonathan was placed in a challenging situation instructing a class with last minute, intensive preparation, at least he fully understood the necessity for doing it. A more traditional supervisor might have requested that a junior librarian do the instruction without much explanation and might have assumed that reasons were irrelevant and that this was simply one of the junior librarian's functions. Although Jonathan would have been glad to do the substitute instruction with or without any explanation, the openness of his Generation X librarian supervisor made him feel more as if he were part of the same team and established a positive note in the work relationship.

Jonathan had a similar positive experience with another Generation X library supervisor. With the typical overzealous attitude of a new librarian, Jonathan approached him about using Google Analytics to track the usage of library Web pages. Unfortunately this idea was not feasible at the time because of impending changes to the library website as part of a university-wide initiative, and he offered an in-depth reasoning of the initiative's thrust and objectives. Instead of minimizing the idea of a younger colleague, Jonathan's Generation X supervisor elaborated more about the organization's goals. He came away from this conversation feeling empowered. In the hands of a less open manager with a different perspective, Jonathan might have felt underutilized.

Two-Way Collaboration: A Tale of Three Projects

The key to creating an open atmosphere, and thereby establishing a positive generational encounter in the workplace, can be underpinned by something as basic as the willingness of Generation X librarians to share their project work with younger colleagues. The success of Generation X librarians in establishing an open atmosphere also comes from an attitude illustrating that they are willing to learn from younger colleagues (Fogg 30). At one University Library, as a freshly hired Millennial librarian, Breanne was given the opportunity to participate in three projects with Generation X colleagues: (1) mass digitization, (2) a transfer student tutorial, and (3) a plagiarism education program. In all these initiatives each generation's ideas and feedback were taken seriously.

For the first project, Breanne's knowledge of Dublin Core allowed her to work closely with a Generation X librarian on creating the metadata for the first digital collection in the academic library. Being an integral part of the mass digitization initiative allowed her to help create a new library resource and be able to visually see the results of my efforts with the Generation X librarian. Combining the Generation X librarian's knowledge of the archives and the history of the University with Breanne's metadata skills allowed them to collaborate on the creation of a digital library. The digital collection is much better than it would have been if either the Generation X librarian or Breanne had tried to complete this project independently.

The second project blossomed into a truly generational-diverse effort where Breanne worked on a tutorial for transfer students to test their information literacy skills with a few Boomer librarians, a Generation X librarian, and another Millennial librarian. They all took different information literacy expectations and wrote scenarios that would test students' skills, sharing them and providing feedback. This resulted in the successful creation of a transfer student tutorial. After the pilot run of this tutorial, they additionally collaborated on creating a follow-up library guide with resources to assist students with scenarios that they had trouble answering. They all had different ways of approaching scenario creation and sharing these different approaches allowed them to create a better tutorial and follow-up library guide.

Subsequently, Breanne took on the role of being one of the go-to librarians for plagiarism cases with a Generation X librarian. They were both new to the area of plagiarism and undertook extensive background research. Professional development was equally important to the two of them and they discussed working on a poster session on plagiarism at a future library conference. Breanne also suggested that they could

complete some research on paper mills and methods used by plagiarism detection software Turnitin or SafeAssign to test for plagiarism. The Generation X librarian agreed
with Breanne and in addition suggested that they could create a library guide to assist
students in defining plagiarism and avoiding it. As a result of their research and collaboration, they are in the process of proposing and planning a plagiarism workshop that
will begin next fall. Due to the Generation X librarian's knowledge of what works well
in their library and Breanne's complementary motivation and energy, they are creating
a new program that will help educate the University's students about plagiarism. Collaborating on this project has been enjoyable since the Generation X librarian has been
open to Breanne's ideas and encourages an ambitious approach. They have worked well
together in coming up with solutions and ideas to combat plagiarism because they function as collaborative equals despite any difference in age or seniority.

Moving from Openness to Flexibility

Generation X librarians create more than just a good management relationship
with their Millennial counterparts. Beyond establishing positive relationships through
openness, they preserve those valuable relationships by fostering a flexible work environment. Although literature stereotypes speak of the rigid Generation Xer who leaves
his or her job promptly at 5:00 P.M., Generation X librarians Jonathan and Breanne
have worked with do not conform to this image. To the contrary, during a mass digitization effort, Breanne worked closely with a Generation X librarian who went out of
her way to make herself available. Since Breanne worked in the evenings, it was difficult
to find shared time for collaboration on the metadata when they could both meet to
discuss the project. The Generation X librarian displayed her flexibility by taking a
later reference shift once a week so that she could work with Breanne in the evening
on the mass digitization efforts. By conveying this work flexibility, she illustrated both
her commitment to the project and a respect for the give-and-take input that allowed
them to be productive together.

Jonathan had a similar experience at another academic library. When his Generation X library supervisor changed the work schedules in the fall, she used Jonathan's
feedback on hours that he would prefer to staff the reference desk rather than giving
preference to seniority alone. In some institutions, seniority entails that junior workers
make all of the sacrifices in their schedule if it is needed to make a project work, but
Jonathan's experience in academic libraries is that a give-and-take exists between Millennials and their older Generation X colleagues.

A flexible work environment also includes the ability to tolerate different
approaches to library work. This means that even in areas where the Generation X
library supervisor and the Millennial librarian have very different perspectives, this does
not interfere with their working relationship or productivity. Millennials seem com-

pletely acclimated to a life where they are "always connected, despite their mobility," and where computers are viewed not as technology, but an embedded, natural part of their world (Skiba 370). Because Millennial librarians feel so comfortable with this ultra-integrated world, the integration of work and personal communications seems logical and even desirable. Conversely, Millennials' Generation X supervisors can feel differently in this area, particularly given their preference for boundaries between their professional and personal lives. This seems to brew with the ominous potential for conflict, but Jonathan's experience in this area revealed compatibility.

After helping students with reference questions at one academic library, Jonathan often gave students his work and personal contact information so that they would have the best opportunity to reach him as soon as possible with future questions. The students were comfortable with this arrangement; it made Jonathan more approachable and Jonathan would often see students that he had assisted come back repeatedly with successive research questions. One of the Generation X librarians used a different approach. She spoke to Jonathan about the issue of mixing work-related and personal email after another Millennial librarian sent a work-related message to her personal email account. She preferred to keep her personal and work-related email accounts deliberately separate. She argued that keeping these different spheres of her life organized separately allowed her to work more efficiently in both areas. Her dedication and helpfulness towards students at the library was no different than Jonathan's, and he acknowledged her approach as equally valid. Reciprocally, she sent work-related email to Jonathan's personal email account at his request and had no reservations about his integrated approach to library business. This case illustrates an important aspect of good management by Generation X librarians: Generation X library managers inured to working with a degree of independence seem willing to tolerate a level of independence in their subordinates. To a Millennial librarian this translates into desirable flexibility in the workplace.

In another library Breanne had a Generation X supervisor that fostered workplace flexibility. The library had acquired an Elmo Document Camera and Projector. As a new librarian, Breanne was excited about using new equipment and requested training on it. Her supervisor was enthusiastic about showing her how to use it for her instruction sessions and requested that Breanne inform her about the experience afterwards. She was flexible and open to change in the regular instruction sessions by making it known that if Breanne thought it was useful, she would recommend that all librarians use it during instruction sessions. This open-minded flexibility allowed Breanne to feel empowered in the possibility that she could improve her work environment and the services she provided.

Workplace flexibility as a generational issue also arises as professional development becomes increasingly important in the ever-evolving library profession. Sometimes small but indelible overtures on the part of Generation X colleagues to their Millennial counterparts can engender positive relations by fostering shared goals of professional development. For example, at one academic library Jonathan and colleagues were given the opportunity to attend a variety of webinars on databases that the library had recently acquired. These webinars were encouraged for librarians at all levels. For one of the webinars regarding Credo Reference, Jonathan did not have the proper space and microphone equipment to fully participate. His Generation X colleague was generous in offering the use of her office and equipment and understood the importance he placed on participating in the webinar.

Whereas more traditional librarians might loathe the idea of a subordinate borrowing one's office for several hours, this Generation X librarian was willing to make allowances for the sake of professional excellence rather than insisting on management prerogatives or privileges. On a related level, a common managerial reaction might have been to downplay the importance of professional development activities without direct applications to immediate library projects, particularly when it calls for the manager to operate outside of traditional comfort zones. Although a place of work, a Faculty Librarian's office is still a personal space and it took flexibility and a willingness to look beyond personal comfort for her to offer Jonathan the use of her office and equipment. Given the scheduling, equipment, and time requirements of the webinar, Jonathan 's Generation X colleague chose the path of being supportive at the cost of privilege or comfort. Jonathan was able to use that webinar experience to more effectively integrate Credo into future instruction sessions, with students becoming the real beneficiary.

Perspectives on Technology: Cooperative Intersections

In addition to creating positive work relationships and flexible work environments, Generation X librarians work well with Millennial librarians through their demonstrated ability to use technology effectively. Insights in the literature lend credence to this idea. Generation Xers are known for using technology to communicate, and they provide learning and mentoring opportunities with their tech-savvy attitudes. In complementary form, the literature finds that Millennials desire clear objectives and view technology as crucial for delivering information (Arnold and Williams 18). How do these two perspectives meet? At one academic library this meeting of viewpoints became a daily strongpoint in library work. On one occasion when Jonathan 's supervisor's meeting ran late and she had course instruction scheduled, she requested that he set up the computer lab for instruction so that she could begin the session on time. They both had similar technical skills required to properly arrange the projector, laptop, and software settings necessary for the presentation. This skill-based level of trust gave them more flexibility and reinforced their work relationship. It is easy to understate the importance of this compatibility. It is not unusual for librarians at a given institution to have varying skill levels in terms of technology. This imbalance can be detrimental to library service. It causes the library supervisor lacking in technical skills to rely too much on their subordinate, even as the subordinate lacks the authority to affect policies that create the technological conditions in which they work.[2] Because Jonathan's Generation X supervisor and he had similar technical skills, this dissonance did not exist. This does not mean that Generation Y librarians should worry whether their Generation X library supervisors have identical skills in using digital tools. Indeed, because Generation X supervisors value a flexible work environment and know how to use technology, they often create perfect mentoring opportunities while working with their Millennial subordinates.

Generation X librarians also have good management relations with Millennials because in the realm of technology Generation X librarians demonstrate lessons from which Millennials can learn. This is underlined by the literature, which identifies a capability among Generation X managers to use technology more intelligently than their younger colleagues. One manager noted a tendency among Millennials to overwhelm their supervisors with emails when one well-crafted message would have been more effective (Fogg 28). At one academic library Jonathan had frequent discussions with his Generation X library manager about the role of technology. One vulnerability among Millennial librarians is that being a tech-savvy generation, they tend to idealize the potentials of technology. Millennials tend to fixate on the newness of technology when we could focus more on the potential to use existing technology more intelligently. Generation X librarians, including Jonathan's supervisor at one academic library, held a healthier and more balanced view of things that informed his work. Her generation is often referred to as "digital adaptives" in the literature because technology changed so significantly between Generation X's coming-of-age years and middle age (Becker 343). Those changes were not necessarily smooth or efficient. Generation Xers are old enough to remember the competing technologies of Betamax and VHS in video formats and understand that new technology does not necessarily connote convenience and success, but also growing pains. Those growing pains were evident in this Generation X librarian's perspective on technology. She felt that new technology should not be implemented in a forced way. Using Facebook, Flickr and other tools as efficient methods to target specific library users had significant potential. However, she felt that too often there existed a tendency to implement technology with the assumption that its 'newness' is what will reach library users, rather than asking the tougher questions that include "how do we reach users, efficiently, and phase in technology gradually if the functionality does not yet meet the library users' needs?"

For example, this college library and many other libraries in its consortium implemented a federated search feature that theoretically allowed their students to search all the databases in one interface. The librarians later discovered fatal flaws in this federated search engine, including the failure to properly search any Ebsco databases. Consequently the librarians made a decision to discontinue the feature until its functionality could actually deliver on what it promised, a truly comprehensive and federated search capability. This is something with which Generation X librarians may have an advantage over Millennials. Since they are more skeptical, as the literature describes, they tend to hold technology to a higher standard.

The Generation X librarian held technology to an even more discerning standard than Jonathan did, ruthlessly identifying weaknesses rather than condoning the technology. This became clear in the way we evaluated databases. Although both of them were adept at identifying desired search features or interface capabilities, Jonathan's Generation X colleague was even more apt to recognize features in the database that only partially delivered their function as advertised. More and more of the databases to which the university subscribed were offering a "formatted citation" template to go with each article, but the reliability of the formatted citations varied. Jonathan's Generation X colleague was one of the first to be aware of the extent to which incorrectly formatted citations hindered our students as much as helped them. As a result they stopped marketing this feature during their instruction sessions.

Effective use of technology cements a good management relationship between Xers and Millennials in ways that can be explained beyond similar technical skills, an Xer's willingness to mentor, and pragmatic Generation X expectations of what technology can deliver. Generation X library managers also understand how to use technology across different library departments. One Generation X library faculty member Jonathan worked with had taken on the responsibility of generating content for the new Open Stacks library blog. When she first asked Jonathan to write an article for the blog he was eager but also surprised. He had not been working at the library for very long, and he felt honored that he had been asked to provide a perspective for the library blog. This Generation X library faculty manager asked Jonathan to write about anything affecting the library that related to library research or library offerings. He ultimately wrote an article about challenges and successes helping a student studying French Christian female identity by using nontraditional French sources. Under her stewardship the library blog became a meeting place of ideas that reflected the library community of faculty and staff, particularly between Generation X and Millennial faculty and staff. Providing a variety of opportunities for workers' perspectives to be shared is crucial, but this requires managers to realize that different settings can be conducive to a particular range of generational preferences (McCaffrey and Garnar 145). As adaptive users of technology, Generation X and Millennial librarians are both comfortable using the online blog as a format for expressing themselves. In the communications-rich world in which Jonathan, Breanne, and their Millennial colleagues have emerged, Millennial librarians gravitate towards their Generation X managers who embrace this kind of connectivity. As the literature demonstrates, Millennials crave meaningful work and recognition. Generation X managers, like Jonathan's colleague in charge of the library blog, make this meaningful work and recognition ever more possible because they are encouraging technological forums of communication in which Millennials can begin to truly feel part of the larger institution. These managers are less interested in the age of the people who work under them than in the ideas and interests they generate. A more traditional approach would call for strict editorial control of any library-wide forum, and allow only supervisors to create content. Generation X, by having an open and collaborative approach to technology, uses that technology to effectively improve employee relations.

Generation X: Diplomats in the Library

The Generation X librarian cohort is also able to construct positive relationships with their Millennial colleagues through their ability to resolve conflict. What makes this skill so important in management? According to literature on generational diversity, Millennials entering the library workplace seldom hesitate to challenge authority when they perceive unfair treatment (Barnes 61). Coupled with this tendency, Millennials also have a propensity to respond poorly to correction through penalties or discipline (Barnes 61). Meanwhile, Generation X has expressed a persona as a "results-oriented" cohort caring little for supervision during their own rise as young professionals (Martin 8). Have Generation Xers, unenthusiastic about being supervised themselves, evolved into effective supervisors in the world of libraries, especially given the demanding Millennial colleagues now entering their workplace? The answer, contrary to conventional wisdom, is "yes."

Almost every academic library has its problematic users. This is inevitable given the large and diverse clientele that the academic library serves. Consequently conflict was not absent in one academic library where Jonathan worked. One professor in particular took a different approach to the library than virtually all other faculty on campus. He interrupted library faculty who were in the midst of helping students with research questions and consistently expected them to give his questions top priority. Librarians calmly refused inappropriate requests in a firm, professional, and non-confrontational manner. After Jonathan's supervisor returned from a long absence, he noticed more drastic improvements in this faculty member's behavior. Jonathan's generation X supervisor earned his respect by the way she defused this potentially divisive situation. As a curriculum committee faculty member with seniority, she provided her full support of the younger librarians, allowing them to politely and consistently correct this faculty member without fearing possible ramifications. She also understood that this faculty member felt emboldened around part-time or younger librarians, and as a result she conscientiously kept younger and part-time librarians informed of the faculty member's behavior. Their collective responses eventually improved the faculty member's behavior, but their success grew from the Generation X librarian's proactive management towards resolving conflict. She alleviated what could have become a significantly distracting conflict by communicating well with those under her and using her authority to bolster the actions of her subordinates.

Another illustration points to the conflict management skills of Generation X librarians. While in library school, Breanne was fortunate to work part-time at the Help Desk. Her Generation X supervisor gave her additional projects after he realized that she was progressing well in her library studies. Traditionally, the library science students at the information desk only answered very basic reference questions, primarily directional questions. Since Breanne was becoming a librarian, she felt prepared for more in-depth reference questions. This lead to a conflict between Breanne, being results-oriented, and the conventional wisdom of the more traditional librarian who worried that library students could not be trusted to work at the actual reference desk.

Breanne's supervisor became a middleman between a Millennial perspective concerned with getting genuine work done and the more experienced librarians who were concerned with the service reputation of the library. By being a willing agent of change in this situation, Breanne's supervisor became an effective force for conflict resolution. She was able to do genuine, in-depth reference work, and her supervisor vouched for the quality of her work to the library director, thus assuring that the library's reputation and service quality remained high. Sometimes resolving conflict requires one party to take a risk. Generation X is in a perfect position to do this in the role of mid or upper management. They have the veteran status and clout while tending to be more connected to their younger colleagues than uppermost management.

Conclusion

Ultimately, if these experiences have revealed different work approaches and perspectives between Generation X and Millennial librarians, these distinctions are complements to be examined rather than disparities to be feared. Generation X librarians practice a style of management that effectively integrates their Millennial colleagues into the profession. Generation X librarians skilled at forming positive relationships, adjusting for dynamic work environments, using technology wisely, and managing conflicts have richly affected Jonathan and Breanne's experiences in academic libraries. When a subsequent generation enters the library profession, Millennial librarians may examine their relationships with Generation X mentors more closely, eventually using these relationships as guides when they manage the next cohort of librarians, bright and brimming with possibilities and ready to be tempered by the hard-won wisdom of elders and experience.

NOTES

1. It is useful to avoid overly zealous stereotypes when discussing a generation. A "generation," however, is meant to connote more than a group of people born during a particular timeframe. The shared experiences and developments of one era create tendencies of perspective in a given population (Martin, 5 & Patterson, 17).

2. This type of dilemma nearly came to fruition at one academic library where I worked. When the IT department made a strong push to remove audio-visual stations from the library and replace them with computers, the library director initially approved the plan, unaware of the technological and cost implications. Realizing that the library would not be able to afford to provide access to essential

materials for the curriculum on a per download basis, the director's Generation X and Millennial subordinates combined in persuading the director to retain the audio-visual stations.

Works Cited

Arnold, Karen, and Kevin Williams. "Playbook: Dealing with Generational Crosstalk." *Parks & Recreation* 43.11 (2008): 18–19. *Academic Search Premier*. Web. 8 Feb. 2010.

Barnes, Ginny. "Guess Who's Coming to Work: Generation Y. Are You Ready for Them?" *Public Library Quarterly* 28.1 (2009): 58–63. Print.

Becker, Charles H. "Student Values and Research: Are Millennials Really Changing the Future of Reference and Research?." *Journal of Library Administration* 49.4 (2009): 341–364. Print.

"Conference call: Gen X bites back; Researcher Arthur Young takes the heat, as GenXer Steve Casburn criticizes the Boomer view of leadership. (Professionalism)(Interview)." *American Libraries* 35.8 (2004): 43–45. *CPI.Q (Canadian Periodicals)*. Web. 19 May 2010.

Drucker, Peter F. *Classic Drucker: Essential Wisdom of Peter Drucker from the Pages of Harvard Business Review*. Boston: Harvard Business Review Book, 2006. Print.

Fogg, Piper. "When Generations Collide." *Chronicle of Higher Education* 54.45 (2008): B18-B20. *Academic Search Premier*. Web. 8 Feb. 2010.

Frandsen, Betty MacLaughlin. "Leading by recognizing generational differences." *Long-Term Living: For the Continuing Care Professional* 58.2 (2009): 34–35. *Academic Search Premier*. Web. 8 Feb. 2010.

Lancaster, Lynne C. "The Click and Clash of Generations." *Library Journal* 128.17 (2003): 36–39. *Academic Search Premier*. Web. 8 Feb. 2010.

Martin, Jason. "I Have Shoes Older Than You: Generational Diversity in the Library." *Southeastern Librarian* 54.3 (2006): 4–11. Print.

McCaffrey, Erin, and Martin Garnar. "Long-range planning across generational lines." *College & Research Libraries News* 67.3 (2006): 144–164. Print.

McGrath, Renée Vaillancourt. "Talking 'bout My Generation." *Public Libraries* 44.4 (2005): 188–191. *OmniFile Full Text Mega*. Web. 8 Feb. 2010.

Patterson, Constance Kindrick. "The Impact of Generational Diversity in the Workplace." *Diversity Factor* 15.3 (2007): 17–22. *Academic Search Premier*. Web. 8 Feb. 2010.

Skiba, Diane J. "The Millennials: Have They Arrived at Your School of Nursing?." *Nursing Education Perspectives* 26.6 (2005): 370–371. *Academic Search Premier*. Web. 8 Feb. 2010.

Generation X Mentoring Millennials

Kathy Shields and Lynda Kellam

"Millennials" has been a consistent buzz word at library conferences, workshops and in journals during the last decade. Many of these efforts have focused on ways to reach, teach, and work with Millennials as if they were entirely new creatures. The existence of different generations is an assumed fact and not problematized. Even outside the library realm, the current literature on the workplace tends to assume that four distinct generations exist — the Traditionals, the Baby Boomers, the Generation Xers, and the Millennials. The focus of the literature is usually on the characteristics that separate these generations from one another and make it difficult for them to work together. Very little attention is given to the overlaps or commonalities between generations. While the generational trope assists us in rethinking our practice as librarians, those points of intersection should be addressed as well. Not all of these generations are as distinct as one may believe.

In this chapter, we explore the intersecting points of commonality between the two most recent generational categories: Generation X and the Millennials. We will primarily focus on the role of Gen X in leadership positions arguing that many Gen X attributes overlap with the newest generation to enter the workplace — the Millennials. As more members of Gen X move into leadership roles, these overlapping characteristics position members of Gen X to be skilled mentors, supervisors, and administrators.

Characteristics of Gen X and Millennials

Although almost every article has a slightly different take when it comes to defining the generations, there are some common themes. Generation X, more commonly known as Gen X, consists of those born between roughly 1961 and 1981 (Strauss & Howe 317). According to a recent Pew Internet and American Life study, twenty percent of the total adult population is within the Gen X generation (Jones & Fox 3). Members of this generation are often described as self-reliant and accustomed to working alone (Ansoorian 35; Gordon 27). They are "global and diverse thinkers, pragmatists, skeptics, and technologically competent" (Gordon 27). As a diverse group themselves, they are more tolerant of diversity than previous generations (Mosley 187). They are not afraid to ask

"Why?" (Mosley 187; Gordon 27). They desire flexibility and prefer to be given an objective and a deadline and then be allowed to execute the task in their own way. Balance between work and personal life is extremely important to Gen X; they do not want to defer personal enjoyment until after retirement (Mosley 187; Gordon 27). In addition, they want work to be interesting and fun as well as meaningful (Mosley 187). Members of Gen X are very straightforward and tend to "call it like they see it" (Mosley 189). They also have a tendency to be impatient, particularly with older employees who are not as comfortable with technology (Mosley 191). They adapt to change quickly and may become frustrated with slow-moving bureaucracy (Gordon 28). They prefer constant feedback rather than infrequent performance reviews (Martin 29; Gordon 28). In addition, Gen X is not afraid to move on when a particular job does not meet their expectations. They are often characterized as bumping heads with members of older generations.

Millennials, generally defined as those born between 1982 and the early 2000s (Strauss & Howe 335), are the current college students and newest entrants into the workforce comprising twenty-six percent of the total adult population (Jones & Fox 3). They share many characteristics with Gen X, as well as some important differences. They are described as "less rebellious" (Slate 11), more optimistic, and more altruistic and civic-minded than their Gen X predecessors (Gordon 28). An even more diverse group than Gen X, distinctions of race, gender, and ethnicity are not important to Millennials. Like Gen X, they want the flexibility to set their own schedules and complete projects in their own way (Gordon 29–30). But although they value independence in some areas, they also value working as part of a group. They recognize their need for support, and as a result, desire regular feedback (Feiertag 458; Fallon 5). Millennials also ask "Why?" and enjoy learning in interactive settings. They are technologically competent, but not necessarily to the level that they or their colleagues may perceive them to be (Feiertag 459). In addition, they value a work/life balance and want work to be fun and meaningful (Fallon 5). They adapt well to change, are discontent with situations that do not meet their expectations and, like Gen X, are not afraid to move on (Martin 42–43).

These categories are problematic; not every Gen Xer or Millennial will display these characteristics. However, these generalizations can be useful for building a greater understanding of the relationship between the two generations and the possibilities for mentoring and collaboration.

Generations in the Workforce

Literature review

Up to now, much of the literature on generations in the workforce has focused on two main areas: the transition of Gen Xers to leadership and management positions and suggestions for improving the multi-generational work environment. Although both mentoring and the similarities between Gen X and Millennials have been touched upon in the literature, neither has been the primary theme of any article, nor have they been discussed together. In addition, most of these articles are not placed within the context of libraries.

Several articles discuss relationships in the multi-generational workforce. The focus is typically on the relationship between Gen Xers and Baby Boomers, particularly the tensions that may arise as Gen Xers move into leadership roles. Gordon and Steele approach the topic within the context of academic advising in higher education. The authors outline the differences between the four generations in the workplace today and suggest ways to recognize and use the "ideas, values, and perceptions" of each to enrich collaboration and create an environment of mutual respect and productivity (30). Ansoorian, Good, and Samuelson describe the characteristics of Baby Boomers and Gen X and discuss how to reconcile the differences between the two generations and prevent conflicts in the workplace, focusing specifically on the educational setting. Houlihan provides suggestions to prepare Gen Xers for taking on leadership roles in the corporate world. Writing from the perspective of the marketing industry, Kennedy discusses how to diffuse conflicts between Boomers and Gen Xers. Mosley examines the impact of Gen X moving into managerial positions in a multi-generational workplace and offers suggestions for smoothing this transition.

Many of these articles also recognize the similarities between Gen X and Millennials. Gordon and Steele's article draws some important parallels between Gen X and Millennials and groups them together in contrast to Traditionals and Boomers. Martin details many of the common characteristics of Millennials and notes a few similarities between them and their predecessor, Gen X. From the beginning of their article, Kehrli and Sopp group Gen X and Millennials together. The authors even go so far as to state that Millennials "[capture] the characteristics of both generations" (113).

Mentoring, in one form or another, is suggested often in the literature as a way to connect members of different generations. Martin provides six "keys" for building strong relationships with Millennials (43–44). One of these keys is to establish a coaching relationship with them, which could be very similar, if not equivalent to, a mentoring relationship. Houlihan, Mosley, and Kennedy all suggest that implementing effective cross-generational mentoring can help Gen X transition more smoothly into leadership positions. Boomers need to mentor Gen X to ensure the emergence of effective Gen X leaders, and Gen Xers are attuned to the need for mentoring (Kennedy 42). Such a program, Kennedy maintains, benefits both groups by allowing each to share information with the other. In addition, "[m]entors slow turnover and increase job satisfaction" (42). Houlihan also implies that the next generation will need similar guidance from Gen X (13). Kehrli and Sopp acknowledge the vital role that informal mentoring can play in building relationships and tearing down misconceptions.

While these articles come close, they do not make the direct link between Gen X and Millennials as ideal mentors and mentees. Similarities between the two groups are highlighted, but none of the articles deal specifically with building a relationship between them. Although Houlihan, Mosley, and Kennedy recognize the value of mentoring, they do not extend it to the newest generation to enter the workforce, Millennials. Martin mentions a "coaching relationship" but does not suggest that Gen X should be the ones to establish this relationship with Millennials (43).

Gen X Mentoring the Millennials

Although a Gen Xer may be in a supervisory role over a Millennial, the focus of this chapter is on the mentoring relationship between the two generations. Supervision has power implications that make it different from mentoring (Manathunga 208). Although neither is necessarily a voluntary situation, supervising is more likely to be an obligation. While mentoring can occur as a result of a formal, institutional mentoring program, it often occurs informally. In either case, it does not carry the same sense of hierarchy that supervising does. Many of the same principles can be applied to supervising Millennials, however, and a mentoring relationship can exist in addition to a supervisory relationship.

As evidenced by the numerous articles that have mentioned mentoring, it can be a valuable tool in virtually any workplace, including libraries. Mentoring can have a tremendous impact on intergenerational communication by providing a bridge between generations (Slate 11). More importantly, it is what both Gen Xers and Millennials want from their work environment. Kennedy claims, "Gen Xers are crazy about mentoring" (42), and Kehrli writes that Millennials "[crave] mentoring" (114). While mentoring does not prevent the mentee from learning some lessons by trial and error, Mosley insists that "[m]entors stop rising stars from making stupid mistakes" (189). This can be invaluable for the mentee's professional growth. Kehrli writes:

> Give them the benefits of your experience, the history and context of a situation, your thorough understanding of the [political] climate, some big-picture thinking, tips on how to deal with that difficult colleague or the inside "scoop." This is the purest form of mentoring you could do without having to label it "mentoring" in the context of a one-on-one formal session [116].

Thus, the mentoring relationship itself does not have to be formal and, in many cases, may be more productive if kept informal.

Mentoring, however, must be genuine. Both Gen Xers and Millennials have a low tolerance for hypocrisy. They do not want a mentor to provide fake praise, give vague, noncommittal answers, and skirt around uncomfortable topics (Mosley 187, 189). They desire and expect clear communication. Gen Xers can meet Millennials' needs for straight answers. However, Gen Xers must be careful that they are not too blunt. Mentees are drawn to mentors "who are warm, good listeners, and unconditionally accepting.

[Mentees] also prefer mentors who are trustworthy, interpersonally sensitive, respectful of values, and able to use and appreciate humor" (Johnson and Ridley 49). Gen Xers need to balance their ability to "tell it like it is" with an understanding of the Millennial's individual personality. By doing so, Gen Xers can build a strong mentor relationship with Millennials that can benefit both groups in numerous ways.

TECHNOLOGY

Technology use, application, and change are the primary areas in which Gen Xers can mentor Millennials. Gen X's familiarity with technology has often been cited in the literature as a cause of tension between Gen Xers and older generations who are less adept with new technology. Millennials, however, expect to use technology and can benefit greatly from the technological savvy of Gen X. Feiertag writes: "Many people in older generations may incorrectly assume that Gen N [Millennials] understands and uses all computer applications when, in reality, the opposite is true" (459). While they may feel confident with certain tools and software for personal and educational use, they need Gen X to share the knowledge that they have gained from using these same tools, in addition to many other ones, in the workplace. Moreover, Gen Xers know how to adapt those tools to the library environment. For example, instead of simply knowing how to use Facebook, Gen Xers can talk about using it effectively for library outreach. Gen Xers can also help Millennials learn how to control their virtual identities through the effective use of social networking and professional blogs and websites.

Gen Xers, as well as newer librarians, have been consistently exposed to new communication tools for professional development. Mailing lists and blogs, such as Beyond the Job (http://www.beyondthejob.org/) or the ALA JobList (http://joblist.ala.org/), are far more effective tools for job searching and professional development than relying on the career sections in the back of print publications. Unlike other generations, Gen X has not had any alternative to these formats. They are comfortable with using them and quick to recommend their favorites to others. In most cases they would question anyone who does not use them for their continuing education and professional development.

As the role of technology in the workplace grows and changes, Gen X can help Millennials develop the skills and gain the experience they need in order to remain marketable. In addition, Gen X can meet Millennials' need to be in constant communication through the use of email, chat, course management systems, social networking, and other means.

LEARNING STYLES

Gen X also has a better understanding of Millennials' learning styles. Like Gen Xers, Millennials want to learn new skills and begin contributing immediately. Gen Xers can allow Millennials to do just that by providing them with challenging activities and projects that have well-articulated purposes and visible deliverables. Although Gen Xers are characterized by their independence, they are accustomed to group work as well and can appreciate that Millennials enjoy collaborating with others. Gen Xers can open doors for Millennials in the professional field by introducing them to other library professionals, co-authoring papers with them, and co-presenting with them at conferences. They can provide Millennials with affirmation when they are on the right track and provide guidance when they falter.

At the same time, Gen X can also appreciate Millennials' need for autonomy at times and their desire to take on increasing responsibility. As they grow professionally, Gen X mentors can help Millennials identify opportunities to expand their knowledge and further refine their skills. Gen Xers also understand that multi-tasking does not necessarily imply a lack of focus on a particular project. Many Millennials, however, do need to learn time management, and Gen Xers can help by providing constant contact to keep them on track without micromanaging. By demonstrating a good work ethic and encouraging mentees to challenge themselves, they can aid mentees in setting a path to professional success.

COMMUNICATION STYLES

Gen X and Millennials also have similar communication styles. Both are quick to ask "Why?" Older generations may incorrectly interpret this as a challenge to authority, particularly from Gen X. In reality, both Gen X and Millennials are curious, especially Millennials. Gen X will answer those questions that others may not, and recognize why Millennials need to ask them in the first place. Furthermore, Gen X will likely provide Millennials with a straight answer and make them feel that they are being included and informed about what is happening in the library

Both generations desire constant feedback and need to be able to communicate in a variety of ways. Gen X can use technology to stay in contact with Millennials and let them know when they are doing a good job or when they may need some improvement. As mentioned earlier, technology can also be a useful tool in keeping Millennials on track and monitoring their progress while still giving them the independence they desire. Gen X may also be more comfortable meeting in informal settings, where mentor and mentee can take the time to get to know one another. Even this small step can go a long way toward building a valuable mentoring relationship.

WORK-LIFE BALANCE

For Gen X and Millennials, work is only part of their identity. They both value a balance between work and their personal lives. As a result, they desire flexibility to manage both. Millennials expect to be able to make their own schedules, rather than be confined to the hours of the traditional workday, and Gen X not only understands that, but has the same expectations. Gen X can also provide counsel to Millennials when they have difficulties juggling their personal and professional lives. While this might be a difficult topic to bring up with a supervisor, the mentoring relationship can provide an outlet for this kind of discussion.

For both Gen X and Millennials, work should be meaningful, but it should also be fun. Both groups are familiar with constant change, and aren't afraid to shake things up and try something different. As leaders and as mentors, Gen X can help create and foster an environment of creativity and innovation that allows Millennials to find both enjoyment and meaning in their work. In some cases, job descriptions and duties could be tailored or shifted to fit both the need of the library and the interests or talents of the individual person. Allowing for creativity and acknowledging their creative insight may also make a Millennial want to stay in a certain position longer.

Workplace Dynamics

Perhaps one of the most valuable areas in which Gen X can mentor Millennials is workplace dynamics. Rather than being a source of conflict, Gen X can instead become a source of cooperation and connection between members of different generations. Gen X has been in the workforce longer and has learned the office culture. Ideally, they have also been mentored by Boomers or Traditionals and can pass on the knowledge they have gained from those older generations to Millennials. In addition, they are in a position to moderate between the Millennials and older generations, since they have an understanding of each. This is especially important for a Millennial who is new to the profession and is not sure how to handle the issues that may arise in a multi-generational work environment. However, even a Millennial that has been in the profession for a few years and is entering a new position can benefit from a Gen X mentor's guidance in navigating a new workplace.

Both Gen X and Millennials are frustrated with slow-moving bureaucracy and have encountered colleagues who are resistant to change. Gen X will, therefore, appreciate Millennials' desire to get things done. They can help them accomplish more because they have an understanding of the internal structure of the work environment — in other words, Gen Xers know how to approach changing practice in their library, which players to include, and which allies to court, both within the library and the larger community or institution. Gen Xers are also likely to treat Millennials as part of the team, valuing their ideas and input, whereas older generations may be quicker to dismiss them as too young and inexperienced to contribute. Millennials need to be included early on, because they have a strong desire and need to contribute to the organization. If they are not allowed to participate fully, then they will likely not remain in the position for long.

Networking

Gen X can also share their network of connections both in and out of the workplace. Gen X can help Millennials utilize the resources of other generations on staff that they might otherwise be unaware of. Hopefully, they have already collaborated with members of other generations, including other members of Gen X, and can help Millennials identify co-workers who might be interested in working on a particular project, or who are already working on projects that the Millennial could join. They can direct them to other members of the staff that may excel in an area or a skill that the Millennial wants to learn more about or develop. In addition, Gen Xers can also connect Millennials with friends and colleagues in the field who could be potential collaborators.

Mentoring, however, is not a one-way street, with all the benefits going to the mentee. Millennials also have something to bring to the table. As Gordon states, Millennials are "optimistic, confident, sociable, moral, altruistic, and civic minded" (28). They are also less individualistic and eager "to celebrate ties that bind rather than differences that splinter" (Slate 11). These attributes can have a positive effect on the more cynical, pragmatic Gen X. While they can benefit greatly from Gen X's experience with technology, Millennials, as "digital natives," can share some of their own knowledge of new tools and trends with Gen X. Moreover, they may provide a perspective on younger library users and their needs and expectations, which could be useful for developing library services and programs.

Conclusion

Gen X and Millennials are certainly not homogenous groups. Although not every Gen X or Millennial will embody all of these characteristics, the similarities that have been noted here should encourage us to shift our focus to the common traits that generations share. As Martin and Tulgan write: "The most successful people in the twenty-first century will be true 'Gen Mixers,' people of all ages who bring to work every day their enthusiasm, flexibility, and voracious desire to learn" (115). In the end, we all want to see our libraries and information organizations succeed. By taking the time to mentor a member of a younger generation, Gen X can promote a collaborative, productive work environment for Millennials and all generations. And Millennials, in turn, will have an example to follow when the next generation is in need of a mentor.

WORKS CITED

Ansoorian, Andrew, Pamela Good, and Dave Samuelson. "Managing Generational Differences." *Leadership* 32.5 (2003): 34–36.

Fallon, Tip. "Retain and Motivate the Next Generation: 7 Ways to Get the Most Out of Your Millennial Workers." *Supervision* 70.5 (May 2009): 5–7.

Feiertag, Jeff, and Zane L. Berge. "Training Generation N: How Educators Should Approach the Net Generation." *Education & Training* 50.6 (2008): 457–464.

Gordon, Virginia N., and Margaret J. Steele. "The Advising Workplace: Generational Differences and Challenges." *NACADA Journal* 25.1 (2005): 26–30.

Houlihan, Anne. "When Gen-X is in Charge: How to Harness the Young Leaderships Style." *Supervision* 69.4 (2008): 11–13.

Johnson, W. Brad, and Charles R. Ridley. *The Elements of Mentoring.* New York: Palgrave Macmillan, 2008.

Jones, Sydney, and Susannah Fox. "Generations Online in 2009." *Pew Internet.* Pew Internet and American Life Project. 28 Jan. 2009. Web. 15 July 2010.

Kehrli, Sommer, and Trudy Sopp. "Managing Generation Y." *HRMagazine* 51.5 (2006): 113–119.

Kennedy, Marilyn Moats. "Learn to Negotiate Office Generational Differences." *Marketing News* 38.7 (2004): 46–42.

Manathunga, Catherine. "Supervision as Mentoring: The Role of Power and Boundary Crossing." *Studies in Continuing Education* 29.2 (July 2007): 207–221.

Martin, Carolyn A. "From High Maintenance to High Productivity." *Industrial & Commercial Training* 37.1 (2005): 39–44.

Martin, Carolyn A., and Bruce Tulgan. *Managing the Generation Mix: From Collision to Collaboration.* Amherst, MA: HRD Press, 2002.

Mosley, Pixey Anne. "Mentoring Gen X Managers: Tomorrow's Library Leadership Is Already Here." *Library Administration & Management* 19.4 (2005): 185–92.

Slate, Brynn Grumstrup. "A Millennial Path to Leadership." *Associations Now* 3.12 (2007): 11.

Strauss, William, and Neil Howe. *Generations: The History of America's Future, 1584–2069.* New York: William Morrow, 1991.

Gen X Takes Over: Managing the Mix from the Middle

Lindsay McVey

It may have been George Bernard Shaw, or more appropriately Dave Sohigian, author of the blog *Gen-X Files*, that said, "The Lost Generation (born 1883–1900) had the unique disadvantage of being young at a time when elders were revered and old at a time when youth was idolized." Generation X (born 1961–1981), or Gen Xers, are caught in the same situation.

Miki Saxon, author of the *Leadership Turn* blog, also comments on the apparent lack of interest in the Gen Xer as a manager or leader. He cites executive retention:

> Two-thirds of executives at large companies were most concerned about losing Millennial employees, while less than half of them had similar concerns about losing Gen Xers ... [but] only about 37 percent of Gen Xers said they planned to stay in their current jobs after the recession ends, compared with 44 percent of Millennials, 50 percent of Baby Boomers, and 52 percent of senior citizen workers. [...] "lack of career progress," was by far the biggest gripe from Gen Xers, with 40 percent giving that as a reason for their restlessness....

Saxon sums this information up by saying, "The economy will turn around. The Boomers may stay in the workforce for now, but they will retire. Millennials are being held back because of the economy and may never catch up, certainly not fast enough to run American enterprise when the Boomers retire. That leaves Gen X, which is being ignored."

But the question is, can Gen X manage across the generations?

Who Are These People and Why Do I Need to Know How to Manage Them?

BABY BOOMERS (BORN 1940–1960)

Baby Boomers love a good cause and believe the world needs change. They love to question authority or rather "they respect authority as long as it is *their* authority"

(Deeken and Webb 213). They are team players and enjoy having meetings to discuss new initiatives. They value in-person communication but don't necessarily like feedback unless it's a monetary bonus or a promotion. "Faced with 80 million cohorts.... Boomers are also highly competitive. Boomers want rewards that show they are getting ahead, whether it meant acquiring a master's degree ... or pushing for that next promotion. Boomers can get flummoxed by the attitude of some Xers who don't care about titles, or who aren't worried about what position they'll hold ten years from now" (Lancaster 37). Probably the biggest hurdle when it comes to managing Baby Boomers is that they have an inability to balance life and work. They live to work (Hammill).

Baby Boomers have begun to feel like the neglected generation. They grew up in a time when it was cool to be them but now they are experiencing misplacement as the library focus shifts to the younger Millennials and what they have to offer. Don't discredit the Boomers before it's too late. This is the generation that redefined the ILS and MARC records by creating the OPAC. They understand the drive and passion that must be dedicated in order to create something worthwhile. Cross-generational mentoring can be very beneficial when working with Boomers. They still want to learn all the time, but they also want respect and to know that they are valued.

GENERATION X (BORN 1961–1981)

Gen X is the smallest generation (approximately 44 million) but also the most educated generation. Gen X is considered the independent generation or "latch-key kids." They're used to coming home and taking care of themselves. They prefer to work independently or collaboratively on projects with constant directional feedback. Gen Xers "are typically comfortable with technology, are independent, are not intimidated by authority, and are creative *but cautious*" (Deeken and Webb 214).

Generation X prefers direct and immediate communication. They don't believe in the corporate structure and they feel everyone should be treated the same. They prefer periodic feedback (when it's convenient!) and for them, monetary rewards can't compare with time off from work or freedom while working. They have the best work-to-life balance of any generation (Hammill). Gen Xers value personal fulfillment and time away from "the job."

Probably the most prominent thing about Generation X is that they are skeptical or cynical about life (think *Reality Bites*) but this in turn has created one of the most defining features of Gen X: They ask questions. Not only do they want to know how to do something, how the OPAC works, how the ILS system works, but Why? (Word to the wise, if you ever encounter a Boomer that responds to "Why?" with "Because that's the way it's always been done" try very hard not to run screaming from the library.) Gen X wants to do things better, faster, stronger and they are very comfortable with change.

Contrary to early stigmas attached to them in the 90s, X is a generation of hardworking and innovative people. Gen Xers are notoriously collaborative workers with an "articulated vision that inspires others, [they] build partnerships within the library or across campus, and recognize interpersonal communication essential at all levels — personally approachable — provide paths — communicate directly when appropriate" (Young, Hernon, and Powell 491).

MILLENNIAL GENERATION (BORN 1982–2004)

The Millennial generation has surpassed the size of the Boomer generation (approximately 72 million) by approximately 3 million and has the lowest parent-to-child ratio. This in turn has made them more family orientated and better at dealing with chaotic situations (Deeken and Webb 215). They value tenacity and are goal oriented. They are very tolerant people having grown up with more cultural diversity and less racism or segregation than generations before them. They are participative decision-making people and enjoy teamwork on projects. They are connected 24/7 to technology and expect their work to follow a similar pattern. They want meaningful work with constant feedback. They have a strong work-to-life balance (Hammill).

The Millennial generation is poised for success. They are constantly complimented for their technological prowess but they lack appropriate mentoring and work-related skills. They are in tune with technology, social networking, and Web 2.0: skills that libraries across the globe are demanding, but Millennials lack structure and boundaries. Millennials need structure and boundaries with freedom. They are a generation that has grown up with locker searches and overbearing parents (Tulgan 65–66). They will need constant reassurance as to their work performance, a need to know they are valued, and a creative license to explore new possibilities. Don't be surprised when, on their second day of employment, they are ready to reinvent the workflow in Tech Services or institute a new policy for research at the Reference Desk. This is a generation that believes it can (and will) accomplish everything before lunch and leave early to go to yoga class.

Why They Like to Work Differently

One of the biggest differences between the generations and their work ethic is the differing opinion of work-to-life balance. Understanding work-to-life balance and how each generation views this will make it easier to motivate and reward library staff. Beginning with the Boomer generation and moving down through Gen X and the Millennials in sequential order, the balance between work and life shifts drastically from one side of the spectrum to the other. The study done by Young, Hernon, and Powell clearly shows that Gen X leaders are "very supportive of employee's work/life balance" (493). But when you are working with different generations, each group has a different idea of a "healthy balance."

BOOMERS

One of the most challenging obstacles when working with and leading Boomers is understanding that they associate their personal identity with their work. "Boomers ... tend to view work as an anchor in their lives and may see Xers as less involved in work because of their work-life orientation" (Beutell and Wittig-Berman 519). Boomers are also notorious for their inability to prioritize their work and say NO! They will take on more than they are capable of accomplishing (and continue to add more and more on top of that). Their lack of time management skills and prioritizing tasks combined with a need to please everyone causes a very unhealthy work-to-life balance.

"So what?" you might say. Let the Boomers work long hours and take on more than they can responsibly handle. This is what they want. As adults, they should know what they can and can't handle, right? Wrong! They aren't aware that they are over-extending themselves. Sure, they're working longer hours, getting less and less accomplished, and not seeing their family, but they don't see it like that. A good manager has to recognize when a Boomer is losing control and step in to help reduce and distribute their workload. Because of the large amount of Baby Boomers vying for employment, they were conditioned to work long hours knowing that if they refused they could be easily replaced. This has also trained them to be people-pleasers and never say no to a job; they are comfortable with over-extending themselves. "If a promotion is available Boomers will tend to take it and then figure out how it affects other aspects of their life while Xers will be more concerned about how everything else is affected before making the decision" (Beutell and Wittig-Berman 509).

A secondary problem caused by their large population numbers — Boomers believe that a 9-to-5 job means coming in early and staying late. They will have a difficult time understanding the supervisor or library director that only works an eight-hour day and leaves each evening promptly at 5:00. A Boomer expects their supervisor to work longer hours because they are conditioned to believe that long hours directly relate to job performance: the longer the day you have, the more work you must be doing. "In their view, the more hours you put in, the more loyal and productive you are" (Houlihan 12). This corresponds directly with their work-overload and lack of prioritizing. Working with a Boomer is a Catch-22; they want the responsibility to work on multiple projects, but the more work they take on, the less they are able to accomplish. Initially this may cause leadership and motivational issues for the Gen X manager, but studies have shown that more Boomers are interested in a healthy work/life balance. They just need someone to show them how to make it work for them. Appropriate mentoring and patience will make it easier for a Boomer to adjust and understand that long hours *do not* equal more productivity. When working with and managing a Boomer, you must help them to prioritize and teach them to say "No!"

Boomers don't like to take time off for fear of replacement or being passed over for a promotion (Hammill). Instead of offering a Boomer vacation time for quality work, a monetary bonus would be a good reward. Many Boomers approaching retirement would like to move into part-time and semi-retirement positions. This concept should be embraced and would greatly help to reduce their loss of knowledge as the largest workforce moves into retirement, effectively taking with them several decades of experience. As a Gen X manager, it will be your responsibility to mentor the Boomers on how to shorten their work hours, take time off, and prioritize their workload.

GEN XERS

Gen Xers probably have the most equalized balance between work and life resting between the workaholic Boomers and the easy-going Millennials. "Gen Xers tend to work only eight- or nine-hour days, they still get the job done because they value results rather than hours." Xers are also comfortable with technology and will use it to provide quicker answers and results (Houlihan 12). When you begin managing Boomers and Xers, this may be a complaint you will hear from the Boomers. Try pairing these two generations together for good mentoring and knowledge exchange on the part of both workers; the older generation will be able to provide valuable experiences and situations for good mentoring and the younger generation can help the Boomers to manage their time more effectively and teach them that longer hours don't necessarily mean better results.

"Xers want challenging work that can be accomplished in a single day working flexible hours" (Beautell and Wittig-Berman 519). Brian Mathews, a Gen X Librarian, comments, "I prefer conversations that are direct and practical. I prefer working on projects over a period of five weeks rather than five years." Gen Xers, as librarians, are more impromptu when it comes to planning sessions and idea sharing. They enjoy constant innovation and brainstorming. Generation X leaders prefer having informal gatherings with small groups than waiting for the larger, formal information sharing sessions that occur with the Boomer manager. "Limit in-person meetings. Offer alternatives like conference calls, video, and web conferencing. For face-to-face meetings, stick to small productive groups and skip long planning sessions" (Auby 63).

Probably the best thing you can do when managing a Gen X librarian is to provide them with empowerment. A Gen Xer prefers to have limited instruction and work their way through, learning from their own mistakes and only asking for guidance when necessary (or in their mind, when they have no other option).

MILLENNIALS

As far as work-to-life balance goes with Millennials, they have swung far to the opposite of their Baby Boomer parents. Not only do they value family life above their work, instead of on equal terms as Xers or as a secondary priority for Boomers, but they want to incorporate their family into their work. And again, just as Boomers are learning to multi-task and prioritize, Millennials have skyrocketed past a healthy ability to multi-task and prefer to do many things at once. Remember, this is a generation raised with instant information and technology that is designed to provide multiple services. (Think cell phones that also play music, go online, check email, take photos, etc.) Millennials are very much the mirror to their technology; individuals packaged to perform multiple functions.

Tulgan discusses how many Millennials are close to their parents and treat them like best friends. Millennials look to their parents for advice about everything. Gen X managers need to recognize this characteristic and understand how to properly motivate a Millennial. In one example, a manager discussed with Tulgan how "my approach is simple: sink-or-swim time now, kids. Just let the real world sort them out" (59). The problem with this, Tulgan explains, is when a Millennial leaves their job (and they will leave and go somewhere else) and you hire a new Millennial, that young person will also bring their parents along too. He says, the irony behind this idea is that the Millennial that is *not* close to their parents may not be a good employee. "Among today's young workers, those who are closest to their parents will probably turn out to be the more able, most achievement oriented, and the hardest working" (59). So on their first day, when they bring their parents in and introduce them to all the staff in Tech Services, Circulation, and Reference, don't be alarmed. They work better knowing they have a good support base at home.

Millennials are comfortable with a rapidly changing environment and this plays well with their need to multitask. Tulgan comments on how "what [they] know today may be obsolete by tomorrow. What is beyond belief today may be conventional wisdom by tomorrow.... A year is long term, and five years is just a hallucination. Short term is the key to relevance. In a world defined by constant change, instantaneous response is the only meaningful time frame" (6). A Millennial employee will expect their work to keep pace with their life. To properly motivate a Millennial they will need room to create and invent but with proper guidance. "Precisely because Gen Yers seem to both disregard authority figures and at the same time demand a great deal of them, leaders and managers often find Gen Yers maddening and difficult to manage" (Tulgan 11). You will need to practice a combination of *In Loco Parentis* as well as empowerment. Provide a Millennial with the structure, boundaries, and guidance they need (but will pretend they don't want) and then step back and allow them to perform and contribute on their own. Don't give up on your Millennial staff. They are very eager to work and want to provide meaningful contributions to your library.

Now What? Management Past and Present

In a study done by Young, Hernon, and Powell, they show that the highest, most valued attribute of Gen Xers as library leaders is to maintain a healthy balance between their work and life. Other highly rated attributes included:

- building partnerships
- strong listening skills
- fairness
- initiative
- trust
- frequent communication and mentoring

Mosley notes, "As they become managers, Generation Xers still put significant value on the balance between their work and personal lives, both for themselves and their employees.... They are concerned and caring toward those whom they supervise and highly tolerant of issues such as family demands and flexible schedules" (Wilcox and Harrell 95). These qualities will provide the support and balance that younger Millennials are looking for: good family values, work that has significance or meaning, and the additional feedback required to keep a Millennial motivated. The more difficult group to communicate with, lead, and manage will be the Boomer group.

The Boomer generation employs a variety of management styles. Probably one of the better management styles is called Management by Objectives in which the goal is "to create empowered employees who have clarity of the roles and responsibilities expected from them, understand their objectives to be achieved and thus help in the achievement of organizational as well as personal goals" (Khilawala). Employee empowerment, communication, and understanding the different values to provide focus and motivation are the keys to good leadership.

POOR MANAGEMENT

- **Autocratic or Authoritarian:** Good luck with this director. They believe that their way is the right way, and more importantly, the only way. (Sound familiar?) This style of management will create discipline, but will quickly "cause dissatisfaction and a lack of creative space." Employees are considered expendable with little interest given to overall job satisfaction. This style of management also holds to the old standard of hierarchical communication from top-level supervisors responsible for reporting to staff.
- **Laissez-faire:** This is the complete opposite of Autocratic. There is no right way with this management style because there is no appropriate leadership or decision-making. Chaos reigns supreme with little thought as to delegation of responsibility. Communication is available but only from all sides and usually in the form of gossip or "Monday morning quarterbacking" without any real substantiation.

BETTER MANAGEMENT

- **Paternalistic:** Similar to Autocratic with authority in the hands of one top individual, but the focus of management is on the employees, not on the library. Again, this style of management is popular with the Boomer generation in that they still maintain total authority but "the employees are the heart of the organization." This management style believes in good communication but lacks appropriate empowerment for employees.

- **Democratic:** For this management style, employees may voice an opinion on company policy, large and small. Representatives from all levels and departments are expected to participate in decision-making and policy implementation for the library. This style of management is often referred to as Participative Management. Communication is an "open-door policy" where confidentiality may not be perfectly adhered to.

- **Collaborative:** This is probably the most popular style of management currently employed by the Gen Xer. It goes against the "command-and-control," or Autocratic type of leadership that the pre–Boomer generation employed, a concept modeled after traditional, military structure. Mike Bawden, on his blog *Fearless Leadership*, breaks down the main points of collaborative management:

   o Listen More: listening shows the employee that you are interested in their work and value them. This will increase their motivation to perform better.
   o Talk Less: "Stop blathering on about how things used to be done." With a new generation of people looking for meaningful work, the worst thing you can do is ignore the future in favor of the past. Focus on the future and talk less.
   o Follow Through: as a part of collaborative work, you need to make sure goals are achieved and when they aren't, make sure poor work and poor employees understand and adhere to the consequences.
   o Step Back: Probably the most difficult part to managing successfully. Empower your employees, let them make decisions, *and support their decisions.* Most people learn best from their mistakes, so let your employees make mistakes and learn from them.

Probably one of the best examples of how Gen Xers work and manage collaboratively can be seen online in technology forums and blogs or more prominently with the company Google. As a leader in technology and innovation, they are not above beginning a concept or project and then turning it over to unknown fellow computer developers around the world to comment, critique, and add to their initial design. In fact, they welcome it in their developer's labs and by beta testing their designs. Gen X librarians as leaders have the ability to reinvent the library workplace in the same manner. A library run by Gen Xers

> would probably be a constant work-in-progress, characterized by a willingness to try new services or organizational approaches with little pre-implementation planning. Individual initiative and self-reliance would be encouraged, with cross-organizational communication an imperative. Formal meetings would be minimal, with more time spent in small and impromptu working groups. All aspects of the organization would be permeated with technology. Rather than being hierarchical, the organization would have

more of a flat structure with different individual schedules and an increase in working from home. Similarly, the administrative and management corps would consist of a larger number of individuals, who rotate roles on a periodic basis, so managers and administrators have a better work and life balance, avoid boredom and fatigue, introduce fresh viewpoints, and enable development of the next generation of managers [Wilcox and Harrell 96].

Conclusion

Management styles aside, communication and understanding how to motivate and reward people correctly will make managing multiple generations less daunting. "Proper communication is critical — the better each generation understands the other, the better they'll all work together" (Jimenez 50). Proper motivation can be understood by recognizing what each generation values in work and how they like to perform. More and more, the future is looking toward a reinvented work day where time will become a key factor; whether that is through part-time work with the Boomer generation, flexible hours for the Gen Xer, or less time in the office altogether for the Millennials.

Gen Xers will be good leaders. They just need positive mentoring from their colleagues and current supervisors to give them the guidance and correct motivation so that, when the time comes, they will be ready to take control. They have the ability to make libraries "innovative, responsive, and flexible ... by trying new approaches to streamline work process, and by rotating workers through different positions to prevent burnout and to take advantage of new ideas" (Wilcox and Harrell 95). These ideas further reinforce our need for a collaborative and open work environment where equality and communication are valued.

With multiple generations working together, the best form of management is education on the part of the supervisor and tolerance to allow people to work as they prefer. "The gap between [generations] isn't about age; it's about their unique experiences of the world" (Lancaster 39). Gen X managers need to be understanding and aware that motivations differ from generation to generation and person to person. A Boomer likes to know that they are still a valued member of the staff and are respected. A Gen Xer likes to know that they can work independently. A Millennial likes to know that their work has meaning and their opinion is valued. A good way to encourage these individuals is through mutual respect and cross-generational mentoring. Putting a Boomer and a Millennial together at the Reference Desk might seem like the set-up for a horror story, but they can work together as long as they understand and communicate with each other.

Works Cited

Auby, Karen. "A Boomer's Guide to Communicating with Gen X and Gen Y." *Business Week* 25 Aug. 2008: 63.

Bawden, Mike. "Collaborative Management." agencymanagementadvisor.blogspot.com. Fearless Leadership, 5 Jan. 2006. Web. 5 Dec. 2009.

Beutell, Nicholas, and Ursula Wittig-Berman. "Work-Family Conflict and Work-Family Synergy for Generation X, Baby Boomers, and Matures: Generational Differences, Predictors, and Satisfaction Outcomes." *Journal of Managerial Psychology* 23.5 (2008): 507–523.

Deeken, JoAnne, and Paula Webb. "We Are All Winners: Training Silents to Millennials to Work as a Team." *Serials Librarian* 54.6 (2008): 211–216.

Hammill, Greg. "Mixing and Managing Four Generations of Employees." www.fdu.edu. FDU Magazine Online, Spring 2005, Web. 1 Jan. 2010.

Houlihan, Anne. "When Gen-X Is in Charge." *Supervision* 69.4 (2008): 11–13.

Jimenez, Linda. "Management Implications of the Multi-Generational Workforce." *Profiles in Diversity Journal* 11.3 (2009): 50.

Khilawala, Rashida. "Management Styles." www.buzzle.com. Buzzle.com, 9 Sept. 2009, Web. 10 Dec. 2009.

Lancaster, Lynne. "The Click and Clash of Generations." *Library Journal* 128.17 (2003): 36–39.

Mathews, Brian. "The Inevitable Gen X Coup." *Library Journal* 131.5 (2006): 52.

Saxon, Miki. "Ducks in a Row: Gen X and Executive Stupidity." www.leadershipturn.com. Leadership Turn, 17 Nov. 2009, Web. 17 Dec. 2009.

Sohigian, Dave. "Generation X: Lost Again." www.thegenxfiles.com. The Gen-X Files, 16 Nov. 2009, Web. 1 Jan. 2010.

Tulgan, Bruce. *Not Everyone Gets a Trophy: How to Manage Generation Y.* San Francisco: Jossey-Bass, 2009.

Wilcox, Kimberly, and Shelley Harrell. "Next-Generation Librarianship: The Revolution Begins." *Christian Librarian* 52.3 (2009): 93–111.

Young, Arthur, Peter Hernon, and Ronald Powell. "Attributes of Academic Library Leadership: An Exploratory Study of Some Gen-Xers." *Journal of Academic Librarianship* 32.5 (2006): 489–502.

Leading the Way into the
Future of Libraries

Jessica Clemons

Librarianship has been around for thousands of years, and for many of those centuries, libraries were defined as places that hold books. This was largely true around the world, and libraries are often still typecast in that light. But now a transition is being made from the brick-and-mortar library to include space and place in the abstract. Traditional library services are being offered online, sometimes at all hours of the day and night. Libraries have brought in cafés, learning commons, and massive digital collections. In many ways the lines between librarian and technologists have begun to blur. Either in merged organizations or collaboration, these two groups will be brought together for the foreseeable future (Cain 181). Despite this innovation and collaboration, there seems to be a weak leadership base to support the evolution that is happening. There is a lack of capability to recruit and retain the strong and dynamic library leaders that will advance the academic library, rather than race to catch up to user demands. There are many opportunities to grow in the librarian profession, yet there are few willing to take on leadership responsibilities. In a time of information glut there is an ever-present need for information professionals to manage, organize, and lead the way into the future. This is detrimental to the library as a growing organism and the process of scholarly communication. A new generation of leadership from Generation X will be needed in order for the library to secure its future in the community. Gen X library leaders will have to take advantage of their ability to thrive on change and forge partnerships to ensure the success of libraries in the future.

Who Is Generation X?

Gen X is a cohort of people born between 1965 and 1981. Gen Xers watched the O.J. Simpson trial, were influenced by President Clinton, and demanded their MTV. Gen Xers also have very different feelings about careers and the role of work in the work/life balance. They tend to operate best under freedom and balance, while maintaining portable career skills. This is in stark contrast to the Boomers (1946–1964) who value money, titles, and recognition in a career that tended to be tied with a single company or institution (Young 146).

What Generation X Desires from Leadership

According to Young, Gen Xers have a decidedly different view of leadership in the library. Essentially, Gen Xers are not looking for a "buddy." Humor, ability to compromise, and broad knowledge of the issues are ranked as some of the least preferable personal traits for leadership. What is expected from leadership is the ability to secure resources, listen and respond to community needs, and build partnerships within the library and across campus (160). Gen Xers seek leaders who are supportive of them as individuals and as professionals, and who recognize their accomplishments. Personal attributes of these leaders include passion for libraries and librarianship, trustworthiness, and superior communication skills of all types. These attributes certainly make sense when put into context; look at some of the major issues that have shaped the generation and the kinds of challenges Gen Xers have faced. In a world where one can lie with statistics, advertisements, and even now with photographs, personal integrity becomes paramount.

What sets Gen X library leaders apart from their predecessors is their lack of fear of change (Hernon and Rossiter 155). Like their desires to create career portfolios rather than getting jobs straight out of college and staying at them to retirement, they are always looking to reinvent, improve, and prove themselves to be dynamic creatures. The linear paths with high emotional investment of their predecessors are likely to become things of the past. Gen Xers are experimentalists and entrepreneurs by nature. They seek to build relationships and secure resources which are important to the vitality of libraries. This is an asset in the library world, where patrons change every year, with different needs and expectations. These leaders need to be able to take advantage of these opportunities and adapt to the changing environment. Since Gen Xers are trying (and potentially failing) at many different opportunities, it is important for them to be recognized as a valued member of the library team. Higher levels of leadership may imply higher risk, and, succeed or fail, they need support just as much as they need to give support.

How Will Generation X Become Leaders?

Librarianship is a decidedly unpopular profession. Rife with negative stereotypes, it is no wonder that there is a so-called looming crisis in staffing the library world. This may be overhyped (to the graduate library school's benefit) but the fact remains that there is approximately the same number of library school graduates today as there were over 30 years ago (Matarazzo and Mika 39). Of these graduates, they tend to be a fairly homogenous group looking for second careers. Not many people dream of being a librarian when they are young, or even as undergraduates. Now, more than ever, this second-career librarianship can be seen as an asset. Experiences outside of the profession should be seen as ways to innovate and invigorate the profession. The small number of graduates from library schools may be due to a lack of strong undergraduate "feeder" programs." This is not necessarily a hindrance; experiences that are seemingly library unrelated help librarians relate to their patrons. Gen Xers may have had similar experiences as library users, not strictly as emerging library professionals. Additional graduate studies and training, particularly in a complementary area, will increase the value of librarians and gain perspective from outside of the library. However, with more education and training it can be easy to be lured into other fields. Easily transferable skills can trump the initial purpose of going to library school. These experienced Gen Xers could be recruited by information technology departments, research consultancies, and other more enticing roles. Of those who do seek out librarianship as a profession, far fewer of them look to leadership roles. Arnold, Nickel, and Williams affirm the popularly held notion that there is a significant deficit of librarians who are willing and prepared to take on leadership roles (445).

Many say that a large portion of learning happens outside of the classroom. This is often referred to as "real world" learning. New librarians learn from the sage, experienced librarians. This relationship can be beneficial as this is how we learn the culture and spirit of institutions, the often-tenuous relationship between librarians and faculty (even for many faculty librarians), and all of the things we were not taught in library school. However, emerging leaders must ask themselves about what things want to remain the same, and what things should change. Is the prevailing style of leadership the best way to keep the library on track? Some Gen X librarians think not ("Gen X Bites Back" 43–45). Leadership institutes and programs may be one way to gain leadership perspectives found lacking in education and personal experience, but this can be expensive and will not replace actual leadership experience. In a sense it only takes one person to get something started and librarians need to be bold enough to take that first step. Rather than going to leadership institutes, many Gen Xers will seek out leadership roles and use the resources at hand to get projects moving. In this manner, they learn and develop leadership by doing, not by attending meetings. Gen Xers should use their abilities, skills, and interests whenever possible to forge paths into the future world of libraries and information.

Leadership cannot function in a vacuum; Gen X leaders need a staff willing to be empowered. Gen Xers may gain leadership strength through perseverance and taking the time to understand the entire library staff. They must ask themselves, "What is the problem?" Older generations may not appreciate a perceived one-trick pony coming in and changing the status quo. This is not simply a dichotomy between *old* and *young* librarians; it is a conflict between established norms and the technological revolution that is literally happening before everyone's eyes. While writing about conviction, confidence, and exploration, it is important to recognize that many unrelenting and forward-thinking librarians do not fit into Gen X. These librarians are certainly leaders in the field, regardless of title. The difference between Gen Xers and these older librarians is that rejection, stalwarts, and the politics that can dominate library work have not beaten Gen Xers down. To this end, at some point they have to find the internal motivation to create initiatives on their own. They must energize the library and make it as lively — while not necessarily as noisy — as the student center. It is necessary to find ways to go around barriers and seek compatible partners. To do so is certainly a large task, but Gen X is ready.

Often, leaders are met with resistance. In the face of adversity or a split staff, Gen Xers must use every tool in their toolbox, especially emotional intelligence. The ability to recognize and assess the emotional state of self and others is a very powerful tool of understanding. Imagine a Boomer or even a Traditionalist (1900–1945) who automated the library. They have been with The Library since before Gen X was out of high school. Gen X comes along talking about scholarly communication, the horror that is MARC, and replacing stacks with community spaces. Developing complementary intelligence that is equipped to handle these emotional minefields is part of the key to succeed as a Gen X leader. They will not only be leading people older than them, but also younger or newer than them. The challenges of mentoring Generation Y (Millennial) information professionals, born between 1982 and 1999, compared to leading Boomers is no small task. Younger professionals will require more training and reassurance, while the Boomers' rigidity will need to be mitigated.

What the library can become has yet to be played out in the scheme of the academic arena. What library leaders cannot be are relenting, submissive people who quietly ask for just a few more dollars in the budget. Especially in tight financial times, where would scholarship be without libraries? The massive amount of scholarly communications that have been produced in the last five decades must be preserved for the future generations of researchers. Gen X leaders may have to rebuild some bridges and redefine the library at some academic institutions, but it can be done. The ability to garner an adequate budget and resources is one of the most important managerial attributes required by Gen X (DeLong 453). New and emerging leaders need to take as many opportunities to practice these business skills as well as the just as important political skills.

Gen X must work to break the stereotypes about librarians (Mosley 168). It is a toxic stereotype to be seen as the friendly face behind a desk. Gen X leaders must prove to be agile, information savvy professionals who show others the way of scholarly communication. As retiring librarians are replaced, there is an opportunity to shape the library in a new direction for all who work there and use the resources that they provide. This is not a simple branding change, but a revolution of the profession. And this will not be easy; in 2009, the Special Library Association (SLA) made a bold move to change its identity to better reflect its mission. They proposed a name change from SLA to the Association for Strategic Knowledge Professionals (ASKPro). Turning out in record numbers, the name change was voted down (Schatz). Libraries must have an identity, but in such quickly changing times, they must adapt and adjust. It is important for upcoming library workers to establish their vision of the library or they may face obsolesce.

What Is the Future of the Library?

Librarianship is no place for the Luddite. Even the notorious cataloging department is in the midst of a revolution. MARC is (or should be) all but dead (Mathews 52). Resource description and access (RDA) will create seamless descriptions and searchability that go beyond traditional metadata in the catalog. It is essential that current and emerging Gen X library leaders pay attention to all areas inside and outside of the library. There can be no more siloing of departments and ideas. Unglamorous jobs cannot be ignored or set apart from typical daily functions. Many library workers are responsible for one small yet all-consuming area within their respective libraries; we must not be blind to the interactions and intricacies of the library organism as a whole.

The library itself is a dynamic institution. Gen Xers are not married to the OPAC. With very few exceptions, library catalogs are insufficient and user-unfriendly. Simple searches can be anything but simple. It can seem that most library catalogs are designed with librarians in mind, not the average user. Catalogs and databases are kinds of languages: some can be a different dialect and others can be like trying to speak a foreign language. Librarians should aim to be multilingual because many library users are not. Changing the library's language, rather than the users, is a goal that should be adopted by all libraries. This is just a small part of scholarly communication that can potentially enable others to communicate and share knowledge more readily. Designing with the user in mind is one of the ways to ensure the future of the library.

The Future of the Library Profession

Librarianship, as it has been known, is dying. During a summer internship at the Library of Congress, I told someone that I was in graduate school for library science. That someone responded with a dismissive, "Oh, so you must deal with books and stuff." This is just not true, yet it is still how we in the profession are stereotyped in the age of full-text databases and information literacy, among so many other things! Library leaders from Generation X will have the task of dispelling these limiting myths and invigorating the profession with a diversity of experiences and beliefs. Because one of the traits of this generation is the desire to build a career portfolio rather than a static resume, they can cross-pollinate academic institutions. Learning from failures and success at one institution will enhance what one librarian is able to enact at the next. This diversity of ideas enriches libraries and the profession.

Traditionally, librarianship is defined as a service profession: librarians support academic curricula and show people how to find, organize, and share information. To change this, librarians should begin painting themselves with a broader paintbrush. They must realize that any somewhat intelligent being with digits can plug in some keywords (Google Scholar) and find something that can be added to the works cited of a paper. Gen X leaders and librarians need to market the new or next generation library as explicitly linked with the business of information. From digitization to information technology, scholarly communication to data mining, Gen Xers can expand their skill sets and become ever more valuable and indispensable to the places where they work.

There are several theories on why librarianship seems to eschew new and emerging leaders. First, just the term librarianship is deeply embedded with stereotypes. Who doesn't think of an old lady with a gray bun, glasses and a sweater, shushing disruptive patrons? Many librarians are trying to dispel these stereotypes by creating YouTube videos. While embracing new forms of media is an asset to libraries, it must be done with the user in mind. I cannot begin to catalog and view all of the videos on YouTube for or by librarians, but I have made a casual observation that some librarians are just recording the same business-as-usual library class. It is disheartening to see wasted opportunities to use technology to connect with patrons. Just because communication technology is available does not mean it should be used merely to mimic the manner in which people interact in real life. Gen X (and younger) librarians must point out to the administration that those quaint YouTube videos about the library and its staff are so passé, and can be a little embarrassing. YouTube or YouTube EDU would better serve communities as access points to resources, exploratory tools, and places to review information not offered in a classroom setting. Web 2.0 technologies should be used thoughtfully and carefully so librarians do not continue to be stereotyped by the people with whom they interact.

The majority of academic libraries' leadership comes from a certain generation that tends to be unfamiliar and uncomfortable with rapid change. If the average librarian or library staff member were to look around at his or her staff meeting, several (if not more) faces might be associated with those characteristics. Changing library operations to benefit the users or make workflows more efficient may mean learning new skill sets or having to do more work. Many Boomer library leaders have been able to keep pace with changes: more study spaces or cafés in lieu of print journals and creating vast digital archives that are accessible twenty-four hours per day, seven days per week, and 365 days per year. As beneficial as these changes may be, they are simply layers over the same library of decades ago. It is as if a clothing designer is using the same mannequin, just adding some thoughtful accessories to what is already there. The library profession must find a new model and some new designers to meet the changing and challenging needs of academe. They cannot expect the corseted structure and guidelines to change the user; the library must adapt to meet user requirements. As Gen X leaders take on and embrace leadership roles they need to be supported, rewarded, and encouraged to succeed, else the profession may lose them (Mosley "mentoring" 191).

The nature of librarianship is essentially information sharing and all of the activities that surround that practice. It is important to attend and participate in library-related conferences for many reasons. Librarians can get to know one another, hear about the success stories, and find support as they endeavor towards their shared goals. But it seems that conference attendance is viewed as important primarily by the organizations that sponsor said conferences. Library conferences and meetings may become less and less influential, especially as virtual communication becomes easier to manage. It is amazing what can happen in any number of the librarian listservs and blogs available. There are tremendous amounts of library journals, peer-reviewed and otherwise, which can be scanned to unveil the comings and goings in the academic library world. All of these forums can be opportunities to discover like-minded people, supportive networks, and gain insights from movers and shakers in the field of all ages.

Gen X library leaders will need to break away from the traditional conference attendance. They must present new and exciting ideas about how to connect and respond to user populations. Increasing contact and sharing experiences with others would enrich the profession like never before. This may become ever more important to do so at non-library conferences. The types of conferences to think about attending are those of the academic departments that librarians enrich and sustain. Discipline-specific and liaison librarians should be going to the same conferences that the departmental faculty attends. And everyone should be going to technology conferences because libraries can no longer function without it.

In the not-too-distant past, books were carefully guarded treasures, chained to desks, and with very limited access. In more contemporary times books are widely available to everyone, cheap, and can be brought just about anywhere thanks to ebook readers and smart phone apps. The model has changed from the library as a kind of roadblock of knowledge to one that tries to keep up with user demand. Librarians have gone from "gate keepers" of knowledge to beacons of light in a sometimes-disorienting sea of information. Gen Xers must illuminate every dark corner of knowledge. Librarians have to embed themselves into the curriculum, and be visible and available. Gen X leaders have to support this revolution and take the risks to make it happen.

Conclusion

In previous decades, librarians may have been able to hide themselves away in service departments and other offices. The new librarians, particularly new library leaders, cannot afford to do so. In the age of the information professional, Gen X librarians are needed to break down barriers and understand the culture, politics and status within an organization. New and emerging Gen X leaders will have to encourage meaningful collaboration, dynamically manage library staff, and alter the image of our profession if we are to transcend into a new century of librarianship.

Leadership is a challenging endeavor. Simple management will no longer suffice in the information rich world in which we all live. As Gen X steps up to the leadership table, as they must, they will be tested and rewarded. To stand up to these trials, the future library leaders must explore the vision for the future as guided by a desire to succeed. Rewards will be the freedom earned and the positive impact they can have as they steer the library, both the physical and virtual spaces, into the future.

BIBLIOGRAPHY

Arnold, Jennifer, Lisa T. Nickel, and Lisa Williams. "Creating the Next Generation of Library Leaders." *New Library World* 109.9–10 (2008): 444–456. Print.

Cain, Mark. "The Two Cultures? Librarians and Technologists." *The Journal of Academic Librarianship* 29.3 (2003): 177–181. Web.

DeLong, Kathleen. "The Engagement of New Library Professionals in Leadership." *The Journal of Academic Librarianship* 35.5 (2009): 445–456. Web.

"Gen X Bites Back." *American Libraries* 35.8 (2004): 43–45. Web.

Hernon, Peter, and Nancy Rossiter, eds. *Making a Difference: Leadership and Academic Libraries.* Westport, CT: Libraries Unlimited, 2007. Print.

Matarazzo, James M., and Joseph J. Mika. "How to Be Popular." *American Libraries* 37.8 (2006): 38–40. Web.

Mathews, Brian S. "The Inevitable Gen X Coup." *Library Journal* 131.5 (2006): 52. Web.

Mosley, Pixey Anne. "Mentoring Gen X Managers: Tomorrow's Library Leadership Is Already Here." *Library Administration & Management* 19.4 (2005): 185. Web.

_____. "Shedding the Stereotypes: Librarians in the 21st Century." *Reference Librarian* 37.78 (2002): 167. Web.

Schatz, Cara. "SLA Name Will Stay: Alignment of Association to Continue." Web. 1 Feb 2010.

Young, Arthur P. "Gen-Xers and Millennials Join the Library Express." *Making a Difference: Leadership and Academic Libraries.* Westport, CT: Libraries Unlimited. 143–167. Print.

_____, Peter Hernon, and Ronald R. Powell. "Attributes of Academic Library Leadership: An Exploratory Study of Some Gen-Xers." *The Journal of Academic Librarianship* 32.5 (2006): 489–502. Web.

A Finger in the Pie:
A Look at How Multiple Careers Benefit the Library Professional

Dawn Lowe-Wincentsen

When a person becomes a chef it is expected that they know how to bake more than one type of pie. Yet in libraries and many other careers, we are often expected to specialize to the field, and within the field. In February 2010, a review of 15 management or higher positions listed in the American Library Association job list required on average a minimum of 5.25 years experience. Some of those even specified what type of library experience. Yet, the average length of time a person of Generation X spends in a job is 6 to 18 months (Gonzales 2). Instead of shunning those who have multiple experiences in their background, we should be embracing the fact that they can make much more than one flavor of pie.

Diversity is something that we, as a culture, speak of in many ways; for example, diversifying our profession, diversifying the schools, having a diverse culture, etc. Despite our need to diversify it is often looked down upon to have a diverse professional background. Until Generation X hit the workforce it was traditional to stay in one profession or even place of employment for your entire working life. Job hopping, or moving between jobs and careers every few years has been deeply frowned upon. But the workforce has changed, and many Generation X and millennial librarians have had multiple careers before they even considered becoming librarians. Where ten years ago librarianship was sometimes a second career, now it is often a third or fourth career.

Literature Review

Research on retaining Generation X employees often suggests providing continuous training (Bova and Kroth 58) and diversity among those learning opportunities. Job-hopping is another way of learning. Generation X employees often want flexibility in their schedule and job duties (Heenan 6). Beatrice van der Heijden writes, "Experience can only lead to occupational expertise when it is neither too congruent or [*sic*] too incongruent with prior experience" (91). Many of the skills developed in previous careers can be transferred into librarianship. Sherry Sullivan and Ryan Emerson call the people who build a career through many skill sets and past work experience "careerists" (4). These people focus on a set of skills as they move between careers to increase their marketability in the end. Van der Heijden goes on to say that it is not the total number of jobs, or the time spent at a particular position that matters, but the career steps that are made (92).

Breda Bova and Michael Kroth state, "Job-hopping is a normal, accepted method of career advancement for Generation Xers" (57). This want of the ability to job hop by Generation X employees is one of the largest contributors to conflicts and tensions between generations (Govitvatana 65). This is often voiced as "disloyalty" and "lack of commitment" by people with more traditional workplace values. Others say there is a lack of work ethics among Generation X employees, often exemplified through movies of the early 1990s such as *Mall Rats* or *Clerks* where members of Generation X are pictured as "slackers." Much of the literature on Generation X characteristics agrees on the "slacker" label (Tolbize 5). Through a survey conducted about librarians' past careers' influence on their current jobs, this chapter will argue that instead of slackers, these people should be considered professionals who have built diverse and full careers.

How does this information fit into current employment trends in librarianship? According to a study presented to the American Library Association's executive board in 2006 more than 40 percent of current librarians are age 50 to 59, and another 15 percent are over age 60. With the expected age of retirement being 65 these statistics herald a huge leadership gap for librarianship in the upcoming 10–15 years (Tordella and Godfrey 3). The same report lists 40 percent of librarians between the ages of 30 and 50, and less than 5 percent of librarians as under the age of 30. Broken into broad generational guides, that is 40 percent of librarians in 2006 were members of Generation X. If, as a profession, we continue to overlook the past experiences of new librarians, we will continue to lose out on all that those experiences can bring.

The Generation X library careerist may have worked in many industries, such as publishing, legal, retail, or IT before becoming a librarian. All of these skills can and often do work together to create a whole case of pies, as opposed to the one pie on the windowsill. A study of what members of Generation X valued in leaders found that scholarly communication, financial management, facilities planning, digital libraries, and planning skills are all areas of knowledge they value (Young, Hernon, and Powell 493). Another survey that looked at characteristics newer librarians expect from themselves as future leaders found inspiration ability, problem solving, innovation, and being a visionary to be important (Byke and Lowe-Wincentsen 50). All of these characteristics can be built through a number of professions and transferred to librarianship.

Though both of the previously cited studies focus on leadership characteristics, the following study did not. The study described below focuses on a broad range of skill sets and whether or not those skill sets are used in librarianship.

Method

In fall of 2009 a survey was developed to determine the past career choices of current librarians, and the skills developed in those careers that they continue to use in librarianship. The average time it took to complete the survey was less than 5 minutes. It was meant to gather initial responses without the respondents overthinking their answers. The questions were meant to be simple and succinct to collect clear data without causing strain on the respondents. (See Appendix A.)

The survey was distributed through list serves such as NMRT-L (New Members Round Table) and Off-Campus Library services list. Respondents were self selected from the members of the email lists. The survey was mainly marketed as a survey on career choices of librarians, and the skill sets associated with those. While the generational information gathered was important, it was placed as demographic information in the survey so as to not alienate any potential respondents.

Though the survey was marketed to a broad range of librarians without taking into account age or generational identification, the majority of respondents self-identified as Generation X. After the initial requests for participants were sent, the survey was left open for one week. The responses were then downloaded into a spreadsheet and analyzed by generational self-identification of respondents.

Results

Of all respondents to the survey, 11 percent self identified as Baby Boomers, 61 percent as Generation X, 20 percent as Millennials, and 8 percent as others, usually described as people who identified with multiple generations' characteristics. The responses were first broken down by generational self-identification, then by age brackets to check the consistency of results. Fifteen percent of respondents identified themselves as age 45–65, roughly corresponding to the generational guidelines of the Baby Boomer generation. Sixty-two percent identified that they were 30–45 years of age, roughly corresponding to Generation X, and 23 percent identified themselves as under age 30. Although the age category of over 65, and the generation title of Greatest Generation were included on the survey, there were no respondents that identified themselves as either.

The greatest differences between these groups' average number of past careers was two-tenths of a percent between those who self-identified as Baby Boomers, and those who were age 45–65. Those who identified as Generation X and those who identified as age 30–45 had the same average number of previous careers to the ten-thousandth decimal place. The consistency in these results is important to the rest of the study as we discuss the previous skill sets of Generation X and whether or not those skills are of use, and being used in the library workplace.

For the rest of this analysis we will only focus on those 61 percent of respondents that self-identified as Generation X. Of these respondents, 75 percent had had one or more previous careers to librarianship, 32 percent had had more than two previous careers, and an astonishing 6 percent had had four or more previous careers, meaning librarianship was at least their fifth career.

GENERATION X LIBRARIANS AND PREVIOUS CAREERS	
first career	25%
second career	43%
third career	26%
fifth or higher	6%

Of the careers that these respondents have had prior to librarianship, accounting and finance are the highest, closely followed by education, and then business. Some respondents commented on how the skills from these two groups fit in to and helped them in librarianship. One such comment was: "Use my problem solving and business analysis skills everyday as a library director" and "I often use data analysis skills for writing reports." The following comment was on the similarities between being a public librarian and a high school teacher: "It surprised me just how similar they are — in the sense of giving instruction, balancing doing a thousand things at the same time, getting interrupted constantly, dealing with behavior problems, making sure everything is running smoothly."

The ambiguous terms of education and business were the ones provided in the survey. The actual results were that "Other" was the most common previous career. The "Other" category requested that respondents enter a career, these and the predetermined titles were then divided into categories, either fitting into the predetermined list, or defining a new list where a category was overlooked such as IT or health care. Some similar careers were grouped together; for example, software grouped with IT, and social work and ministry grouped with counseling. The "Other" category in the table below includes research and assessment, legal, insurance, and janitorial careers.

Respondents were allowed to check all that applied in this question, sometimes making for very diverse lists such as one person who has worked in education, food service and healthcare, and another who has worked in education, arts, hospitality, graphic design, and retail. Although impressive on an individual basis, what truly grabs the attention is the diversity of these skill sets; from engineering and food service to arts and business, each skill set needed to accomplish these careers is vast, and the ability to then roll these past experiences into current career needs is quite impressive.

CAREER FIELD PRIOR TO LIBRARIANSHIP	
Accounting	18
Business	12
Education	17
Engineering	2
Arts	11
Food Service	10
Logistics	4
Health care	3
Hospitality	3
IT	4
Journalism	5
Marketing	6
Non Profit	3
Publishing	2
Counseling	4
Retail	6
Other	4

Examples include a librarian who used theatre design skills to create a kids drama program and to design informational posters at her library, and the former social worker who uses her skills to calm stressed out students.

After identifying their past careers, respondents were asked to rank how often they used skills they had learned in the following areas in their current library positions. The areas were the pre-identified career categories:

- Accounting
- Education
- Business
- Marketing
- Journalism
- Arts (listed as fine arts and theatre on the survey)
- Hospitality
- Janitorial
- Food Service
- Engineering
- Construction

The most frequently used skill set was education. This may be attributed to the overall most common library type of respondents being academic libraries. Among those self-identified as Generation X, 59 percent identified themselves as working in an academic library. The second most frequently used skill set was marketing, followed closely by hospitality and business. These all averaged as either used "very often" or "often." For all respondents of the survey, the most commonly used skill sets were education, marketing, business, and then hospitality; a slight variance in order from Generation X.

For Generation X, the least most frequently used skill sets were food service, followed by engineering, and construction. All three skill sets were either infrequently used or never used according to respondents. For all survey respondents these three were still the least used skill sets, but the order was construction least used, followed by engineering, and then food service — though one respondent did mention that their previous food service skills were very handy when prepping for openings and special visitors in a special collection. On average all other skill sets were either somewhat often used, or infrequently used for both the self-identified Generation X respondents and the overall survey respondents.

The final question of the survey asked respondents to share any tales that they may have about using knowledge and skills from past careers in their current librarian positions. These were not divided out by self-identified generation, or by age range, but they do give some powerful advice on skills sets used outside "what you learned in library school." The most commonly mentioned skills are those in customer service, and people skills. These are mentioned for working with library patrons and coworkers.

One person, formerly in real estate says, "I've found the skill of determining what people tell you they want vs. what people ACTUALLY want to be invaluable." Another person takes his people skills in a different direction: "I used my people skills developed as a bouncer in an inner-city branch library."

Other skill sets mentioned frequently among the comments fall into the leadership realm, including project management, business management, marketing and public relations. A third skill set mentioned is IT skills, and developing and helping others with the technologies that continue to grow in libraries. Others include those who use presentation skills on a regular basis such as a former marketing professional that uses presentation skills as an outreach librarian, and a music performer who channels their skills into classroom teaching. The comment that most clearly states the overall feeling of the survey data is "I think most of being a librarian involves 'outside skill sets.' The skills I employ as a librarian could be employed in other fields, but I choose to do my work in librarianship."

Conclusions

The workplace on a whole is changing. We are at a point in history where the world is changing, sometimes fast, and sometimes not. By the time this article sees print some of the careers and skill sets that the respondents have developed will have become obsolete. They will have adapted and learned new skills, or moved to using other skills that they knew already. Librarianship on a whole is a vastly different place in 2010 than it was in 2000, or 1990, or in 1970 when the generation previous to Generation X was trying to set themselves apart. The profession and the modern work place will continue to change, even as Millennials come into it and try to define themselves. New to Generation X is the ability, and the want of flexibility and diversity in skill sets, careers, and positions. The skill sets that this generation is developing, and will continue to develop by job-hopping will shake up librarianship, and other careers. Generation X will change things because they have diverse backgrounds, and because they don't spend that much time in any one position.

As a profession we need to look at these skill sets and past careers when people apply for jobs and consider how these skills may augment what the applicant learned in library school. On the other side of this argument, those who have had multiple careers and who have skill sets beyond librarianship should highlight how these skills are useful in the library workplace. Do not, as tradition tells, take those past jobs off your resume because they clutter it up. Leave those jobs on so the libraries you apply to know that you know how to bake more than one flavor of pie.

WORKS CITED

Bova, Breda, and Michael Kroth. "Workplace Learning and Generation X." *Journal of Workplace Learning* 13.2 (2001): 57–65.

Byke, Suzanne, and Dawn Lowe-Wincentsen. *A Leadership Primer for New Librarians*. Oxford: Chandos Publishing, 2009.

Gonzales, Candace. "Job-Hopping: Generational Trend or Employment Trend?" MA Thesis, University of Denver, 2009.

Govitvatana, Wipanut Venique. "Generation Gap in the Workplace Between Baby Boomers and Generation X." MS Thesis, University of Wisconsin–Stout, 2001.

Heenan, David O. "The Right Way to Downsize." *The Journal of Business Strategy* 12.5 (1991): 4–7.

Sullivan, Sherry E., and Ryan Emerson. "Recommendations for Successfully Navigating the Boundaryless Career: From Theory to Practice." *Midwest Academy of Management Proceedings*. 2000. Web. 8 Feb 2010.

Tolbize, Anick. *Generational Differences in the Workplace*. University of Minnesota. Research and Training Center on Community Living. 16 Aug. 2008. Web. 19 Jan 2010.

Tordella, Stephen, and Tom Godfrey. "Librarian Retirements and ALA Membership." American Library Association Annual Conference. McCormick Place. Chicago, IL. 13 July 2009.

Van der Heijden, Beatrice. "The Relationship Between Career Mobility and Occupational Expertise." *Employee Relations* 25.1 (2003): 81–109.

Young, Arthur P., Peter Hernon, and Ronald R. Powell. "Attributes of Academic Library Leadership: An Exploratory Study of Some Gen-Xers." *The Journal of Academic Librarianship* 32.5 (2006): 489–502.

SECTION THREE

TECHNOLOGY

Twitter My Glitter:
A Dialogue on the Technological Expectations of Library Users

Rachel Williams and Jennifer Cromer

How do you define yourself? Perhaps you define yourself by your profession, your personal hobbies, your family, your age, the generation you belong to. Oftentimes when trying to define ourselves, we think about our generation. Whether a Traditionalist, Baby Boomer, Generation X, or Millennial, these brackets of time encompass years of history and culture within a single word or phrase. Of particular interest is the relationship between Generation X and Millennials, especially in technology use and expectations among library users.

Is the culture of technology generational? Through a dialogue between a Generation X and Millennial library school student and a survey of two local public library communities, this article addresses the implications of technology as a culture among several generations. Tweeting, updating statuses on Facebook, and emailing friends and colleagues YouTube videos all indicate that technology has taken hold of our communities. Snowball states that "many libraries and authors of books have a profile on MySpace" (30). Libraries are environments that have embraced this cultural shift in technology use. With this growth of technology sharing, however, comes a decrease in expectations of privacy and personal identity — we are in fact becoming a culture of sharing. In acknowledging these diminishing expectations of privacy in constantly evolving technology, it is vital to examine the cultural impact of technology trends and the loss of personal identity in the shift from Generation X to the Millennial generation.

Of equal importance in addressing the individual cultural needs of Generation X and Millennials in the library is understanding how librarians from these two generations work together to provide library services to the public, no matter what the generation. This cultural shift, as well as changing expectations in privacy and personal identity is seen, not just within the library user community, but among librarians as well. Generation X and Millennials are required to work collaboratively, while their predecessors,

Baby Boomers and the Silent Generation, were not required to. This collaboration enables Generation X and Millennials to be more open to changing technology, though at times librarians from these generations may be frustrated by those less flexible and open to an "evolving environment." In her article "A Neo-Modern Summary of the Futcha," Jane Scales questions our inherent assumptions about the role of libraries as "evolving environments" when she asks:

> If the library is changing as much as it seems to be, how can we be sure that the proce-
> dures, practices, and philosophies established twenty to thirty years ago are right for the
> evolving environment? Is it possible to look at these issues in an objective way — or are
> our views irrevocably shaped by a certain point in our professional careers? [25].

To address concerns of technology use, privacy, programming expectations, and user needs, a survey covering these topics was performed. Both Pullman, Washington, and Moscow, Idaho, are unique in that they are agricultural as well as university communities and provided an interesting backdrop for this particular analysis. To get an adequate sample size, surveys were made available at Neill Public Library in Pullman as well as at all seven branches of the Latah County Library District. Surveying these two communities provided an opportunity to acquire a wide range of respondents. These communities are comprised of agriculturists, university professors and staff, students, and families.

Surveys were available for completion for three weeks at both Neill Public Library and at all branches of the Latah County Library District. The surveys were also available in either a paper or online format through SurveyMonkey, and respondents were encouraged to take the survey in the format most appealing to them. Though the surveys were available in both formats, every action was taken to ensure that the formats of the survey were very similar to elicit the most honest answers possible from survey respondents.

Results

A total of 130 respondents participated in the fifteen-question survey, with 45 percent taking the survey in paper format. The 15 questions covered several subjects related to technology use, frequency of library visits, and purpose for visiting the library. Responses were divided into four generational categories according to the Municipal Research Services of Washington general definitions as outlined by Sweeney (166). Using these definitions, four generational categories were defined for the purposes of this survey: Millennials (born 1982–2000), Generation X (1961–1981), Baby Boomers (1944–1960) and the Silent Generation (1922–1943).

Shown in Table 1 are four major generations and survey responses as to when users visit the library. Response totals are shown in percentages relative to other generations

TABLE 1
GENERATION AND NUMBER OF VISITS TO THE LIBRARY PER WEEK

Age Range	Once	Twice	Three Times	Four Times	Five Times	Six Times	Seven Plus
Millennial	12	13	23	33	0	50	29
Generation X	40	26	23	17	29	0	0
Baby Boomer	31	45	23	17	57	0	14
Silent	17	16	32	33	14	50	57

Number of visits to library per week, as shown in percentages of responses of generation per total responses of day visited.

that gave the same response. For example, those ages 11–26 comprised 12 percent of the total respondents who visit the library once per week. Calculating relative frequency in this manner best illustrates when each generation is visiting the library. The largest number of respondents who visit the library six or more times per week is either the Millennial generation or the Silent generation. Baby boomers visit the most, either twice per week or five times per week, compared to other generations. Generation X patrons, interestingly, seem to be more evenly distributed in their visits to the library, although they visit the most once per week compared to other generations.

While respondents tend to visit the library a variable number of times per week based on their generational designation, there is less variance in *why* respondents visit the library. Table 2 demonstrates that, no matter what the age group, respondents tend to visit the library to 1) browse materials, and 2) pick up materials. A predominant percentage of respondents within each generation (at least 48 percent and up to 63 percent) agreed that they visit the library to browse materials. Combined totals indicate that 91 percent of Millennials, 76 percent of Generation X, 64 percent of Baby Boomers, and 76 percent of the Silent Generation felt it was at least "Very Important" or "Most Important" to them to visit the library to browse materials.

Relative frequencies for Table 3 indicate that picking up library materials is "Most

TABLE 2
GENERATION AND IMPORTANCE OF BROWSING MATERIALS

Age Range	Most Important	Very Important	Important	Slightly Important	Not Important
Millennial	58	33	8	0	0
Generation X	48	28	21	3	0
Baby Boomer	57	7	29	0	7
Silent	63	13	13	0	13

Importance of visiting the library to browse materials, as shown in percentages of each generation's total responses.

TABLE 3
GENERATION AND IMPORTANCE OF PICKING UP LIBRARY MATERIALS

Age Range	Most Important	Very Important	Important	Slightly Important	Not Important
Millennial	23	38	15	15	9
Generation X	44	25	17	11	3
Baby Boomer	50	34	13	3	0
Silent	68	21	5	5	0

Importance of visiting the library to pick up materials, as shown in percentages based on total responses for each generation.

Important" or "Very Important" to respondents. Relative frequencies were determined by calculating a sum of the total responses for each generation and then calculating the percentage of responses within each category. For example, 38 percent of those identified as Millennial responded that they feel it is very important to visit the library to pick up materials.

Although these results are not surprising, what is fascinating is that the data illustrates that, despite generational differences, library patrons have relatively stable expectations when it comes to browsing for and picking up materials. Whether Millennial or Generation X, library patrons feel it is important to look for and get materials that interest them. At a time when librarianship is focused intensively on digitization and Web 2.0 technologies, it is clear that library patrons still expect print material services.

Interestingly, 91 percent of the Millennials responded that they use internet computers while at the library (Table 5), but only 33 percent felt it was important to offer this service (Table 4). Additionally, 28 percent felt that having internet computers was not important at all, although almost all respondents from this generation indicated that they use them. Compared to the other three generations, Millennials use the internet computers and wireless services substantially more, yet feel that offering them is not as important.

TABLE 4
GENERATION AND IMPORTANCE OF INTERNET USE

Age Range	Most Important	Very Important	Important	Slightly Important	Not Important
Millennial	33	17	17	6	28
Generation X	7	10	7	20	57
Baby Boomer	16	10	6	32	35
Silent	13	19	19	25	25

Importance of internet use shown in percentages calculated by number of responses per category divided by number of total respondents within each generation.

TABLE 5
GENERATION AND COMPUTER USE AT THE LIBRARY

Age Range	Internet	Catalog	Wireless
Millennial	91	30	70
Generation X	38	82	33
Baby Boomer	46	64	31
Silent	73	86	50

Computer use shown in percentages calculated by number of responses per category divided by number of total respondents within each generation.

Although library programming is an integral part of providing library services to the public, it is clear from survey respondents that there is a fairly even distribution of opinion. There is no obvious opinion in how important library programming is to each generation based on the data gathered from the respondents to this survey. However, for the Millennial generation, library programming seems to be the least important, closely followed by the Baby Boomer generation (Table 6). Those who fall into Generation X appear to most strongly feel that library programming is important.

A correspondence analysis using STATA was performed to get a better understanding of the relationship between technology use and generation. As acknowledged by UNESCO, "correspondence analysis remarkably simplifies complex data and provides a detailed description of practically every bit of information in the data, yielding a simple, yet exhaustive analysis." The use of Web 2.0 technologies — specifically social networking sites such as Twitter, Facebook, MySpace, and YouTube — initially appeared to be evenly distributed within the correspondence analysis. However, this analysis created fascinating results as shown in Figure 1. The strongest correlations are between r1, or the Millennial generation, and technology use at the library, and between r2, or Generation X, and YouTube at the library and Facebook at home.

TABLE 6
GENERATION AND IMPORTANCE OF LIBRARY PROGRAMMING

Age Range	Most Important	Very Important	Important	Slightly Important	Not Important
Millennial	15	15	15	23	31
Generation X	38	6	18	18	21
Baby Boomer	13	20	20	17	30
Silent	13	44	19	19	6

Importance of library programming shown in percentages.

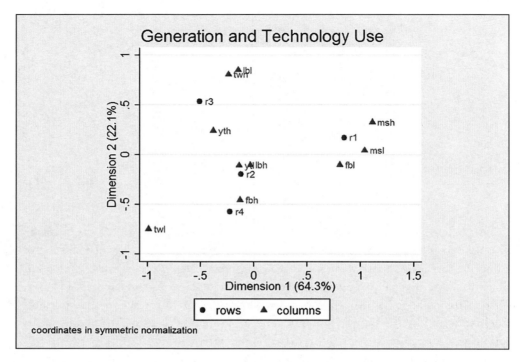

Figure 1. Correspondence Analysis illustrating technology use related to each generation. r1=Millennial, r2=Generation X, r3=Baby Boomer, r4=Silent, fbl=Facebook at the Library, fbh=Facebook at Home, ytl=YouTube at the Library, yth=YouTube at Home, msl=MySpace at the Library, msh=MySpace at Home, twl=Twitter at the Library, twh=Twitter at Home, lbl=Library Blog at the Library, and lbh=Library Blog at Home. Figure 1 illustrates the correspondence between r1 and fbl, msl, and msh, as well as the relationship between r2 and ytl and fbh.

Discussion

In "Talkin' 'bout My Generation," Lowe and Skarl state that "the electronic landscape is a fertile field for exploring and comparing a wide range of issues across age groups" (400). The responses of the sample survey have facilitated exploration into some of the issues facing generations, especially Generation X and the Millennial generation. These concerns include how often and why library patrons visit the library, how varying generations utilize Web 2.0 technology, and computer and internet use while at the library.

Library uses per week are dominated by Millennials and the Silent Generation, with variability in the number of visits per week by Generation X. With recent shifts in the economy, however, there is likely in an increase in visits overall for all four major generational groups. No matter when each generation visits, however, it is clear that it is "Most Important" or "Very Important" to all respondents to visit the library in order to browse and pick up library materials.

Computer use (internet, catalog, and wireless) provided insight into the habits of

Generation X and Millennials. While Millennials use the internet computers and wireless service substantially more than other generations, they also do not feel that these are important services. This could perhaps be the result of growing up with internet and computer technology with them.

The correlations between generations and Web 2.0 technology use as graphically demonstrated in Figure 1 suggest differing perspectives on privacy, as the Millennials appear to feel more comfortable using personal social networking sites at the library than other generations. While Generation X appears to be comfortable using Web 2.0 technologies such as YouTube at the library, they are more reserved in using personal social networking sites at home. R3, or the Baby Boomer generation, makes use of YouTube and Twitter at home. R4, the Silent Generation, appears to only be comfortable using Facebook at home and shows no correlation with other Web 2.0 technologies, whether at the library or at home. Despite the fact that, overall, Americans have been atwitter with the idea of tweeting, the use of Twitter within the communities surveyed was minimal at best. This was a surprising result for two fairly large university communities. Even though the two library systems surveyed serve what could be perceived as very technologically savvy library user populations, it is clear that Twitter does not dominate in this instance. In fact, only 10 percent of respondents even acknowledged that they use Twitter. Of those respondents who said they do tweet, only 5 percent tweet on a regular basis, or at least three to four times per week.

Privacy was addressed subtly through the survey and through a specific question asking respondents whether they had experienced any problems with internet filtering. While only 3.3 percent of respondents stated that they had experienced a problem due to filtering, respondents who answered "yes" to this question were asked to explain further. These explanations indicated that in all but one case, filtering was not the problem — the problems were due to outdated computer hardware and software, tight network security, and user error. These statistics indicate that, for the most part, library users are satisfied with the minimal filtering common in many public libraries and that users understand the limitations inherent in utilizing computers in a public setting.

Beyond the survey statistics relating to privacy are the personal experiences of librarians in their interactions with library users. In May 2009, one library surveyed acquired six new internet terminals. This acquisition resulted in the necessary movement of computer terminals and new furniture to house the computers. The older furniture provided more space between computer terminals, as well as dividers to provide users with, at the very least, the perception of privacy. This change in furniture as well as the closer space and increased number of computer terminals resulted in library patrons attempting to haphazardly cover their computers or assert personal space in other ways. Patrons have covered up their computers with notebooks, books, papers, and even their hands in an effort to create a sense of privacy for themselves as they utilize computer stations.

When reference librarians walk past computer stations, patrons often cover up their computers to avoid scrutiny from librarians. This behavior is observed more often from patrons who are from the Baby Boomer or Silent generations. These age groups were also the most vocal when stating their concerns about the lack of privacy and space that resulted from the reconfiguration of the computer stations. Several even said they would rather have fewer internet stations available than less privacy and space. While internet filtering is the most transparent privacy issue, it is clear from the anecdotes of librarians that personal privacy, especially in relation to technology, is something library users feel is important.

For librarians as well as patrons, it may be difficult to embrace a less privacy oriented, more socially networked, Web 2.0 library environment. However, as Caudron points out, it is possible to train, not only Generation X librarians, but all librarians to utilize new technology by employing several key techniques. These include focusing on what is really important, being flexible in scheduling and maintaining a variety of training resources, emphasizing visuals, and by providing continual education (Caudron 4).

Conclusion

As Saw and Todd assert, "[many] dimensions and properties of th[e] electronic frontier [are] unfamiliar and uncharted and our survival depends on how well we adapt our values and skills" (10). Generation X and Millennial generation librarians are in a distinctive position to ride the waves of the changing culture of technology in order to contribute to the continued relevance of libraries. Young and Powell further state that "the need for a creative and constructively engaged library work force is imperative for the coming decades" (501). A creative, engaged librarian will be better equipped to handle generational differences as technology continues to evolve within the library environment.

Although the initial expectation was to see substantial gaps between generations, after examining the data, this simply is not the case. Despite the fact that there is some variation in expectations regarding technology use and services, library users of all generations had similar expectations regarding programming and what is of prevailing importance when they visit the library. Limitations to the survey include the fact that the survey size was fairly small and performed within an insulated community setting. Because adult library programming in this area is limited to book-related events and book clubs, the response for this particular question could be biased. Additionally, prior approval from the libraries surveyed was required, and the survey was censored more than the authors expected. The inability to market the survey well also could have resulted in the small sample size for the survey. As with any survey, due to the fact that the sample size was fairly small, there is the possibility that the survey is not fully representative of the population. However, overall, the survey provides an excellent snapshot into a typical library community.

While this particular sample survey provided some intriguing insight into the perceptions and expectations of library users across generations, future studies could result in a more detailed analysis of privacy use or certain technologies. Specifically, a study involving examination of social networking and expectation of privacy and personal disclosure levels could result in fascinating generational variances.

Regardless of one's generational affiliation, collaboration on every possible level is the only way to secure the role of libraries as continuingly relevant institutions within the paradigm shifts occurring in the technological expectations of library users. As Pixey Anne Mosley states, "If librarians and administrators want to play an active role in the future, they must work to develop a shared vision of the paths they wish to follow and take an active role in creating their destiny" (170). How do librarians accomplish this? Mosley continues by admonishing librarians to "reach beyond the walls of the library" (170). Whether Millennial, Generation X, Baby Boomer, or a member of the Silent Generation, it is imperative that librarians take Mosley's advice. Reaching beyond the walls of the library and into the realm of technology will facilitate the library's continued relevance as a welcome environment for change.

WORKS CONSULTED

Caudron, Shari. "Can Generation Xers Be Trained?" *Training and Development* 51.3 (1997): 20–24.

Kipnis, Daniel G., and Gary M. Childs. "Educating Generation X and Generation Y; Teaching Tips for Librarians." *Medical Reference Services Quarterly* 23.4 (2004): 25–33.

Lancaster, Lynne C. "The Click and Clash of Generations." *Library Journal* 128.17 (2003): 36–39.

Lowe, Sidney, and Susie Skarl. "Talkin' 'Bout My Generation: Exploring Age-Related Resources." *College & Research Libraries News* 70.7 (2009): 400–403.

Mosley, Pixey Anne. "Shedding the Stereotypes: Librarians in the 21st Century." *The Reference Librarian* 37.78 (2002): 167–176.

Saw, Grace, and Heather Todd. "Library 3.0: Where Art Our Skills?" *Conference Papers—World Library and Information Congress: 73rd IFLA General Conference and Council 2007*. 19–23 August 2007. Web. 20 May 2010.

Scales, B. Jane. "A Neo-Modern Summary of the Futcha: An Explanation of the Generation X in Our Midst." *The Reference Librarian* 30.64 (1999): 21–30.

Snowball, Clare. "Enticing Teenagers into the Library." *Library Review* 57.1 (2008): 25–35.

Sweeney, Richard T. "Reinventing Library Buildings and Services for the Millennial Generation." *Library Administration and Management* 19.4 (2005): 165–175.

UNESCO. "6.5 Correspondence Analysis." *UNESCO.org*. n. d. Web. 26 February 2010.

Young, Arthur P., Peter Hernon, and Ronald R. Powell. "Attributes of Academic Library Leadership: An Exploratory Study of Some Gen-Xers." *The Journal of Academic Librarianship* 32.5 (2006): 489–502.

The Transitioning Library Collection: Is the Gen X Librarian the Right Librarian at the Right Time?

Wil Weston

"If you have always done it that way, it is probably wrong."— Charles Kettering

Academic library collections in the United States are rapidly evolving as serial collections become almost exclusively online; more ebooks are being added as a proportion of the overall monographic budget; and an increasing number of libraries are venturing into the creation of digital repositories. Additionally, as a dramatic backdrop to these exciting technological changes in libraries, the United States is trying to stumble its way out of a global economic crisis; often forcing libraries to make difficult decisions about their collections. I can almost hear the Greek Chorus of Baby Boomers cheerfully humming along to Bob Dylan's "The Times They Are a-Changin'."

Currently, academic libraries are scouring the horizon trying to divine some sign about their future identities. The academic library is transitioning into and, in some instances, surging toward an undefined future. For those who currently make materials decisions for the library; some may feel, perhaps, a bit like an Antigone listening to the Chorus when they sing their *parados*. But despite these challenges and the speed with which they are occurring, ignore the choral parade. Generation X has been here before. It will be those who remember the lessons learned from the lean experiences of the early nineties that will be able to deal with this seemingly chaotic and fiscally troubled time for libraries.

"Where am I? Who am I? How did I come to be here? What is this thing called the world?"— Søren Kierkegaard

Personally, I've always resisted ideas about generationalism; in particular, those about Generation X. Granted, being bombarded, for a brief decade, by car commercials, soda advertisements, and other products that could only further enhance my generation's perceived sense of detached, slacker cool didn't really improve my skepticism about whether or not I could be, or ever was, so nonchalantly disengaged. But then, that is a part of the Generation X mythology, isn't it? Gen X isn't really disengaged; they only want to appear that way. "Just leave me alone, okay? I got this," they supposedly gripe at those wayward, forever backwards-looking Boomers. Disengaged is only a fitting description in the same way that a daily horoscope vaguely fits. Mine said this morning that a project I'm working on will get all my attention. Whoa! It is like they know me! Which only begs the question; is sarcasm another Generation X trait?

The real question is "do the currently accepted ideas of generationalism really exist?" Allen Ginsberg's *Howl* might have been a little less poignant if he referred to his generation as "the people who were born about the same time period, within approximately a decade and a half of himself, and experienced similar cultural experiences — destroyed by madness." It doesn't really flow, does it? Yet, even the Boomers, perhaps the best chronologically defined generation, had different life experiences based on socio-economic conditions, race, gender, or based on different cultural regions within the United States. But for Generation X it is even worse; it is still just a wee bit too ambiguous on who is even a part of the generation.

So who is in and who is out? Was Gen X born in between 1965 to 1978, 1960 to 1977, or 1961 to 1981? All of these time periods have been used, at one time or another, to define when the Gen Xer was born; however, I actually like this last grouping the best. The generation would begin with John F. Kennedy taking office and Dwight Eisenhower's farewell address, warning us of the increasing power of a "military-industrial complex." Then four decades later — Hello Halliburton! The Gen X generation would then end with Ronald Reagan taking office and the visionary horror film *Evil Dead* hitting the big screens in 1981. With the demon-possessed character, Cheryl, perhaps prophetically looking into future and saying, "Soon all of you will be like me.... And then who will lock you up in a cellar?" (Actually, that might have been a little too dark and stereotypically Gen X of me to quote.)

The short answer for "when was Generation X born" is 1991. The novel *Generation X: Tales for an Accelerated Culture* was published that year and soon thereafter the media and marketers got a hold of it, packaged it up in a lovely Volkswagen Cabrio, and then labeled almost every music album produced afterwards "alternative," audio pabulum for the Xer. What Coupland later tried to explain was that Gen X was more of a sensibility or way of finding a path in difficult times. The Gen Xer mindset was born in the recession of the early nineties. Born of necessity, were ideas about living on a smaller scale, community building, and incremental change (as opposed to the previous Boomer "change the world" mentality). It was four years after the publication of his novel that Coupland said in a short piece for *Details* magazine that "X is over. I'd like to declare a moratorium on all the noise, because the notion that there exists a different generation — X, Y, K, whatever — is no longer debatable." He sums up Gen X by saying that "the media refers to anyone aged thirteen to thirty-nine as Xers. Which is only further proof that marketers and journalists never understood that X is a term that defines not a chronological age, but a way of looking at the world" (Coupland). And I would argue that this is true for every generation, including the Boomers, because all generations are affected by the times and environment that they live through. It wasn't just one generation that was looking for a job in the early nineties, nor was it just the Gen Xer who was looking at living within reduced means. Certainly, the recession in the early nineties was transformative for many college graduates expecting a delivery upon life-long promises of more than their parents had and a good paying job. But, this recession in the late 2000s will be just as transformative for college graduates hoping to enter the workforce with, perhaps, even more time accelerated ambitions than any previous graduating class has had before. And past generations will be transformed by this generation and these times, both Boomer and Gen Xer. Some are adapting, changing, and learning new ways. Others will do what they have always done, reflexively look back for those mythical "good ole days." All generations must learn from the past, but look to the future. The Generation X toolbox that was created in the nineties has suddenly become relevant again and now it is time for all of us to apply those intellectual stratagems.

The Generation X toolbox is filled with those lifelong experiences of having to do "more with less," simplifying processes, and living a smaller life. And while Generation X did generationally shepherd in the World Wide Web and its application for social media, it is also one which is conscious of its misapplication, demonstrated by witnessing the bust of the dot com businesses. It is toolbox filled with the skills of the computer savvy, the desire for sustainability, the need for practicality, and the critical eyes of the consummate skeptic. Additionally, it is also fitted with a coffee grinder and strange fondness for the movie *Willy Wonka & the Chocolate Factory* (the one with Gene Wilder), but that has only resulted in a nicely caffeinated sense of morality.

"Things do not change; we change."— Henry David Thoreau

The academic library has undergone massive changes since the mid-nineties and this change was heralded by the advent of the World Wide Web. It is very important to remember that the internet and its creation are intimately tied to the Generation X mentality. Marc Andreessen's launching of the Netscape internet browser, Jerry Yang and Dave Filo's launching of Yahoo!, and, of course, Larry Page and Sergey Brin's launching of Google are just a few of the internet's Generation X game changers. But for most academic libraries the first major use of the internet was to put their library catalog online (Millsap 98); then indexes and databases followed; library guides sprouted up; full-text journals appeared online; reference tools like Gale's *Literary Criticism* series and *Dictionary of Literary Biography* went online and searchable; and, now on the horizon, ebooks will someday be taking a larger percentage of the monographic book budget (Everton). Recent research done by Swets indicates that ebooks constituted approximately 9 percent of total book expenditures in 2009, and that number is expected to double within the next three years (Van Gisenberg). This shift from paper books to ebooks is now not so much technology driven, but economically driven as well. Ebooks are cheaper in the long run, particularly in space and maintenance. Additionally, ebook databases are well suited for libraries with current space issues, reduced staffing for stack maintenance, and lend themselves to long-term storage (Kolowich "E-Library Economics").

But none of these evolutionary online steps are a surprise to those who currently work in libraries. In fact, most academic libraries are already a large part of the ebook discussion; speaking with publishers about some of the pitfalls and procedural difficulties faced in the acquisition of ebooks. Issues with Digital Rights Management (DRM), licensing, multi-user versus single-user, perpetual access, and workable acquisition solutions for libraries with separate Monographic and Serials Acquisitions Units are some of the current obstacles. However, some are hopeful that many of these issues will be solved in the very near future. In a 2007 article, Zsolt Silberer and David Bass prognosticated an imminent future in which libraries will no longer see ebook delays in acquisitions and may even see pre-print databases like in the e-journal world. Also, they anticipate a significant improvement of DRM software and distribution capabilities for electronic interlibrary loan and electronic course reserves (Silberer 26–28). And, perhaps, libraries and publishers are slowly moving toward solving many of these solutions. Blackboard announced July 2010, that it is partnering with a major publisher and two major e-textbook vendors to make it easy for professors and students to assign and access e-textbooks and other digital materials directly through its popular learning-management system (Kolowich 2010). Additionally, standards for e-publishing DRM are evolving, in July 2010, drafts of the electronic publication (EPUB) version 2.0.1 standards appeared on the International Digital Publishing Forum (IDPF) website hopefully improving future interoperability and transport of electronic content (IDPF). Perhaps, these changes are not "imminent," given a three-year perspective since Silberer and Bass's article was written; however, there appears to have been some forward progress.

Nevertheless, the point is that current library patrons are increasingly relying on internet resources and have an expectation of desktop (or laptop) deliverability. Studies like one done by Kelley and Orr in 2003 indicate that student usage patterns are shifting toward increased use of online resources and a preference to accessing library material from home (Kelley 176). To meet these new demands, in matched step, the library has been keeping up with these remote and, now, often mobile needs for information with the same economy and Generation X initiative that has already swept the United States fully into the Information Age. Libraries and librarians have already moved online and they are there to meet their users' information needs.

Libraries are also physically changing their spaces to reflect their users' academic and, even, social needs. Books are being pushed aside for digital learning centers. "Quiet Spaces" are being set aside for what are increasingly becoming louder, more public spaces where students can engage in collaborative learning and work on group projects. Academic libraries have always been a social space to meet between classes, but now it also is a place to check email, connect online via social media, play computer games, and work on personal or academic related digital projects. The idea of the "Library as

Place" is still important, yet finding a balance that serves all library users is still a challenge facing libraries (ACRL 290). In fact, at some universities the library isn't even called the library anymore. In August 2008, the University of Nevada, Reno opened its doors to the Mathewson-IGT Knowledge Center, combining the traditional library with digital and multimedia technologies. The idea behind this move was to pool the expertise of library and information technology professionals in order to remove stumbling blocks to accessing an increasing complex and fast paced world of online information (University). This online environment was born in the nineties and was created by those who had a Generation X sensibility. Its creation and, ultimately, its navigation were by those who found a new, simpler way to do things. The Mathewson-IGT Knowledge Center, in this instance, very much represents Generation X sensibilities of community, practicality, innovation, and a coffee shop.

New buildings are, of course, not a foreseeable reality for most of the nation's academic libraries. Many universities have been hit very hard by the recession and have had to dramatically reduce their materials budget (ACRL 287). In several states, library staff and faculty have had to go on furlough (Muggeridge). But this does not mean that academic libraries cannot take part in technological advances or provide core services to their patrons. It may mean that not all services are offered all of the time and it may also mean increased selectivity for materials purchases. But it is in precisely this kind of environment that the Generation X sensibility excels.

> *"The most certain way to succeed is always to try just one more time."*
> — Thomas Edison

So, how is the Generation X sensibility applied to library collection development and management? First, rethink everything! Allow every wild idea to be aired and don't think about the money. I know that is difficult. But it is important not to kill an idea before it has a chance to develop. Economically things are certainly different than they were a decade ago; however, technologically, things have changed as well. Work the technological advantage. Librarians have done an excellent job transitioning from a print to a digital world and they can't afford to lose the momentum, regardless of budgets. And, frankly, these are the two most practical and influential experiences in the Generation X toolbox, the experiences of having to think creatively about technology and about a living on a reduced budget.

So, rethink the library's web presence! Often library catalogs and "blah" library websites are very static, un-engaging, and overly complicated. This may be the only interaction a patron might have with the library's collection — a virtual one. How a patron successfully navigates or fails to navigate through a library website to their desired information is an increasingly important part of collection development and management. Simply stringing lists of links to databases with cursory explanations of their function is unacceptable. Management of the collection involves facilitating access to the electronic resources. Collection Development should not only focus on procurement of the resources, but also ensure that resources are organized for optimum access, with adequate navigation structures to help patrons deal with the exploding body of electronic resources (Moyo 58).

For instance, broken ebook links in an online catalog are now often an invisible frustration because, at least, with the paper book missing from the shelf there was a chance that the patron, once in the building, would report the book missing. Now, the patron may just get frustrated and try something else; or give up entirely without reporting the broken link at all. Libraries cannot assume that a resource will be used or discovered in the same way; nor can it be assumed that a patron's behavior towards an information resource will be consistent across varying formats.

How can libraries involve the patron in the care and stewardship of the virtual library? How can libraries make these tools more appealing to use? How can libraries use them to invite participation from patrons in an ongoing dialogue about literature, research, and life-long learning? Make the catalog and the library website an active part of library outreach efforts and actively seek partnerships from other departments on campus, not just Academic Affairs, but Student Affairs as well. Wikipedia is an often used example of "collective action" and I would never suggest that a library catalog ever be edited in a public commons way like Wikipedia. However, making it easier for users to report broken links would be a good first step toward fostering a sense of stewardship of the library catalog and website.

Student persistence literature has demonstrated that a sense of belonging and integration into a university, both socially and academically, are critical to the successful persistence of that student (Tinto). A library could help further promote that sense of belonging by helping to create a sense of ownership of the library and library's website, by seeking active participation in its growth and maintenance. The catalog and the library website are pathways to the library's digital collections. Simply having a thing never was a guarantee of its use and this is even truer in the virtual world. The Gen X sensibility actively seeks out close knit, local communities; often actively buying local produce and supporting local businesses. The Gen X sensibility looks to the library's immediate surroundings to forge new relationships, new jointly supported services, and new ways to assist users in the navigation of the virtual and physical collection.

Rethink the library's materials budget! Carefully consider the users and the content they want. For ebooks, based on content, consider whether access only is sufficient, instead of acquiring perpetual access. Carefully consider the audience, perhaps request a Library Journal Usage Report to see what the university faculty cites in their published research. Examine usage reports for use trends. Try to tailor the library collection to the current research needs of faculty and students (Grigg). Perhaps, even survey the academic departments on their top used journals or resources. Also, if a university independently negotiated terms and conditions for a database go back and revisit those licenses. If a resource was consortially obtained, speak with the consortium about options the library would like to see in future. There is always the potential for libraries to become disenfranchised with the consortium if the needs of the institution are being ignored (Kinner). The bottom line is to always negotiate and adjust. Finally, when it does come to cutting resources, be equitable; however, also be transparent in the process. Have a clear rationale and the data to support the decision. The days of core lists, acquiring for just in case, and gut feelings are gone. Libraries must be accountable to their users and show not only their value to student learning and persistence, but also of the library services and the collection of resources which are offered (ACRL 287).

The Generation X sensibility is in place and ready to take on new leadership roles in libraries. It is a sensibility that is able to deal with the complexity of the new economic and technological challenges currently facing library collection development; and one that encourages a diversity of points of view. Additionally, a Generation X sensibility seeks economy and practicality in problem solving. Douglas Coupland said that X is a way of looking at the world and, so, potentially everyone can be a little bit of Generation X. Boomers too. So, turn off the Beach Boys and Britney Spears, you Boomers and Millennials; put on an Elvis Costello album and brew a pot of coffee. The Generation X librarian is the right librarian at the right time.

WORKS CONSULTED

ACRL Research Planning and Review Committee. "2010 Top Ten Trends in Academic Libraries: A Review of The Current Literature." *College & Research Libraries News* 71.6 (2010): 286–292.

Blair, Skylar. "Classes Canceled, Faculty Furloughed." *Daily Titan* 12 Aug. 2009. Web. 30 Sept. 2010.

Coupland, Douglas. "Generation X'd." *Details Magazine* June 1995. Web. Sept. 30, 2010.

Everton, Kelsey. "Are Libraries Dying? Ebooks and the Future of Libraries." *The Book of MPub* 19 March 2010. Web. 17 July 2010.

Grigg, Karen S., et al. "Data-Driven Collection Management: Through Crisis Emerge Opportunities." *Journal of Electronic Resources in Medical Libraries* 7.1 (2010): 1–12.

IPDF. Home page. *Ipdf.org* International Digital Publishing Forum. n. d. Web. 17 July 2010.

Kelley, Kimberly B., and Gloria J. Orr. "Trends in Distant Student Use of Electronic Resources: A Survey." *College & Research Libraries* 64.3 (May 2003): 176–191.

Kinner, Laura E., and Alice Crosetto. "Balancing Act for the Future: How the Academic Library Engages in Collection Development at the Local and Consortial Levels." *Journal of Library Administration* 49.4 (2009): 419–437.

Kolowich, Steve. "Blackboard's Bid to Galvanize E-Texts." *Inside Higher Ed* 15 July 2010. Web. 17 July 2010.

_____. "E-Library Economics." *Inside Higher Ed* 10 Feb. 2010. Web 17 July 2010.

Millsap, Larry. "A History of the Online Catalog in North America." *Technical Services Management, 1965–1990.* New York: Haworth Press, 1996.

Moyo, Lesley M. "Collections on the Web: Some Access and Navigation Issues." *Library Collections, Acquisitions, & Technical Services* 26.1 (2002): 47–59.

Muggeridge, Tessa. "Crow Announces Mandatory Furloughs for University Employees." *statepress.com* 28 Jan. 2009. Web. 30 Sept. 2010.

Powers, Rosie. "Campus Faculty Association to Take Furlough Day." *Daily Illini.com* 15 Feb. 2010. Web. 17 July 2010.

Silberer, Zsolt, and David Bass. "Battle for eBook Mindshare: It's All About the Rights." *IFLA Journal* 33.1 (2007): 23–31.

Tinto, Vincent. *Leaving College: Rethinking the Causes and Cures of Student Attrition*, 2nd ed. Chicago: University of Chicago Press, 1993.

UNR Libraries. Home page. "University Libraries" University of Nevada, Reno. n. d. Web. 17 July 2010.

Van Gisbergen, Maxim, Elyse Profera, and Christine M. Stamison. "A Librarian's View of Ebook Acquisitions." *Information Today* 26.11 (2009): 14–15.

Hackers vs. Librarians:
Some Thoughts on the
Privilege of 2.0 Thinking

Jessamyn West

I do a lot of things for a job, but I'm a technologist career-wise. I'm into this whole technology thing. I like technology and I think understanding and using technology can solve problems for libraries. However, I don't think this viewpoint, and the implications behind it, are entirely value neutral. Part of this is the digital divide issue, how technological solutions to problems will be necessarily leaving some people behind, and part of this is the unspoken aspects of class dynamics generally. There's a lot of back and forth arguing about the value of so-called 2.0 technology but I'd like to talk about an aspect of it that I think rarely gets discussed: how the advocacy of technological solutions can create invisible divides that need to be addressed along with the purely technical aspects.

Please don't get me wrong, I am fully in favor of libraries using technology to address and solve problems. I think the "Should we have public access computers in libraries?" ship has sailed and we are firmly on it and that this is good news. That said, this course is bumpier than anyone expected; my feeling is that this is partly because people are somewhat unaware of the many levels of social adjustment that are required to get people used to a 2.0 networked world. I'm going to mostly look at management and employee issues as one arena that I think is familiar and understandable to many people. This is not about "hacking the library" though several great librarians do talk about those themes. This is about hackers in the library, and how they do or don't work there.

The Shifted Library

I'm a bad employee. Or maybe I'm a good employee. The difference depends on who you ask, and more importantly what their workplace expectations have been. I'm a hard worker and pretty good with patrons. I'm also a casual dresser and don't like waking up early for meetings. I expect fairness and consistently applied rules. I'm polite enough but possibly not a team player. I'm a scorekeeper; if you ask me to stay late one day I'll want to leave early some other day. In some places this makes me a dream employee, in others, a nightmare.

Just as libraries are experiencing a shift in what patrons are expecting of them, so too are employees and managers experiencing a changing of roles. Depending which libraries you work at or patronize, you may see a wide range of employer and employee expectations. How these expectations are met or not met can be a fairly good predictor of people's job satisfaction, and reflect other people's impressions of the profession as a whole.

Lately, I don't work in libraries as much as I used to, though I speak to hundreds of librarians around the world every year. I'm also fairly plugged into the world of librarians online. More than "books vs. ebooks," more than "f*cking computers, how do they work?" ("F*cking Magnets, How Do They Work?") there seems to be a large chasm between people who look at their libraries as creative and interesting places to work, versus stagnant lifer-types who see the work as a paycheck. I see it as hacker culture versus library culture. And while this may not be an oppositional relationship necessarily, I frequently see it manifesting itself in this way.

This divide affects many other aspects of the library profession generally, including technology uptake, website usability, vendor offerings and even faithful chestnuts like library hours and library signage. Our patrons take our cues from us. They see our libraries and think "This is what a library is. This is how a library works." We have a responsibility to that image. Not to our personal images per se, a bit of a red herring if you ask me, but the idea of what a library is and how the business of managing information works: whether it's easy or hard; whether we are intelligent or a bit dim; whether we are hard workers or lazy. We pass on these messages to patrons without necessarily saying anything. I think we need to examine what we talk about when we talk about technology and how what we are saying is affecting what is actually heard.

Corporate Culture for Non-Corporations

I'm going to speak in generalities here. One of the differences in management styles and thus corporate culture between that generation and this generation — ignoring briefly the specific delineations of *this* and *that*— is the wide gap between the command and control style of getting things done, contrasted with a more consensus-based approach to doing the work of the library. I'm 41, if that's helpful. That said, this isn't strictly an age-based distinction, it can also be a cultural one. And since culture- and knowledge-preservation is at the center of our work and why we do it, having a meta-discussion about the assumptions that underlie the way our institutions work is a helpful exercise.

When I'm not working with libraries and librarians, I'm running a fairly large internet community, a giant weblog called MetaFilter ("MetaFilter | Community Weblog") that also has a fairly hopping Q&A part of the site ("Ask MetaFilter | Community Weblog"). It's got some similarities to library work in some ways but our "corporate culture" such as it is, is entirely different. Working at this website is my full-time job. Here is how it works. I am a community moderator which means my main job is customer service and keeping things running smoothly. I answer email, help people with broken HTML links, talk a lot about site policies and guidelines, and occasionally delete posts or comments that run afoul of those guidelines. I make jokes that my online job is not entirely different from my lifeguarding job which is also very similar to the library jobs that I've had in three ways:

1. I spend a lot of time telling people to behave.
2. I help support and maintain an institution that is owned by the public/group, not by me.
3. Very few people know that I have training or experience in doing my job.

Hacker Culture

The thing that makes this job so different from my past jobs in public and academic libraries is the extraordinary amount of leeway I have to make my own decisions, to determine my workload, and my workflow. I work from home or anywhere with an internet connection. I do the work when it needs doing, which can mean evenings and weekends. The people who populate the website are, in many cases, the people I also interact with in real life either at home or when I travel for other work.

When people ask me what my hours are I say that I don't have a regular schedule but that I work about ten to fifteen minutes an hour. The response is often "Oh that doesn't sound like much" to which I reply "Every hour I'm awake, that is." The work determines the hours, at some level. If there are some tumultuous discussions happening, or if we're launching a new feature, then I may need to stick around more. If things are looking pretty well taken care of, I can wander off somewhere and check back in a few hours. I can do most of my job via my phone.

The job pays more than every other library job I've had. I mention these details not to be bragging or hectoring people about their own workplaces, but to say that this sort of thing works for me. It is possible to get the workplace that you want. I'm not a magical genie, I just held out for a job where the work, hours, and dress code suits me. This environment, one that is task-centered and flexible and not very schedule-dependent, is typical in software environments, atypical in many other office jobs. People sometimes refer to it as "hacker culture" (Riemens) and depending who you talk to, they may think it's the wave of the future, or the worst thing to happen to the workplace since casual Fridays.

The thing that I think is not discussed much about hacker culture, and I would extend this to 2.0 culture, is that in many ways it's a culture of privilege. People who have jobs writing software are often decently paid people with marketable, transferable skills. There are barriers to entry which are both educational and financial before people make their way into hacker culture. In my situation, I am a second generation technologist. I grew up in a household that was familiar with and supportive of technology. I could hold out until I found the perfect job while not having to worry about raising a family or keeping a roof over my head. Some of this, certainly, was making decent choices, but a lot of it was the background that I came from.

Library Culture

When I compare and contrast my current workplace with library workplaces I have been in, I remember things like memos that went to all staff to make sure we had taken our coats off *before* we sat down at the reference desk and not afterwards. I remember filling out paper ILL forms by hand and putting them in a folder for the staff who did ILLs two days a week. I remember being asked to do shopping for library supplies on my lunch break. I remember that we weren't allowed to have a coffee maker because we had one once and someone left it on and we weren't allowed to get another one. I remember being fidgety and unhappy and feeling that people didn't care about the quality of my work as much as whether I was in the door at 8:58 or 9:02.

I redesigned the website at one of those libraries and have watched it slowly degrade over the years through a series of bad edits until it now looks like what I would call broken. It took me a long time to realize that when the people who work at that library now look at the website, they don't see it as broken. They see it as their library information, online, that they put there. They're not online enough to really grok the idea of web design, much less usability or accessibility. They don't come from a tech background and they don't see the web as a networking and transparency tool. This is not to say that they can't, but they're coming from a different sort of library background, where librarians are stewards of not just information, but culture. While they may use the web as a tool to promote library events and list library policies, they don't see the web as a fertile medium where the business of librarianship is done.

Again, I am over-generalizing to make a point. It's clear to me that when I speak to some librarians that my talk of installing Firefox and using Greasemonkey and running scripts (all of which can be done with pointing and clicking, I'd like to mention) they see me as someone coming, as we say in Vermont, "from away" to somehow tell them that my culture is better than their culture. And this is a problem. The question I get asked more often than any other question when I go to give talks is "Where do I find the time to do this sort of thing?" The statement that I hear most often is "We're not allowed to use that software in our libraries."

I feel that what they are really saying is that their library environment is not conducive to 2.0 sorts of things for whatever reason, but there are other reasons as well:

- They are not deputized to make technological decisions at their library.
- They are not given time to learn new technologies at their library.
- They are not in a library that encourages technological innovation and change.

But most importantly, I think what they're saying is that **they don't have the leverage to change this state of events**, either through applying pressure or changing jobs. Or that they don't care. And again, this is something that I feel is a class issue. Lack of job mobility for social or financial reasons, is something that can be outside of people's ability to change. And yet I believe it's one of the larger issues that affects our nationwide system of libraries (I can't speak as much to the library environment in other countries) and why many of them seem content with status quo technology. And why is there pushback against the technophiles among us as being people promoting a culture that is antithetical to librarianship? Or is it?

2.0 Culture and Beyond?

I'm a person who enjoys computers and the internet and would like other people to enjoy these things too, particularly if they have a problem to solve. I like to listen to other librarians talking about how they've solved their problems with technology. I think there are a lot of people for whom free or cheap tools really do solve a problem. But I think we've focused on the money issue at the expense of the cultural issue. We all know that computers cost money. But it's equally true that smart phones and text plans cost money and might not be consumer choices made by people who are on a budget. Having jobs where you can spend a lot of discretionary time on Facebook or Twitter for your company is a mark of privilege. Being able to freely leave a job because your boss objected to something in your personal blog is also something that many people, even librarians, don't have the freedom to do. As much as we proclaim the benefits of our increasingly networked and online world, they're available for many fewer people than I think we sometimes imagine. And many of these people are our colleagues.

I'm increasingly aware that while I don't feel that I have any particular skills that make me more able to interact with and enjoy technology, I definitely have the freedom to experiment and the free time to experiment in and, most importantly, the freedom to fail. This marker, above most others, indicates that I occupy a privileged position in the world of work. I've been fortunate enough to be able to leverage this into a situation where I can actively help people who need it — my online job subsidizes my community technology job locally — and I'm aware that a lot of this for me has been luck of the draw. There are other 2.0 advocates who speak frequently about the experience gap that we are seeing in users of 2.0 technologies. Danah boyd gave a great keynote presentation at SXSW 2010 discussing why it is the responsibility of those who understand the systems to ensure the security of privacy of those who use but do not fully comprehend the systems they are using.

> Sure, it's great to say that everyone SHOULD be comfortable being in public, but that's not the world in which we live. Many people are just trying to get by. We cannot expect marginalized folks to always be fighting for their right to speak and we shouldn't accept the marginalization of folks just because of the roles that they play. The "public by default" environment that we are so proudly creating isn't always the great democratizer; for many, it's exactly the opposite. Just because technology allows us to speak up in public doesn't mean that everyone is comfortable doing so or, for that matter, will be heard [boyd].

We've seen that the network effect of 2.0 technologies hasn't immediately leveled the playing field in the U.S. in terms of providing not just access but instruction in how these technologies work, even as the tools get simpler and, we're told, user-friendly. I believe that before we can fully manage the issues wrapped up in the mostly explicable and discussable digital divide, we have to look further inward at our own mostly unstated cultural divides and the assumptions that go along with them in order to better understand each other and be able to move forward into our technological future together.

WORKS CITED

"Ask MetaFilter | Community Weblog." *Metafilter.com* n. d. Web. 1 Sept. 2010.
boyd, danah. "Making Sense of Privacy and Publicity." *SXSW* Austin, Texas. 13 March 2010. Web. 1 Sept. 2010.
"F*cking Magnets, How Do They Work?" *Know Your Meme* 1 May 2010. Web. 1 Sept. 2010.
"MetaFilter | Community Weblog." *Metafilter.com* n. d. Web. 1 Sept. 2010.
Riemens, Patrice. "Some Thoughts on the Idea of 'Hacker Culture.'" *Cryptome* 3 June 2002. Web. 1 Sept. 2010.

SECTION FOUR

POP CULTURE

Watchers, Punks and Dashing Heroes: Representations of Male Librarians in Generation X Mass Culture

Rafia Mirza and Maura Seale

> *"Who you are? The Watcher? Sniveling, tweed-clad guardian of the Slayer and her kin? I think not. I know who you are, Rupert. And I know what you're capable of. But they don't, do they? They have no idea where you come from."*—"Halloween"

> *"I think it only fair to warn you that I am a Librarian."*—*Curse of the Judas Chalice*

> *"I am the Punk Librarian Deluxe. Parents, beware."*—Niffenegger 178

It might be said that librarians are a little obsessed with their public image; how the profession and its practitioners are portrayed in mass culture have been the subject of numerous articles and books. While these analyses have investigated in detail how libraries and librarians are depicted in films, television programs, novels and short stories, comic books, advertisements, websites, and material culture, few have explicitly examined the role of gender ideologies in these representations. Most merely observe that librarians tend to be portrayed as women, perhaps unsurprisingly given that the profession has been dominated by women since the early twentieth century, and note that depictions of male librarians in mass culture have historically been quite rare (Dickinson 104–107). This has changed, however, as the most prominent mass culture representations of librarians currently are male: Rupert Giles the Watcher from *Buffy the Vampire Slayer*, Flynn Carsen in the *The Librarian* series broadcast on TNT, and Henry DeTamble from both the novel and film versions of *The Time Traveler's Wife*. The emergence and popularity of these characters during the last decade of the twentieth century and the first decade of the twenty-first, which have been characterized by massive changes in the information landscape, in the field of librarianship, and in dominant understandings of masculinity, is striking. In this essay, we argue that these texts and characters negotiate power disruptions within the realms of gender and information/knowledge. From the 1970s on, traditional definitions of masculinity have been challenged socially, by the emergence and mainstreaming of the feminist movement, and economically, by the shift to a service economy (Kimmel 17–18). Generation X is the first generation to come of age amid these changes, and these texts exemplify this generation's attempts to reconcile these changes and create a new model of masculinity. This new model acknowledges feminism's critiques but simultaneously resurrects and authorizes masculine power in order to stave off the sense of powerlessness left by the breakdown of clear-cut notions of masculinity and manhood (Kimmel 42). While the male characters in these texts retain some traits associated with earlier, female representations of librarians, the narratives work to construct them as powerful, authoritative, and masculine gatekeepers, whose role in limiting access to knowledge is necessary in order to control the irrational and, implicitly, the female, as embodied by the paranormal elements in these texts.

In "Old Maids, Policeman, and Social Rejects: Mass Media Representations and Public Perceptions of Librarians," Seale argues that representations of librarians can be roughly grouped into five distinct but often overlapping categories: the old maid librarian, the policeman librarian, the librarian as parody, the inept librarian, and the hero/ine librarian (Seale). Although Giles the Watcher, Flynn Carsen, and Henry DeTamble do considerably differ from previous representations of librarians, they do share some characteristics such as bookishness and social awkwardness. *Buffy the Vampire Slayer* revolves around the eponymous heroine fighting against the forces of darkness, such as vampires and demons, with the aid of her friends and her Watcher, Rupert Giles. In order to provide Buffy with information and guidance in her fight, Giles takes a job as a librarian at her high school. Giles is often made fun of for his stuffy, librarianish ways, with various characters remarking that he was probably upset math was not "mathier" in high school and likely wore tweed diapers when he was a baby ("The Dark Age"). He tends to refer to computers as "dread machines" ("The Harvest"). Buffy sums up one of Giles's lectures as "blah blah biddy blah, I'm so stuffy, give me a scone" ("Inca Mummy Girl"), while his main love interest makes fun of him by telling him she dog-eared a book he leant her, wrote in it, and then spilled coffee on it. When Giles, who has become increasingly horrified throughout this conversation, points out it was a first edition, she says she was just teasing and calls him a fuddy-duddy, albeit a sexy fuddy-duddy ("The Dark Age"). Although Giles himself is not explicitly Generation X — he is really more of a father figure to Buffy, who is — his attitude towards the occult is embedded in the new model of masculinity created by Generation X and prevalent in Joss Whedon's work. Giles seeks to "hide the heterodox knowledge from the world in order to protect them from the truth of what lies beneath; but also protect the orthodox knowledge from those from the Hellmouth who would seek to destroy it" (Pateman 32). This is analogous to what Anthony McMahon refers to as the "New Father," which emerged in the 1980s and 1990s as a mode of masculinity (McMahon 116). The New Father is an expert, likes Giles, with a superior understanding of the world and its workings, and incorporates both nurturing and male right, thereby resolving the contradictions of Generation X masculinity.

When *The Librarian* series begins, Flynn Carsen is working on a Ph.D. in Egyptology to complement his twenty-two other academic degrees. In *The Librarian: Quest for the Spear*, Flynn's professor tells him to leave college and gain real world experience; he then receives a magical invitation to apply for the position of the Librarian, and begins traveling the globe for magical artifacts to bring back to the Library. Immediately after this, a women that his mother is trying to set him up with points out that he's in his thirties, still in school, and lives with his mother. She is not interested in him, and this comes up a lot with the women he interacts with as Flynn. Flynn is a resident of "Guyland," Michael Kimmel's term for the social space inhabited by young men of Generation X and Y prior to full adulthood (Kimmel 34). He is depicted as the stereotypical overeducated and underemployed Generation X slacker. Until he exits Guyland and its physical manifestation, his mother's house, he is not seen as a fully masculine sexual partner. Flynn prizes theoretical knowledge but the female characters are more impressed when he can use that knowledge for practical purposes, such as Flynn using his knowledge of geography, biology, and botany to triangulate his and Nicole's position in the Amazon. In *Return to King Solomon's Mines*, Flynn cannot reconcile himself to his father's memory, thinking all he has of him are his "silly bedtime stories" until he realizes that the stories were actually clues to prepare him for this movie's central quest. Despite possessing a great amount of book knowledge, Flynn is lacking something. His immaturity and conflicted relationship with his father embody the struggle within Generation X understandings of masculinity to embrace domesticity to some degree while retaining some of the trappings of traditional masculinity.

The Time Traveler's Wife tells the love story of Henry DeTamble and Clare Abshire; Henry is afflicted with involuntary time traveling and first meets Clare when she is a child. Time is key to this novel; each section begins with Clare's and Henry's ages, and Henry must discover what year it is after he time travels. Henry was born in 1963, Clare in 1971, and the majority of the action takes place from 1991 to 2007. The constant references to dates, combined with cultural references — a pivotal scene at a Violent Femmes concert (Niffenegger 154), Prince's song "1999" (Niffenegger 213), the dotcom boom and bust (Niffenegger 145) — emphasize the position of the characters as members of Generation X. While Clare grows up in a somewhat dysfunctional nuclear family, Henry's mother is killed in an accident when he is a child, and his father subsequently falls into alcoholism and ceases to be a good parent; this, too, locates the characters within Generation X, which is characterized by "less stable and settled family lives" (Kimmel 32). Henry is a rare books librarian at the Newberry Library in Chicago and somewhat surprisingly, his work is occasionally mentioned although not depicted at length; he catalogs materials, lectures and presents, and assists researchers using the library's collections. These brief mentions of his work, however, are less integral to the narrative than two scenes that take place in the Newberry. The first chapter opens with Henry meeting his future wife as an adult, when she travels to the Newberry to conduct research. In the second lengthy scene set in the Newberry, Henry time travels into the

Cage, which "is four stories tall and runs up the center of the stairwell" (Niffenegger 304–305). When Henry is stuck in the Cage, he is forced to explain his time traveling to his colleagues and supervisor: "I explain about trying to have a normal life. 'And part of having a normal life is having a normal job,' I conclude" (Niffenegger 463). While the emotional and social aspects of Henry's work are acknowledged and even briefly depicted, his work as a whole is downplayed. The novel intensely focuses on the relationship between Henry and Clare; their alternating roles as narrator propel the plot. Despite the bittersweet ending, this novel fits most closely with the genre of romance, which is characterized by an almost singular focus on the hero and heroine.

In contrast to Flynn, Giles and Henry interact with users. For Henry, the interaction is not seen as significant within the novel. Instead, it is just one more way in which Henry is attempting to have a normal life and analogous to scenes of Clare at work, Henry and Clare interacting with friends and family, and so on. It is this normalcy that is Henry's higher purpose. As he notes, "All my pleasure are homey ones: armchair splendor, the sedate excitements of domesticity" (Niffenegger ix). This domesticity is a crucial part of the redefinition of masculinity that began in the 1970s, during the childhood of Generation X, and continued throughout the 1980s and 1990s, and is exemplified in McMahon's "New Father." While Henry becomes a literal father, Giles and eventually Flynn function as metaphoric fathers. In *Buffy the Vampire Slayer*, Giles is often irritated by students' request for his time and clearly believes that his role as a Watcher is more important than his work as a librarian. When the principal forces him to interact with students, he remarks, "I did try to explain that my vocational choice of librarian was a deliberate attempt to minimize said contact, but he would have none of it" ("The Puppet Show"). While Giles is a librarian, it functions primarily as his cover, so that he can interact with Buffy and not arouse suspicion. *Buffy* plays with genre for comedic effect, but it functions mainly as action adventure series. The genre itself gives the action hero Buffy agency as a character, while dominant discourses give Giles primacy as an older, more knowledgeable man. Cultural expectations and genre often battle for supremacy throughout the series, and this battle is made explicit through the many clashes Buffy and Giles have over duty, knowledge, and destiny. For example, in "Prophecy Girl," both Giles and Angel are convinced Buffy is going to die because of a prophecy, but she is determined to escape her fate by quitting her job as Slayer. Interestingly, neither is proved to be wrong by the narrative — Buffy does die, so the unavoidable prophecy is completed, but she is brought back to life when Xander performs CPR on her, thus proving the prophecy incomplete at the very least. Giles acts as a father figure to Buffy and her friends and in fact becomes a more effective Watcher due to his parental instincts. In *The Librarian* series, Flynn has to distance himself from his mother in order to become a man. As the series progresses, he moves out of his mother's house, realizes that the surrogate father she chose is corrupt and also the murderer of his father, and replaces the figure chosen by his mother with a father figure of his choosing, Judson, a former Librarian. In taking these actions, Flynn both matures and creates an ideal family, and is validated by Judson, when he tells him his father would be proud of him. There is a sense of a heroic, masculine legacy here.

Giles and Flynn also desire the pleasures of domesticity, or at least the pleasures of a heteronormative relationship, but struggle. While *Quest for the Spear* deals primarily with Flynn becoming The Librarian, *Curse of the Judas Chalice* and *Return to King Solomon's Mines* deal with the cost that being the Librarian has had on his life. This series primarily fits into the action adventure genre, and Flynn, like Henry and Giles, puts effort forth to maintain a secret identity. Women who do to know his secret cannot deal with Flynn's lifestyle, and women who do know have their own extraordinary destinies to deal with and cannot be with him. In both *Return to King Solomon's Mines* and *Curse of the Judas Chalice*, Flynn wants to continue his relationships with Emily Davenport and Simone Renoir respectively, but they turn him down. Flynn repeatedly has minor breakdowns over the cost of being the Librarian and wants to quit because of the effect on his personal life, and the movies go on to show how Flynn cannot escape his destiny of being the Librarian. Giles similarly mentions that the "tedious grind" of studying the occult and the "overwhelming pressure of [his] destiny" led him to rebel ("The Dark Ages"). Unfortunately, the demon Eyghon he summoned while a rebellious youth disrupts his relationship by possessing his girlfriend Jenny; while she is eventually freed, she tells Giles that she needs time and cancels her date with him.

Although Henry and Clare's adult relationship spans from 1991 to 2006, a period of massive changes in information and communication technology that impacted both librarianship and basic social interaction, Henry is not depicted as technologically savvy or even much engaged in technology. He does advise his friends Kimy and Gomez to invest in the internet and technology stocks prior to the dotcom boom of the late 1990s, but his work and his personal life with Clare remain unaffected by these changes. This evokes earlier representations of librarians as averse to technology and parallels Giles, an active Luddite, and Flynn. In "I, Robot ... You, Jane," a book containing a demon is scanned, freeing the demon to roam the Internet and Giles remarks, "Things involved with a computer fill me with childlike terror. Now, if it were a nice ogre or some such I'd be more in my element." Technology is not merely unnecessary; it is the enemy of the librarian in that it cannot contain the paranormal or understand the context in which the paranormal should be fought. While Jenny and Willow are both technologically savvy and have experience with the paranormal, their affinity for technology cannot save them. Humans and particularly women attempting to use technology to control the supernatural always ends poorly in the Buffyverse.

While Flynn mentions in passing that he is familiar with RSS feeds, technology is in no way significant to his character. He relies on ancient parchments and books to track down the treasures he hides or destroys. In *Quest for the Spear* Flynn tells his mother that his books are "not just books.... These books are slices of the ultimate truth ... they speak to me.... Like nothing else." The entire series hinges on Flynn's affinity for books. In *Quest for the Spear*, Flynn has a book written in the Language of the Birds, and he is the only one who can decipher the book and thus locate the Spear of Destiny; the film revolves around his ability to successfully find the truth in a book that no one else can read. In *Return to King Solomon's Mines,* the successful resolution depends on him having the knowledge to refuse to read King Solomon's book and in *Curse of the Judas Chalice,* he also must interpret texts to obtain the Chalice. Dracula himself tells Flynn that he would have made "one hell of an historian."

Like both earlier representations of librarians and both Giles and Flynn, Henry is occasionally portrayed as socially awkward, although this awkwardness is primarily connected to his time traveling. When Henry time travels, he simply disappears and then reappears in another time, naked and helpless: "When I am out there, in time, I am inverted, changed into a desperate version of myself. I become a thief, a vagrant, an animal who runs and hides" (Niffenegger ix). In order to survive, he often ends up breaking social norms and being arrested and held by the police. Similarly, his inability to control when he time travels can potentially lead to other forms of social embarrassment, as when he time travels during his first visit with Clare's parents, his wedding, and the birth of his daughter. Henry's vulnerability and powerlessness are constant and unpredictable, so much so that he eventually loses his feet to frostbite due to time traveling to Chicago during the winter. These repeated episodes of helplessness and lack of control echo the dearth of markers that define and validate masculinity for Generation X (Kimmel 42). Yet this vulnerability and lack of power are balanced and subverted in several different ways. Henry may be helpless to control when he time travels, but he can predict it somewhat — "Exhaustion, loud noises, stress, standing up suddenly, flashing light" often precede an episode — and he does work with a geneticist to determine the causes and possible ways to treat it (Niffenegger ix). Although he is naked following his time traveling, he is portrayed as quite skillful at surviving; he is an excellent pickpocket and thief, he is more than able to defend himself, and he continually thwarts the efforts of the Chicago police department by disappearing once he in custody. Henry is portrayed using almost stereotypical traits of conventional masculinity in these moments — he fights, runs, and subverts authority — that are echoed by his intense sexual drive and multiple girlfriends. His twenties are a "blur of women, breasts, legs, skin, hair" and his sex life with Clare so active that she eventually says, "there are days when I can't sit down" (Niffenegger 66, 229). These moments of traditional masculinity evoke Kimmel's Guyland, which, "rest[s] on three distinct cultural dynamics: a culture of entitlement, a culture of silence, and a culture of protection" (Kimmel 59). Violence, misogyny, and rape are often implicated in Guyland, and while Henry is not a rapist and generally commits crimes in order to survive, the text does gesture towards the reclamation of masculine power through these acts. According to one character, "[Henry] treats her bad, drinks like they ain't making it no more, disappears for days and then comes around like nothing happened, sleeps with anything that stands still long enough" (Niffenegger 159); in another scene, Henry "stomp[s] the living shit out of a large drunk suburban guy who had the effrontery to call [him] a faggot" (Niffenegger 137).

Henry's time traveling actually invests him with power, as do his relationships with his father and Clare; as with Giles and Flynn, this power stems from knowledge and as such, Henry functions as a gatekeeper. His relationship with his father is conflicted and often unpleasant due to his mother's death and his father's subsequent alcoholism, and there are very few scenes between Henry and his father. In perhaps the most significant scene, Henry reveals how he sees his mother when he time travels: "I see her on a regular basis. I've seen her hundreds of times since she died. I see her walking around the neighborhood, with you, with me. [...] I see her at Juilliard. *I hear her sing!*" (Niffenegger 226) This knowledge establishes Henry's authority; this is echoed by Henry paying his father's rent, coercing him into giving up drinking, and generally taking care of him. Henry's relationship to Clare also ascribes power to him, although it is more balanced than his relationship with his father. Henry first begins appearing to Clare when she is a child and in general, he keeps knowledge about the future from her and she even notes, "It's not fair that you know everything about me but you never tell me anything about you" (Niffenegger 67). He possesses knowledge about time traveling — about what he can and cannot do, whether things will or will not change. In some moments, he is depicted as omniscient, as in this discussion of how he repeatedly returns to the scene of his mother's death: "My mother dying ... it's the pivotal thing ... everything else goes around and around it.... I dream about it, and I also — time travel to it. Over and over. If you could be there, and could hover over the scene of the accident, and you could see every detail of it, all the people, cars, trees, snowdrifts — if you had enough time to really look at everything, you would see me. I am in cars, behind bushes, on the bridge, in a tree. I have seen it from every angle" (Niffenegger 114). This is countered by instances in which Clare possesses more knowledge than him; when she meets him at the Newberry, for example, she has known him for twelve years and knows many things about him, while he has not yet met her in his adult life. Most significantly, Clare experiences his death as a teenager and it is she who first realizes that that was when he died. Ultimately, however, the power embedded within knowledge is understood as residing in Henry; while Clare recognizes the moment of Henry's death, he is the one who is ultimately able to travel to the future and learn the exact date. These power dynamics around knowledge evoke the conflict within Generation X definitions of masculinity, which simultaneously seek to acknowledge feminism and incorporate the nurturing and domestic into masculinity through the figure of the New Father (McMahon) while reinscribing traditional notions of masculine power and authority, as seen in Guyland (Kimmel). Henry's relationship with Clare is generally egalitarian; he takes care of his father and daughter. He also occasionally behaves violently and misogynistically and controls the access of knowledge.

Similarly, Flynn derives authority from his interactions with the paranormal. In *Return to King Solomon's Mines*, Flynn discovers that his father was a Mason and intended for him to follow in his footsteps. His mother is unaware of this, and refers to his father's stories as "silly." This is the movie where Flynn fully becomes a gatekeeper, deciding not only what should be put in the Library, but that Solomon's book should be destroyed, and what information he will share with his mother about his father's life. In order to protect his mother from violence and betrayal, he keeps his father's life a secret, essentially reversing the relationship of parent and child. Although Flynn primarily relies on trickery, he, too, can be violent. In *Curse of the Judas Chalice,* he is able to kill Dracula while KGB agents and the heroine, despite being a vampire herself, have failed. As described earlier, Giles's relationship with Buffy is similar to that of a father. He is also a member of the Watcher's Council, which trains Slayers and determines whether or not a Slayer is worthy through a test called the Cruciamentum. Like Henry, Giles often resorts to violence, although it is depicted as justified. In "The Gift," Giles secretly kills Ben, a human possessed by the demon Glory in cold blood, because Buffy essentially cannot: "She's a hero, you see. She's not like us." Giles's knowledge of the occult, his role on the Watcher's Council, and his metaphoric parenting of Buffy invest him with authority and power. Like Flynn and Henry, he is a New Father in Guyland; entitlement, silence, and protection are all at work in the ways in which these characters interact with information. They feel entitled to take any artifact or action they feel they have to. They decide who needs to know what and often decide that no one else can handle it. And finally, they do it to protect those around them, who are understood to be weaker and less capable.

These three male librarians do not sit comfortably in any of the five categories identified by Seale. They are policemen in that their power derives from the possession of knowledge and heroes in that they are the protagonists of these texts. We contend that these characters represent the formation of a new category within mass culture representations of librarians: the gatekeeper. The gatekeeper's predominant role is the limiting of access to potentially harmful information and as such, acting as a figure of benevolent and even necessary authority. Unlike the policemen, they operate outside of the law, answering to a higher authority and purpose. In *The Time Traveler's Wife,* Henry strives for a "normal life" and in order to give this to Clare, he intentionally and repeatedly withholds knowledge from her and everyone else in his life for their own good: "If you are in time not knowing, you're free. Trust me" (Niffenegger 145). Henry operates outside of human law, by constantly thwarting the Chicago police and usurping his father's authority, and the laws of physics, by time traveling. Flynn's role as the Librarian is to seek out fantastical and powerful objects and either bring them back to the Library where they are hidden away from the world, as in the case of Spear of Destiny and the Judas Chalice, or destroy them, like Solomon's book. The treasures that Flynn gathers from around the world for the Metropolitan Library in New York could never be legally brought to the United States; they are the world's greatest and most powerful treasures. The Spear of Destiny gives the holder the power to never be defeated in battle, the Judas Chalice possesses the power to control and heal vampires, and Solomon's Book can resurrect the dead. Giles is supposed to keep the Slayer and her mission secret and while his success in keeping this secret is debatable, he is also successful in other ways. He keeps the secret of the Slayer's test, which determines if a Slayer is worthy, from Buffy because the Watcher Council decrees it. Giles refers to it as "an archaic exercise in cruelty" ("Helpless") and in the end, rejects the decision of the Watcher's council and helps Buffy with the test. This is one of Giles early heroic moments — when he becomes not just a representative of the Gatekeeping organization but the embodiment of gatekeeping himself. Giles is shown as standing outside of human and Watcher law, and is eventually removed from his position as Watcher. No longer does the Watcher's council dictate his actions or what information he shares; only his own conscience and morals can do that.

The gatekeeper, in contrast to the other categories of librarian representations, is also specifically male. It echoes the very earliest stereotypes of librarians in the United States, in which librarians were portrayed as "grim, eccentric and male" (Dickinson 98). This stereotype is related to the initial role of what were then referred to as "library keepers": enforcing rules regarding borrowing and returning privileges and thus restricting access (Dickinson 100). In contrast to these current incarnations of male librarians as gatekeepers, the role of the library keeper was perceived as thankless, low status, and feminized (Dickinson), while Giles, Flynn, and Henry are depicted as powerful, knowledgeable, and extremely masculine. This masculinity, however, is not the masculinity of John Wayne or Dirty Harry; it is a combination of dominant Generation X models of masculinity that acknowledge the impact of feminism but ultimately seek to reify male power in a post-feminist age. These male characters yearn for and seek out the domestic, like McMahon's New Father, but still reside in Kimmel's Guyland and deploy violence and control knowledge in order to regain and retain power. Giles's past life as Ripper was extremely sexual and violent, Henry is "moderately notorious" due to his sex life, and Flynn is the romantic lead who ultimately saves the heroine with his knowledge (Niffenegger 141). These gatekeeper librarians, then, control access to knowledge, but rather than being perceived as emasculated and lacking in prestige, they are viewed positively: as fully masculine individuals whose control of knowledge is benevolent and necessary. The powerlessness that resulted from the collapse in traditional notions of masculinity beginning in the 1970s is reversed through the tropes of the New Father and the creation of Guyland and this is celebrated. This shift in representation seems tied to the rapid pace of change within the information landscape during the past twenty years, as "information overload" has become the predominant way of describing it.

In "Power, Knowledge, and Fear: Feminism, Foucault, and the Stereotype of the Female Librarian," Radford and Radford argue that the library functions as a "metaphor for rationality" within the Western literary tradition (254). They note that "the library and librarians are a prevalent metaphor of power and knowledge within popular culture" and argue that the library "guards and controls discourse" — that is, what can be known and said (259). The stereotype of the female librarian, then, acts to defuse the power embodied in the library: "there is nothing to fear: there is only a woman" (261). In an age of information overload, however, knowledge begins to behave irrationally, and escapes the rational confines of the library. Radford and Radford do not explore this, but rationality tends to be associated with masculinity, while irrationality — the madness that is the alternative to the library, according to Radford and Radford — is associated with the feminine (255). Irrationality is not the only trait stereotypically associated with women; the body is as well and these texts duplicate this association. In *The Time Traveler's Wife*, Henry repeatedly muses about Clare's body: "Clare reading, with her hair hanging over the back of the chair, massaging balm into her cracked red hands before bed" (Niffenegger x). Clare's paper art is physically demanding and the final third of the book focuses on her repeated pregnancies and miscarriages. In *Buffy*, the Slayer embodies physicality; her power is both physical and paranormal, as it is demonic in origin. The heroines in each of *The Librarian* films are physical and sensual; while they are depicted as physically and intellectually capable, they all rely on Flynn to complete their quests. These male librarians act to tame and regulate the irrationality of information overload and of the permeable and mutable gender roles that have characterized the post-feminist, Generation X decades. Ultimately, these texts reject feminism, even while incorporating some of its critiques of masculinity; the initial promise of gender egalitarianism in each of these texts is abandoned by their conclusions. Flynn is unable to maintain relationships with any of the heroines, due to his role as the Librarian, as well as the desires of the women. Giles leaves his position as Buffy's Watcher and moves to England in order to reform the Watcher's Council. Henry dies young.

The male librarians in *Buffy the Vampire Slayer*, *The Librarian*, and *The Time Traveler's Wife* derive power and authority from their knowledge, their ability to regulate the flow of knowledge, the rationality ascribed to them by their positions as librarians, and their modified but still potent masculinity. Their control over knowledge is depicted as altruistic and paternal. What does it mean, then, that these characters are repeatedly forced to interact with the paranormal, which in these cases, embodies the irrational? While Radford and Radford describe the female librarian as dominated by the rationality of the library (261), these male librarians are able to control and dominate the paranormal. In *The Time Traveler's Wife*, Henry eventually discovers that his time traveling has a genetic basis; a geneticist is able to sequence his DNA, identify and copy the faulty genes, and then use them to breed mice that can then be experimented on. By the conclusion, Henry's daughter Alba is able to identify herself as "Chrono-Displaced Person" and the geneticist continues to work on treatments (Niffenegger 389). In this way, rational science is deployed to if not vanquish, then to dominate the paranormal and an easier future is implied for Alba, even if the horror of Henry's death lingers (Niffenegger 390). In *Buffy the Vampire Slayer*, it is eventually revealed that the Slayers were created by a group of magic users who later form the Watcher's Council. The Watcher's Council does not partake in paranormal and irrational power, but instead controls it through the Slayers, who they train, control, hide, and destroy. Technology and scientific rationality are, in the Buffyverse, insufficient to control the paranormal and so control must be exerted in other ways, such as hiding or destroying it (Pateman 15–37). This is similar to the control of the paranormal in *The Librarian* series; the book of Solomon, for example, cannot be allowed to exist and cannot be scientifically explained.

The recent appearance and dominance of male librarians such as Giles from *Buffy the Vampire Slayer*, Flynn from *The Librarian* series, and Henry from *The Time Traveler's Wife* embody contemporary renegotiations of power relations within the realms of gender and knowledge/information. Male librarians became possible in American mass culture as technology became to be seen as central to the profession in both mainstream discourse and within librarianship itself (Tancheva 542). Ultimately, these texts are reactionary, as they endorse the need for an authoritative, masculine figure to act as a gatekeeper to knowledge and information and to conquer irrationality. This vision is complicated by a modified masculinity that is based on the Generation X models of the New Father and Guyland and by these characters' relationships with female characters, but it remains. These texts simultaneously reveal a discomfort with this gatekeeping figure, as these male librarians are forced to confront the irrational as embodied in the paranormal elements of these texts; however, these male librarians are ultimately able to control the paranormal, even if only to a degree. Unlike female librarians, burdened by the domestic and the bodily and dominated by the rationality of the library, these male librarian gatekeepers are to be admired. They are manly, powerful, and act for the forces of good; they are cool.

WORKS CONSULTED

"The Dark Age." *Buffy the Vampire Slayer: The Complete Second Season*. 20th Century–Fox, 2002. DVD.
Dickinson, T. E. "Looking at the Male Librarian Stereotype." *Reference Librarian* 78 (2002): 97–110.
"The Gift." *Buffy the Vampire Slayer: The Complete Fifth Season*. 20th Century–Fox, 2003. DVD.
"Halloween." *Buffy the Vampire Slayer: The Complete Second Season*. 20th Century–Fox, 2002. DVD.
"The Harvest." *Buffy the Vampire Slayer: The Complete First Season*. 20th Century–Fox, 2002. DVD.
Helms, B. L. *Reel Librarians: The Stereotype and Technology*. MSLS Thesis. University of North Carolina at Chapel Hill (2006).
"Helpless." *Buffy the Vampire Slayer: The Complete Third Season*. 20th Century–Fox, 2003. DVD.
"Inca Mummy Girl." *Buffy the Vampire Slayer: The Complete Second Season*. 20th Century–Fox, 2002. DVD.
"I, Robot ... You, Jane." *Buffy the Vampire Slayer: The Complete First Season*. 20th Century–Fox, 2002. DVD.
Kimmel, Michael S. *Guyland: The Perilous World Where Boys Become Men*. New York: Harper, 2008.
The Librarian: Quest for the Spear. Dir. Peter Winther. Perf. Noah Wyle, Sonya Walger, Bob Newhart. 2004. Turner Home Ent., 2005. DVD.
The Librarian: Return to King Solomon's Mines. Dir. Jonathan Frakes. Perf. Noah Wyle, Gabrielle Anwar, Bob Newhart. 2006. Turner Home Ent., 2006. DVD.
The Librarian: The Curse of the Judas Chalice. Dir. Jonathan Frakes. Perf. Noah Wyle, Stana Katic, Bob Newhart. 2008. Sony Pictures, 2009. DVD.
McMahon, Anthony. *Taking Care of Men: Sexual Politics in the Public Mind*. Cambridge: Cambridge University Press, 1999.
McNeilly, Kevin, Christina Sylka, and Susan R. Fisher. "Kiss the Librarian, but Close the Hellmouth: 'It's Like a Whole Big Sucking Thing.'" *Slayage: The Online International Journal of Buffy Studies* 1.2 (2001). Web. 1 Feb. 2010.
Niffenegger, Audrey. *The Time Traveler's Wife*. Orlando: Harcourt, 2003.

Pateman, Matthew. *The Aesthetics of Culture in* Buffy, the Vampire Slayer. Jefferson, NC: McFarland, 2006.

"Prophecy Girl." *Buffy the Vampire Slayer: The Complete First Season.* 20th Century–Fox, 2002. DVD.

"The Puppet Show." *Buffy the Vampire Slayer: The Complete First Season.* 20th Century–Fox, 2002. DVD.

Radford, M. L., and G. P. Radford. "Power, Knowledge, and Fear: Feminism, Foucault, and the Stereotype of the Female Librarian." *The Library Quarterly* 67.3 (1997): 250–66.

Seale, Maura. "Old Maids, Policeman, and Social Rejects: Mass Media Representations and Public Perceptions of Librarians." *E-JASL: The Electronic Journal of Academic and Special Librarianship* 9.1 (2008) Web. 1 Dec. 2009.

Tancheva, K. "Recasting the Debate: The Sign of the Library in Popular Culture." *Libraries and Culture* 40.4 (2005): 530–545.

Pinko vs. Punk: A Generational Comparison of Alternative Press Publications and Zines

Jenna Freedman

In her article about the Salt Lake City Public Library zine collection, proto zine librarian Julie Bartel quotes Chip Rowe's definition of zines as "cut-and-paste, 'sorry this is late'" publications (Bartel 232). That's also a good description of this essay. I'm putting it together in a last-minute deadline-conscious frenzy, having read over a hundred articles. Therefore, I'd like to begin with disclaimers and explanations.

I wouldn't be a good iconoclast if I didn't take a moment to say that even though I'm contributing to a book about Generation X, I'm not crazy about the whole generations discussion. Tom Eland put it well in an email: "I consider the entire construct of 'generations' bankrupt. To lump people into categories of every 10 to 20 years regardless of class, race, gender, religion, political ideology, and geography and then extrapolate a common set of values and viewpoints is nonsensical" (Eland). Most of the conversation about "Baby Boomers" and members of "Generation X" is primarily about middle and upper class white people, and men more than women. Only when other groups are specifically referenced, can we assume the topic to include them. But such is much of recorded history, right? I just had to acknowledge it. As you'll see in my conclusion, I also think age has a lot more to do with behavior than generation. Even so, I have gamely attempted to make generalizations about people from the Baby Boom and Generation X.

There is a lot I would like to cover but have deemed out of scope in the interest of time and space. What I will attempt to do in this essay is to compare zines, which were spawned from and are still rooted in anarcho-punk movements with their antecedents: the underground, alternative and independent presses, and little magazines, using alternative press most often as a catch-all descriptor. The various alternative presses have characteristics more closely resembling communist and socialist principles and practice. In their 90s heyday zines were almost exclusively created by people born in this book's designation of Generation X, 1961–1981. Now there are Millennials in our

147

midst (some of them are, like, almost 30 now!) along with the occasional Baby Boomer (I can recall reading only two zines by members of the Baby Boom Generation: *The Visible Woman* and *The Ken Chronicles*).

The Alternative Press

Most of this essay will be about zines and zine librarianship, but I want to provide some background on today's underground print culture's forerunners. Let's look at what exactly the alternative press was in its days as the underground press. In "The Underground Press in America: 1955–1970" Donna Lloyd Ellis recounts Columbia professor Thomas Pepper's assertion that the papers had a local focus: providing event listings and artistic and political commentary, supported by ads, which made them not so different content-wise from suburban newspapers (Ellis 121). The newspapers' viewpoints and perhaps which cultural and political events they addressed may have been widely divergent from those expressed in mainstream publications, but essentially they were just filling a void left by the corporate media. Talking of both national and local underground press titles, librarian John Van Hook said at a lecture at the Civic Media Center in Gainesville, Florida, "So there had to be a *Rolling Stone*, there had to be a *Village Voice*, an *East Village Other*, because *The New York Times* had no idea what was going on. They weren't ignoring it, they were just ignorant of it — and nobody wanted to wait around until they caught up" (Van Hook). He went on to comment that there was a generational component: "It felt like people who were twenty were communicating with people who were twenty all over the country for the first time" (Van Hook).

Presuming these twentysomething consumers of the 1960s underground press were hippies, it's important to note that while some of them were just in it for the sex, drugs, and rock 'n' roll, others were deeply committed to effecting social change. Patricia Case gives examples of a newspaper handed out at the 1972 Republican National Convention, a publication by the George Jackson Brigade, and the Eat the Rich Collective's cookbook as some of the radical material in the Contemporary Culture Collection. (Case 4) She goes on to contend that the commercial press waited for the underground publications to cover new or potentially controversial topics first, and that they did so from entirely different viewpoints. "In 1982 [the alternative press] surveyed the state of the economy by looking towards the poor, women, and the middle class while the commercial press watched Wall Street.... The Union of Concerned Scientists were documenting the sloppy inspection practices at the Nuclear Regulatory Commission and accidents and safety defects at nuclear power facilities before the near-meltdown in Harrisburg when the commercial media discovered the question of safety of nuclear power" (Case 4).

Based on Ellis's rundown of underground press titles and their editors, and on the "Woman Question" chapter of *A Generation Divided: The New Left, the New Right, and the 1960s* (Klatch 158–185), I contend that the movement was dominated by men (*The*

Village Voice, The Realist, The Los Angeles Free Press, The Berkeley Barb, etc.), which would be in keeping with how business was done by 1960s and 70s Baby Boomer activists before women's liberation movement began to educate them (Alpert 10). I also observe that true to the communalist ethos of the era, some underground press titles were edited by one person backed up by staff writers and editors, but others had editorial collectives (Ellis 103).

Zines

Zines, in contrast, tend to be the work of one person, though there are some exceptions such as collective projects like *Grrrls of Gotham* published by the NYC chapter of Riot Grrrl or edited anthologies called compilation zines, like Mimi Nguyen's *Evolution of a Race Riot.*

Most definitions of zines include one or more of the following descriptors: self-published, small print run, motivated by a desire to participate in or contribute to a community rather than for fame or profit, on activist or counter culture topics, and created in the do-it-yourself (DIY) tradition. The genre terms I use at Barnard College, in addition to compilation or comp zine are art zine, DIY zine, fanzine, literary or lit zine, mamazine, minicomics, and perhaps most importantly personal or perzine. As 1970s and 80s punk fanzines morphed into what we now call zines, they became less subject oriented and more personal, or autonomous, documenting the writer's daily life along with political and social analysis, anarchist-style.

For those who think of punks and imagine only black-clad smashers of chain store windows and spiky-headed hardcore matinee moshers,[1] consider this definition of punk that better describes zine publishers' perspectives: "Being punk is a way of critiquing privileges and challenging social hierarchies. Contemporary punks are generally inspired by anarchism, which they understand to be a way of life in favor of egalitarianism and against sexism, racism, and corporate domination" (Clark 19).

Though characterized by an activist spirit and the desire for social change, punk zines embody the "personal is political" philosophy. While I'm spouting worn slogans, let me also say that for zinesters (a word to describe zine publishers that no one likes but that is widely used) the medium is the message. Zinesters choose to self-publish because they want total control of their work and don't want or need a commercial publisher's approval. "The act of creating a work without any financial motivation (any zine-maker will testify to the fact that 'zines are a great big hole into which you throw your money'), from materials that are cheap, commonplace, and often illicitly come by (many zine-makers are experts at scamming photocopies from big box stores), is a *de facto* critique of a materialist consumer culture, and also a rail against a taste culture that tends to esteem high production value. Further, zine-making, with its absence of editors, critics, and concerns for marketability assumes as implicit the idea that every voice has value, and factors such as money, status, and even talent are not limiting to the ability to create a zine" (Levanthal 3). The notorious riot grrrl media blackout, where young feminist punks refused to talk to a press that insisted on ignoring, misinterpreting, and fetishizing the movement also speaks to zinesters' disdain for the corporate media (Rothenberg 826).

Some of the articles I read place zines in a continuum with the underground and alternative press, but others liken them to pamphlet culture from colonial America and 1930s science fiction fandom (Bartel 232). Though many zines are serial in nature—published continuously, but irregularly under the same name and with numbered issues—they don't address the same topics from issue to issue the way a typical corporate or even underground magazine might. In the still-developing cataloging practice, many zine librarians (myself included) choose to catalog one-off and distinctly titled serial issues as monographs. Others (e.g., Salt Lake City Public Library) catalog all of their zines that way (Bartel 237).

Zines in Libraries

In public libraries, zines are often targeted to a teen audience (Bartel 232; Hubbard 351; Thompson) and heavily programmed with readings and make your own zine workshops. "Zines can help you attract and serve an underserved population—namely teens and adults in their 20s and 30s—particularly those interested in alternative culture or who many feel that the library has nothing to offer them.... Teenagers are attracted to zines because they feel they can relate to the authors, because the writing is on their level, on their terms. They feel marginalized. In zines, they find a reflection of their own voice, their own feelings and perceptions (Thompson 2–3). Zine librarian Travis Fristoe's experience as a punk teen bears out Thompson's assertion. "Around the time I discovered punk (which I thought was just music and fashion), a friend showed me a zine he had done. We were 15, and I was incredulous that someone I considered a peer had created such a thing. Never mind that all he did was photocopy some pages at the local copy shop—the important thing was that a new world seemed possible, and within our grasp" (Hoyer).

Public librarians do outreach to schools and to youth detention facilities (Winter). Even as an academic librarian I host high school classes, giving them an overview of zines, giving them a chance to handle the materials for themselves to form their own idea of what zines are about. Some public libraries circulate their zines, and others don't. Some don't bother to catalog them. To be fair, cataloging zines is a struggle. There are rarely records to copy, and zine metadata is notoriously scant and inconsistent. The challenge is no excuse, mind you. Just because zines tend to cost only a dollar, doesn't mean they're not valuable. They are primary sources on the culture of groups otherwise underdocumented and underrepresented on library shelves. Typically, teenagers only appear in the stacks as fictional characters or case studies — rarely with the agency of authorship, as they have in zines.[2] Same with anarchists, young mothers, and sex workers. Their zines are more consciously wrought than diaries and more descriptive than scrapbooks. Academics are even beginning to catch on, partly because former zine publishers have gone to grad school (Dodge, "Collecting" 670). Also, as Dodge wrote in an earlier article, zines cover events that the mainstream media doesn't: "Is corporate press coverage severely lacking for events like New York City's Dyke March or the Transcontinental Peace Walk? Look to zines to cover these kinds of countercultural activities more thoroughly than the daily papers do" (Dodge, "Pushing" 27).

Academic libraries are more likely to treat zines as a special collection, though one that I know of (mine) circulates a discrete zine collection, as well as maintaining first copies in a climate-controlled, acid-free, retrievable-by-page archives collection. The archivists at the Sallie Bingham Center for Women's History and Culture at Duke University have been particularly successful at engaging faculty and students with class projects (Micham). In addition to outreach to faculty, academic zine librarians attract patrons with zine readings and exhibits, and table at zine fests, anarchist book fairs, Ladyfests, and other zine friendly events.

While the librarians who work tables at these events are likely to be from Generation X or Millennials, some of zine librarianship's strongest proponents and practitioners were born in the 1940s, 50s and early 60s. They include, but are not limited to Cathy Camper, who founded a collection at Minneapolis Public Library (Hubbard 353); Chris Dodge who, though he didn't preside over a public or academic library zine collection, has probably served as a mentor to nearly every zine librarian in the country, and who also did much to raise zines' profile during his tenure as librarian at *Utne Reader*, and whose comprehensive zineology was an important resource for zine scholarship until it disappeared with its GeoCities hosted website, may it rest in peace; Andrea Grimes who rescued the San Francisco Public Library's Little Magazine collection and expanded it with a slash to the Little Maga/Zine Collection (Hubbard 352); Tom Eland of the Minneapolis Community & Technical College zine collection (MCTC); Cristina Favretto, who presided over zine collections at Duke ("Editor's Donation") and San Diego State (and also established a surfing focused collection at the latter) (Carlson); and finally Jim Danky, now retired from the Wisconsin Historical Society. Danky, who is renowned for collecting alternative press materials of all kinds, including from the radical right (Dodge, "Collecting" 670), collects zines because "they're the latest self-defined print genre that's produced" (Bradford). He doesn't think it's necessary to be part of a culture in order to preserve it. He doesn't even have to like it. Danky is interested in zines that speak to social change movements, but he's not that into perzines (Bradford). Perzines, which personify the autonomy of anarchism and Generation Xers' separation from their Baby Boom and Silent Generation parents, are perhaps less appealing to a Baby Boomer like Danky. But just because he's not drinking the Kool-Aid, doesn't mean that he's not buying it.

Compare and Contrast

One important difference, perhaps because I oversee a collection comprised almost exclusively of zines by women, is that zines are much more girl friendly than the underground press. Let us compare the program from the first Underground Press Conference (UPC) that focused on literary publications, and the print media programs from the 2010 Allied Media Conference (AMC), which is not exactly the UPC's exact successor, but as close as we're going to get. The 1994 UPC offered six workshops, and guessing the participants' genders by name and in the case of ambiguous names internet photographs (this is problematic, but gives us a general idea), there were thirty male presenters and eight women, one of whom is represented twice, both times as a moderator rather than as a panelist (Wachsberger 54–55). I culled through the AMC's heavily online and audiovisual media oriented program and found six more or less print focused sessions. They were led by ten women and three men, though that count is too binary for the several of them that appear to identify as transgender (AMC2010). Even in zine culture, until riot grrrl transformed things, you'd only ever hear about zines by men like *Cometbus* and *Dishwasher*. Both zines deserve their reputation, but if zines and the alternative press are to reflect the community from which they come, we need to talk about *Citronella* and *Doris*, too, not to mention the numerous zines by people of color, including *Evolution of a Race Riot*, which I mentioned earlier. The change in numbers of workshops, thirteen down from thirty-nine, also gives us some idea of how the culture has evolved. The AMC workshops are less panel-driven and more participatory.

Although called "underground," the 1960s and 70s movement was if not mainstream, more popular than today's heterogeneous alternative culture. As Van Hook put it, "I am a member of the largest generation in the history of the world and because we were all — almost everybody we knew — coming into maturity, becoming adults, becoming self-sufficient, and becoming part of the counter-culture at the same time. It was like everyone that you knew was, you could presume, interested in alternative ideas and alternative cultures" (Van Hook). Fellow members of Generation X, I ask you, has that been your experience? Other than people I know from zines or political activism, very few of my friends would even know what a zine was if they didn't get one in the mail from me every year. Several alternative press library collections were originally suggested or supported by academic departments.[3] So far that has not been the case with zine collections.

Because of the greater awareness of alternative culture when the Baby Boomers were in the power of their youth, they were able to create infrastructure such as the United Press Syndicate (UPS), which coordinated ads, subscriptions, and distribution for member publications. In exchange, members had to pay a small fee, agree to send other members copies of their magazines and to notify the UPS if it wasn't okay to reprint a particular article (Ellis 112). The closest comparable operations we have in zinedom are distros, which are individuals and organizations that more or less buy zines wholesale from zinesters and sell them online and via mail order. The best known of these in English-speaking North America, and I suspect the world, Microcosm Publishing, has office space, a store, and a paid staff collective (About), but most distros are kitchen table operations that don't sustain their proprietors.

Even with distros, along with independent bookstores and infoshops (and until a few years ago Tower Books), serving as intermediaries between zine publishers and some of their readers, in my experience nearly all zinesters also do their own distribution. Many if not most zinesters will trade their zines with other publishers. Occasionally zines are offered only for trade, requiring that the authors must deal with each other fairly intimately. Zine etiquette requires that the author include at least a short note with her zine, if not a letter. I haven't found anything to indicate that issues of the *Los Angeles Free Press* came with a handwritten greeting from the editor, written on Hello Kitty stationery, so I'm guessing that there was less intimacy between Baby Boom writers and readers. Of course the scale was completely different, so the pen pal relationships favored by zinesters, whose print runs are generally in the low hundreds, would not have been possible with a circulation of 68,000, as Ellis reported of the *Los Angeles Free Press*, presumably in 1970 (Ellis 107). With their higher circulation and production expenses, alternative press titles are more likely than zines to not only have, but to be dependent on, paid ads. For the most part, zine ads are free or for trade. They plug zines, distros, and small record labels. Per Ellis, underground publications' ads were for music and sometimes sex related items and dating services. They also ran classified ads (Ellis 114). Their reliance on advertising made them vulnerable to exploitation by record companies that had figured out that underground press rates were cheap, and that the publications reached an important demographic (Ellis 109). Zines aren't impervious to cooptation, but they rarely if ever rely on advertising to survive, so it's not much of a problem.

Returning to the issue of intimacy, an important element of many zines, especially since internet publishing became popular, is a handmade feel. Zines can have silk-screened covers (*The Borough Is My Library*), letterpress (*Ker-bloom!*), crayoned in graphics (*Sugar Needle*), intricate bindings (*Parfait*) and many other artistic touches that distinguish them from the one upload reaches all/blog template nature of online communications. That's not to say that alternative press titles don't sometimes feature cool covers and high production values. Leonard Kniffel observes, "Other small press publishers operate elaborate letter-press machines, often producing handprinted and carefully designed texts on elegant paper (Kniffel 13). Crafty zine girl Erin Fae writes about the tactile nature of zines and how it is passed from the creator to the recipient,

> On the back of a postcard I sent in 2005, I wrote, "I'll hold this, then you'll hold this."
> I didn't know at the time that the phrase would be something that would stay with me.
> ..."I'll hold this then you'll hold this" also influences how I understand myself as an artist, especially a book artist. It's important to me to make art that is tactile, that people can hold. I define the book as something with information however that may take shape.

I want to make books that rip you apart. These books might make you feel enveloped and exposed, but will also feel like they belong to you once you hold them. You can give the book back to me, but you have it now, too [37].

That quote reminds me that as I print, assemble, fold, staple, color in, and rubberstamp each and every copy of my zine, that inevitably a little of myself—some tiny bit of DNA goes out with each copy, and that most zines in the Barnard collection, too, were handled personally by their creators.

Another important distinction is that while both the underground press and zine movements are youth driven, zine youth are younger, or were in the 1990s. I've encountered fewer zines by 16-year-olds published in the 2000s, but in the 90s, it was common. High school zinesters even put together a zine yearbook zine called *School Schmool*, with issues published by Theresa E. Molter in 1996 and 1997.

Giving voice to teenagers and getting those voices unmediated onto library shelves is a crucial part of the mission of zine librarianship. Zines and alternative press publications also bring into the library other people who are underrepresented on our shelves — "Feminists, environmentalists, anarchists, socialists, racial minorities, gays, lesbians, and the poor..." (Bartel 234). Although alternative presses may be better than their corporate counterparts at including underrepresented groups, they're not perfect. My observation, especially of the alternative press, but also of zines is that minorities and women can be proportionately underrepresented in projects other than those specifically made by or marketed to their population.

Shinjoung Yeo accuses "libraries as social institutions — often an integral part of the dominant system — neglect knowledge that is not legitimized by the dominant knowledge culture and consciously or unconsciously whittle away the communities that they serve" (Yeo). Responding to the claim that zines aren't authoritative, Chris Dodge writes, "Dubious credibility? Since when have popular novels (or magazines for that matter) been examined under bright lights? We're talking popular culture here, not medical reference sources" (Dodge, "Pushing" 27). Bartel wants public libraries to seek out alternative materials proactively and points out that most collection development policies exclude them by omission. "For example, a typical collection development policy often includes the following: 'select items useful to patrons' (but with no explanation of what is 'useful'); 'select based on demand for the material' (even though demand can be manufactured and people can't demand what they don't know exists); 'select based on the reputation of the author and publisher' (often not known in the case of alternative materials); and 'select based on popular appeal and the number and nature of requests from patrons'" (Bartel 234).

Written about zines, but relevant to all alternative press materials Richard A. Stoddart and Teresa Kiser state that "a library's purpose is not to act as arbiter of culture, deciding what it is or not. A library is an access point to the information in a culture. As such, a library's holdings should encompass a wide range of materials to provide as accurate a picture of a cultural time period as possible. The print zine is well within such a range of materials" (Stoddart and Kiser 196). Numerous other articles in my works cited question how anyone could write a reasonable history of Vietnam War era protests, for example, without the underground press and that if we rely on mainstream media to document today's music scene, all future historians will learn about is *American Idol* (Carlson).

Small press publisher turned librarian Jason Kuscma underlines this point, "I ask you to imagine doing historiographic work on the social revolution of the 1960s without access to such print capital as the *Berkeley Barb* or the *Village Voice*. How complete would an analysis of the times be without the crucial dissenting voices that were amplified in the pages of underground newspapers and magazines.... Unfortunately, today there are few academic libraries that could claim a substantial collection of the underground press of the 1960s, and we can learn some valuable lessons from the mistakes made by past librarians" (Kucsma). Administrators can be blamed who are reluctant to allocate time and money for alternative press and zine collections, and librarians without the imagination or temerity to suggest doing so. Alternative materials take more time and effort to acquire, process, and catalog than other items, and if not housed in a special collection they may be among the first to go in times of budget crises, due to comparatively poor use or the fact that they're less likely to be indexed in online databases.

Regrettably, inclusion in a resource like the Alternative Press Index (API) is no guarantee of a title being held by even an Association of Research Libraries library. An MLS thesis case study reported on API titles held in any format by "Natick" University (presumably Duke). They were pretty good in certain areas, e.g. gender and multicultural studies, but lacking in more overtly political topics like anti-racism and class struggle (Sylvain 33–39). I am painfully aware that shelf space and money are important concerns in libraries, but as Celeste West points out, "Whatever our budget, we always have money and staff for some things and not for others. We can enshrine, for example, the 'ready-reference' function or the investor's services, but have no money for a database to provide local survival (life and death) information. Some things are simply more equal than others in our minds. We often use lack of funds as a cop-out for exclusion" (West 1651). To me this is particularly surprising when a small press magazine subscription might cost $20 a year. I agree with West about reference materials. Don't buy the next $1,200 encyclopedia set or *Europa World Yearbook* for $1,400 and subscribe to all of the API publications you don't already have, or at least the twenty least held in your region, with the savings.

Unfortunately, even when an institution does begin an alternative press collection, it doesn't always maintain it properly. When Joseph Labadie gave his political ephemera to the University of Michigan instead of selling it to the highest bidder, he asked only that they make it publicly available. The university left the materials sitting in boxes for 12 years after receiving it, until a local anarchist rescued the collection. After she died the collection went untended for nearly another ten years. Though it is now, as of the 2000 writing of the article I'm citing, tended by a dedicated and talented archivist, the university does little to promote their world-class collection (Cornell 13). I have seen zine collections meet similar fates, due either to workplace dysfunction or lack of institution level buy-in. A collection is launched to much acclaim only to be forgotten or dismantled when the librarian who originally championed it falls into disfavor with or leaves the institution.

Conclusion

The librarian as alternative press collection champion is a good segue into my conclusion. As I've mentioned, alternative press collections sometimes originate from faculty or local support, but ultimately a collection's success or failure depends on the librarians and archivists who care for them — and to the administrators who allow them to, or at least don't get in their way. When I wrote my zine collection proposal, one of the pros in my pros and cons section was that if I was granted the collection, I wouldn't ever want to leave it. I learned later that this argument was one of the most convincing to my library dean. Unlike members of preceding generations, Generation X workers are not known for staying in one job for a long time, but our loyalty can be bought one $2 zine at a time. What can't be bought, though, is our dedication. That's free. West advises, "Hire librarians to do the job who have a taste for social change, primary sources.... If you choose activists for the job, they will be cheerfully collecting resources even on their own time" (West 1653). Writing about sound archives in 1972, Carlos Hagen bemoaned that librarians' hesitation regarding new media was "doing immense damage to our cultural heritage." He goes on to complain specifically about how librarians failed to collect underground press publications despite how obviously important they were. He ascribes to librarians an attitude of "this is junk, and as such has no place in any respectable library" (Hagen 49). Chris Dodge claims to be able to put a face to the librarian associated with most of the alternative press titles sparsely represented in WorldCat (Dodge, "Collecting" 668). Juris Dilevko is concerned that subject specialists are honing their expertise at negotiating license agreements, at the expense of in-depth subject knowledge (Dilevko 699).

Each library, and maybe every librarian, needs to pick a niche, perhaps one that supports (or expands!) its institution's mission statement, or one that they identify as not being handled anywhere else, and cover it. That is how you preserve the output of your generation, be it Generation X or any other. Two library school students observe an unfortunate change in the archives community's commitment to contemporary collecting: "The 1955 Archivist's Code begins with an exhortation that speaks to the heart of how zine archives, in particular, emphasize a personal as well as professional commitment to the documentation of contemporary culture: 'the archivist has a moral obligation to society to take every possible measure to ensure the preservation of valuable records, not only those of the past but those of his [*sic*] own times, and with equal zeal'"[4] (Woodbrook and Lazzaro). The Society of American Archivists (SAA) updated code doesn't reference contemporary collecting at all, which I can't imagine can have been accidental. The 1955 code was presumably written by members of the Silent or Greatest Generation, whereas we have to hope the bland 2005 update from the SAA Council that ends "Archivists must uphold all federal state, and local laws" wasn't written by my fellow Gen Xers. It wasn't written by anarchists; that's for sure! Case reminds us that "Libraries can be and should be controversial, inspiring, and infuriating" (Case 5).

In an article about Jim Danky around the time of his retirement, Chris Dodge begged that the next generation produce another Danky ("Collecting" 676). I hope there's not one, but a hundred Generation X librarians and archivists who go out of their way — and convince their institution to allow them to — collect the uncollected. We can't always wait for approval; in the internet age information has a short half-life, so we need to seize it as it comes. I also wonder if doesn't help to do it while we're relatively young. As I said earlier, I find the generations discussion to be problematic. The Baby Boomers who were supposedly all aware of and into the counterculture when they were in their twenties in the 1960s and 70s don't necessarily have their fingers on the pulse of the alternative music scene or the latest hip publications any more, and they're not always above telling Gen Xers that our cultural outputs are stupid or inferior. Those of us in Generation X are beginning to reach middle age. Not everyone can stay on top of every trend like the indefatigable retired cataloger Sandy Berman can. Some of us might not be able to or even want to hang out in bars seeing bands as late or as often. Some of us have kids or partners or parents who take our time. Some of us spend our money on mortgages and savings instead of music and magazines. Personally, I don't get to Critical Mass bike rides every month like I used to, and I've declared that this year's zine may be the last one I make. Our cohort will probably be just as annoyed at and mystified by the music, cultures, and operating styles of Millennial and the Internet Generation librarians as previous generations are of ours. It's important that we all remember what it's like to be young, and to value the contributions of the librarians who succeed us.

We must also remember that, as Stoddart and Kiser put it, "information is a perishable resource. It can be forgotten, lost, deleted, or destroyed" (Stoddart and Kiser 196). It is up to each of us, working together like hippie Baby Boomers, or autonomously like Gen X anarcho-punks, to apply our librarian superpowers to identifying, preserving, and providing access to the materials that define us as such.

Acknowledgements

Although the focus of this essay is on traditional academic and public libraries, I want give a nod to the many non–MLS librarians who have founded and maintained alternative press and zine collections. Among those who have lead and continue to lead the way are the English department at Temple University that called for the founding of the Contemporary Culture Collection there (Case 4), the English professor and the small press publisher who pushed for the zine collection at DePaul University (Chepesiuk), the Minneapolis psychiatrist whose experimental literature holdings launched the Little Magazine Collection supported by the English faculty at the University of Wisconsin-Madison (Kelley 154), Southern California Library for Social Studies and Research founder Emil Freed and the students and faculty members who supported the collection (Cooper 48), Joseph and Sophie Labadie, whose collected ephemera formed the basis for the Labadie Collection at the University of Michigan and the local anarchist Agnes Inglis who was its first curator (Cornell 12), the non-librarian librarians who guided the Rand/Tamiment collection until trained librarian Louise Heinze took over in 1948 (Danky 159), zine librarians at institutions like the Queer Zine Archive Project, the Independent Publishing Resource Center in Portland, OR; the ABC No Rio Zine Library, and the Zine Archive and Publishing Project in Seattle, the editors of the zine review zine *Factsheet 5*, and finally to the hardworking, multigenerational indexers at the Alternative Press Center who have been putting out the *Alternative Press Index* since 1969. I know that is a lot of name-dropping, but really, it's not enough. I hope in the future to write an article about these capable and inspired finders and keepers of public knowledge and picker-uppers of balls dropped or never even seen by degreed librarians.

NOTES

1. I ran a LexisNexis search on <punk! AND anarchis!> to identify media portrayal and reporting of anarcho-punks. Of the subjects assigned to ten or more articles, other than those pertaining to music, or with broad headings such as "Humanities & Social Science," the remaining categories were Crime, Law Enforcement & Corrections (13); Criminal Offenses (10), and Government Bodies & Offices (10). The search returned merely three articles assigned to the subject Civic & Social Organizations, but there were also three results for Substance Abuse.

2. I currently have 275 zines cataloged at Barnard with the subject heading Teenage girls, typically meaning the zine was written by a teenage girl. I introduced that subject heading to the catalog fairly recently, so it doesn't represent all of our cataloged holdings, much less those in our backlog.

3. See acknowledgement at the end of this paper for a brief list.

4. Woodward & Lazzaro are quoting U.S. National Archives & Records Administration and Wayne C. Grover, Archivist of the United States, 1948–1965, *The Archivists Code*, 1955.

WORKS CONSULTED

"About." *Microcosm Publishing*. n. d. Web. 11 Aug. 2010.

Alpert, Jane. *Growing Up Underground*. 1st ed. New York: Morrow, 1981.

Alternative Press Center. Home page. "Alternative Press Center: History." *Alternative Press Center*. n. d. Web. 11 Aug. 2010.

"AMC2010 Sessions! × Allied Media Conference." *Allied Media Conference* 2010. Web. 11 Aug. 2010.

Bartel, Julie. "The Salt Lake City Public Library Zine Collection." *Public Libraries* 42.4 (2003): 232–8.

Bradford, Michaele. "Jim Danky Talks About Zine Culture/a Response to Jim Danky." *Counterpoise* 11.2 (2007): 47–54.

Carlson, Scott. "Not-Yet-Rare Collections: Libraries Preserve Pop Culture." *The Chronicle of Higher Education* 51.41 (2005): A.25.

Case, Patricia J. "An Antidote to the Homogenized Library." *New Pages* 2.2 (1983): 4–7.

Chepesiuk, Ron. "The Zine Scene: Libraries Preserve the Latest Trend in Publishing." *American Libraries* 28.2 (1997): 70.

Clark, Dylan. "The Raw and the Rotten: Punk Cuisine." *Ethnology* 43: 1 (2004): 19–31.

Cooper, Sarah. "The Southern California Library for Social Studies and Research, Los Angeles." In "Resources for Scholars: Collections of Alternative and Left Materials: Part I" edited by James P. Danky. *The Library Quarterly* 59.1 (1989): 47–54.

Cornell, Andrew. "Reclaiming Radical History in the Labadie Collection." *Alternative Press Review* 5.3 (2000): 11–13.

Danky, James Philip. "Resources for Scholars: Collections of Alternative and Left Materials: Part 2." *The Library Quarterly* 59.2 (1989): 148–161.

Dilevko, Juris. "An Alternative Vision of Librarianship: James Danky and the Sociocultural Politics of Collection Development." *Library Trends* 56.3 (2008): 678–704.

Dodge, Chris. "Collecting the Wretched Refuse: Lifting a Lamp to Zines, Military Newspapers, and Wisconsinalia." *Library Trends* 56.3 (2008): 667–77.

_____. "Pushing the Boundaries: Zines and Libraries." *Wilson Library Bulletin* 69.9 (May 1995): 26–30.

"Editor's Donation Adds 'Zine' Collection to Library." *Campaign News* The Campaign for Duke. 1 Aug. 2001. Web. 30 Aug. 2010.

Eland, Thomas. "Generational Identification." Message to the author. 10 Aug. 2010. Email.

Ellis, Donna Lloyd. "The Underground Press in America: 1955–1970." *Journal of Popular Culture* 5.1 (1971): 102–124.

Fae, Erin. "I'll Hold This, Then You'll Hold This." *Imaginary Windows* 4 (2009): 35–41.

Hagen, Carlos. "The Struggle of Sound Archives in the United States." *Library Trends* 21.1 (1972): 29–52.

Hoyer, Kristin. "An Interview with Travis Fristoe, Zine Librarian." *Counterpoise*. 6.3 (2002): 7–11.

Hubbard, Colleen. "DIY in the Stacks: a Study of Three Public Library Zine Collections." *Public Libraries*. 44.6 (2005): 351–354.

Kelley, Carol. "The Little Magazine Collection at the University of Wisconsin–Madison." *Serials Review* 28.2 (2002): 153–5.

Klatch, Rebecca E. *A Generation Divided: The New Left, the New Right, and the 1960s.* Berkeley: University of California, 1999.

Kniffel, Leonard. "Libraries and Small Presses: Opening the Doors." *New Pages* 1.4 (1981): 13–18.

Kucsma, Jason. "Countering Marginalization: Incorporating Zines into the Library." *Library Juice* 5.6 Supplement (2002). Web. 30 Sept. 2010.

Levanthal, Anna. "The Politics of Small: Strategies and Considerations in Zine Preservation." *Graduate Student Panel: Preservation of New Media, McGill University* (October 2006): 1–15. Web. 30 Sept. 2010.

"MCTC Library — Zines." Minneapolis Community and Technical College. n. d. Web. 11 Aug. 2010.

Micham, Laura. "The Sallie Bingham Center for Women's History and Culture, Rare Book, Manuscript, and Special Collect..." *Celebrating Research*. Web. 11 Aug. 2010.

Rothenberg, Jessica, and Gitana Garafalo. "Riot Grrrl: Revolutions from Within." *Signs* 23.3 (1998): 809–843.

"SAA: Council Handbook (App. K — A Code of Ethics with Commentary)." Society of American Archivists. Web. 11 Aug. 2010.

Stoddart, Richard A., and Teresa Kiser. "Zines and the Library." *Library Resources & Technical Services* 48.3 (2004): 191–8.

Sylvain, Matthew C. "The Collection of Alternative Press Materials by a Member of the Association of Research Libraries: A Case Study." Thesis, 1999.

Thompson, Jerianne. "Zine: It Rhymes with Teen: How a Zine Collection Can Help You Connect with Young Adults." *Tennessee Libraries* 57.1 (2007): 1–10.

U.S. National Archives & Records Administration and Wayne C. Grover, Archivist of the United States, 1948–1965. *The Archivists Code*. 1955.

Van Hook, John. "The Selection of Alternative Materials: Building a Library Collection." *Counterpoise* 13.3–4 (2009): 76–79.

Wachsberger, Ken. "Underground Press Veteran Discovers Thriving, Self-Described Underground Press Scene." *Serials Review* 20.4 (1994): 53–60.

West, Celeste. "The Secret Garden of Censorship: Ourselves." *Library Journal* 108.15 (1983): 1651–3.

Winter, Laural. "Zines Free Teens: Zine Outreach to Incarcerated Teens." *Zine Librarian Zine 3: DIY-IYL Do It Yourself in Your Library* (2009): 18–19.

Woodbrook, Rachel, and Althea Lazzaro. "'How Are [We] to Bring Such Wayward Creatures into the Bonds of Organization' Zine Archives and the Archival Tradition." MA, University of Washington, 2010.

Yeo, Shinjoung. "The Importance of Alternative Libraries." *Counterpoise* 9.2 (Spring 2005): 5–8.

Section Five

Social Responsibility

Remaining Responsible, Remaining Relevant: Gen X Librarians and Social Responsibility

Peter Lehu

The library profession contends with the unique contradiction of being both treasured by American society and, as Patti Clayton Becker writes, being "plagued by the problem of purpose" (1). Doctors have always healed, janitors have always cleaned, but American librarians have served almost as many roles as decades that they have been considered professionals. Not only are there a wide variety of library science specializations, there are also numerous interpretations of librarians' mission: from impartial curator to community educator to social critic and defender of democracy. Hence, throughout the twentieth century, professional debate routinely returns to the fundamental questions: what is our role, and how do we stay relevant?

Even as they are eager and ready to apply their new proficiencies, today's younger librarians who are members of Generation X and Generation Y (or, the Millennial Generation) have had to grapple with these questions early in their careers. Many even have faced them before becoming librarians as family and friends may have looked askance at their decision to pursue graduate study in library science in the age of personal computers and the Internet. Lengthy job searches, which have become a reality for most new members of the profession, can also lead to career doubts. Then, when finally hired, librarians must deal with dwindling budgets and patrons that seem to need more help using email and copy machines than with answering substantive reference questions. It can all be quite discouraging, especially when retirement is decades away. Yet it is through negotiating similar "problems of purpose" that librarians throughout the last one hundred years have discovered their relevance to social issues and carved their niche as public servants and advocates.

Some Gen X-aged librarians are embracing the role of society shaper, but many, for various reasons, are not. Younger librarians may be too busy, complacent, or worried about defying traditional occupational boundaries to get up from behind the reference desk. Rutgers professor Jana Varlejs rightly views this as a concern, writing that "the dominant conservative, technocentric ethos among the profession has obscured many of the tenets espoused by the 1960s/1970s generation, and therefore more recent recruits to librarianship seldom confront the old social responsibility issues" (24). These issues, however, are key to debates on librarians' roles in contemporary society and on how to position ourselves as important community members. Indeed, Gen X librarians must embrace the mantle of participation in societal change in order to remain relevant in this one-click information age.

Game-changing innovations such as the Internet, online catalogs, and centralized material selection threaten the traditional roles of librarians, leaving those new to the profession forced to take on new roles or risk becoming glorified computer attendees or, worse, being deemed dispensable by administrators under pressure to cut jobs. Whether through implementing instructive programming, community outreach, or adopting social causes, Gen X librarians must revisit the ideals that gave purpose to previous generations and be willing to adopt nontraditional roles. This will not only preserve their own relevance but keep the profession healthy in future years as Gen Xers play greater supervisory roles to younger generations. This article will first examine the ways in which earlier generations of librarians defined the profession by adopting new responsibilities in response to American society's needs. It will then consider how some Gen X librarians are applying this ethos to a new era and call on more to follow this example in order to thrive in a new period of occupational reckoning.

A Tradition of Social Responsibility

The cultivation of a mission of social responsibility among librarians was gradual, and young librarians instigated most shifts in that direction. While American libraries initially served the elite and promoted a narrow ideology, by the turn of the twentieth century librarians began to base their services on the wants and needs of society. These mostly male librarians took up the cause of advancing American minds through the selection of materials they deemed enlightening. But first they had to get these minds through the library doors and so libraries began to lend out vocational training materials and fiction for recreational reading with the ultimate goal of eliciting interest in canonical texts. Soon after, world events began influencing librarianship. During World War I, the American Library Association (ALA) ran programs to provide books to the military and raise money for government fund drives (Becker 9). The Great Depression drained state and city budgets of funding for libraries but because of an increased need for social services this did not initially prevent a large increase in library patronage across the country. When, however, circulation rates began to drop in 1934, ALA leaders could not settle on a cause — although a suspicion was that the diminished library budgets were starting to seriously affect the quality of service (Becker 17). This problem may return in the twenty-first century as librarians are again encountering shrinking budgets in the face of a national recession and an increased reliance on libraries by the poor and unemployed.

The debate over making room on library shelves for user-demanded materials soon turned into the beginnings of the intellectual freedom movement. These new ideas developed among young librarians in the ALA Junior Members Round Table, which formed in 1931 (Samek 7). The members of the Round Table, which consisted of librarians 35 years old and younger, not only discussed social issues, but they called for a more democratic ALA in which younger members had more input in policymaking. By 1937 there were twenty-nine state-level junior member groups throughout the country, all involved in various projects to improve library service in their states (Ireland 156). In 1937, the Progressive Librarians' Council (PLC) was formed in response to ALA's silence when a member was fired from his library without due process (Samek 8). A breakthrough moment was ALA's defense of John Steinbeck's *Grapes of Wrath* which was being censored by libraries across the country for its explicit language and critique of capitalism. But Toni Samek points out that ALA's decision to create the Library Bill of Rights in response was the result of years of activism "by young members involved with issues such as peace, segregation, library unions, and intellectual freedom" (7).[1]

It was also during the thirties that ALA leaders and many librarians began to speak of themselves as defenders of democracy, largely in response to the rapid rise of totalitarianism in Europe. Meanwhile, other librarians, led by the PLC, protested U.S. involvement in the European conflict, arguing that war was antithetical to democratic ideals. The ALA, led by director Carl Milam, called on librarians to build ties to community organizations to proactively encourage civic engagement (Becker 57). Notably, although librarians began to take up the cause of democracy, librarianship in the United States was not a particularly egalitarian institution as women and minorities were only beginning to take on leadership roles. Social conditions very much guided the ethos of a developing profession. While some historians view the library's willingness to adopt political ideals as opportunistic, it is also testament to the loosely defined role of librarianship in American society and how each influenced each other.

During World War II libraries were redefined as not just part of the national education system, but as facilitators of American freedom. In a letter to the ALA in 1941, President Roosevelt thanked librarians for serving Americans and, significantly, for being "useful and effective in national defense" (Becker 62). ALA conferences during the war were dominated by debate over how to best serve the war effort, and how to procure funding to do so. A minority criticized the profession for so quickly falling in line with the government's pro-war agenda. At the ALA midwinter meeting in 1943 — when the ALA's pro-war campaign was in full swing with many libraries operating "war information desks" and complying with the FBI's directive to restrict access to books that might aid communist infiltrators — some librarians questioned whether the status quo they were protecting would benefit all Americans equally and whether it was the job of the library to be a propaganda tool of the government (Becker 150). The PLC pressured the ALA in the early forties to lobby for federal funding for libraries and increase services to neglected communities (McReynolds). While library activism up to this point mainly supported the government, the seeds were being planted for librarians to play a role in progressive resistance.

In the 1950s the librarian community firmed up its support for intellectual freedom as it met challenges to the Library Bill of Rights, which was edited to emphasize the equal rights of all library users. The "Statement on Labeling" and The School Library Bill of Rights were adopted in response to McCarthy-influenced calls to censor controversial materials. While librarians were not a seminal population in the counterculture movement of the 1960s, some inevitably embraced it, since it challenged librarians to be more inclusive of radical ideas. Sixties social movements that challenged the government, social mores, and traditional family structures were largely disseminated through a burgeoning alternative press. For libraries to be considered nonpartisan they would have to include these publications and many young librarians were happy to take up the cause. Samek points out that many activist librarians, such as Celeste West and Sanford Berman, "radicalized" through their careers (41). Their public roles as librarians led them to be activists, rather than inhabiting these roles independently. In the late sixties, alternative librarian journals, such as *Synergy* and *Sipapu*, encouraged readers to take political stances, select countercultural publications, and promote certain literature (Samek 48). At the 1967 ALA conference in San Francisco, some librarians picketed outside Gen. Maxwell Taylor's speech promoting war in Southeast Asia while others turned their backs to him as he spoke (Berry).

The organizing of a new breed of young, activist librarians from around the country led to the creation of the ALA Round Table on Social Responsibilities of Libraries in 1969 and local "SRRTs" throughout the country. These groups promoted the role of libraries in actively supporting the Library Bill of Rights, overcoming racial and sexual orientation prejudice, distributing anti-establishment materials, offering research services to striking workers and other activist organizations, and taking stances on nontraditional issues like the Vietnam War. About 200 librarians marched under a "Librarians for Peace" banner at the Vietnam Moratorium rally in Washington in November 1969 ("Related..." 3). Activist librarians also reignited discussion of purpose among ALA membership as a whole, with the eventual formation of groups such as the Activities Committee on New Directions for ALA (ACONDA), the Task Force on Alternative Books in Print, and the Black Caucus.

While opposition to change was strong and prevented a codified redefinition of librarians' role, it was the activism of young librarians that precipitated the ALA to, by the end of the decade, take official stands against discrimination based on sexual preference, and for the active defense of librarians whose welfare was threatened by standing up for intellectual freedom (Joyce 41). This activism was followed by a flood of books and articles published in mainstream journals in the seventies and eighties that advocated for social responsibility over passive impartiality in the profession (Joyce 49). Meanwhile, in the eighties, the Librarians for Nuclear Arms Control organized against Cold War threats. In 1990, left-leaning librarians formed the Progressive Librarians Guild through the shared belief that libraries are "one of the principal anchors of an extended free public sphere which makes an independent democratic civil society possible" ("Statement of Purpose").

A Need for Social Responsibility

While there are countless national and global issues for librarians to take a stand on today, Gen X librarians need not stray far from established librarian causes in order to continue the cultivated tradition of social responsibility. The global recession that began in 2008 has forced local governments to cut budgets and in many cases public libraries are the first agency to suffer, even though they are the last resort for many of our municipalities' most vulnerable residents. Meanwhile, while the digitization of information sources and means of communication broadens opportunities for the young and educated, many are left on the wrong side of the digital divide as even applying for a service sector job today usually requires computer proficiency. Librarians are needed to fight for funding and to work harder with less funding to reach underserved and undereducated populations.

Librarians are also needed to challenge society's leaders. The federal government has challenged the librarian community's tenets on intellectual freedom through the high-profile USA PATRIOT Act and less publicized ways such as the Pentagon enlisting retired generals to give biased interpretations of military performance on national television, and the Obama administration's retaining of the Bush policy to keep "state secrets" from the public and the courts.[2] Private companies also require information watchdogs, as most recently demonstrated by the health insurance industry's shameless "astroturfing"— secretly funding an anti-reform movement so that it appears to have grassroots origins. When journalists uncover these attempts to trick the public, librarians are needed to promote these reports, especially when they are overlooked by mainstream media. It is also librarians' social responsibility to steer patrons towards reliable and unbiased information sources beyond the holdings of the library on television, radio, and the Web, especially since most get their news and information from media companies which are more concerned with what Rusciano describes as the "simulacrum of objectivity" than relaying the truth.[3] Gen X librarian Sandy Iverson writes, "As our global society becomes increasingly based on the commodity of information, power becomes increasingly focused and managed by those with access to information." She continues, "Librarians have been trained in the management of information. Therefore, I see their role as inherently political" (25). Durrani and Smallwood believe libraries risk "blindly walking into extinction" by feigning neutrality in today's information marketplace ruled by profit-driven corporations (122).

Furthermore, the opportunities for librarians to take on social causes without fear of social condemnation or risking one's career, while not boundless, have never been greater. Previous generations of librarians struggled against a strict social culture whereas today the range of acceptability is much broader. There are still gender, race, and sexual orientation biases but it is not seen as radical or aberrant to fight against such discrimination. There is still censorship in libraries but the ALA and other professional organizations unanimously take stands against it. A public library that expresses criticism of a federal policy like the USA PATRIOT Act may be criticized in local press but few would argue that protecting democracy is not one of the public library's roles.

Continuing the Tradition

The good news is that many Gen X librarians have carried the social responsibility tradition into the twenty-first century. A good example of how young librarians have brought new ideas and energy to a library system is at this writer's place of work, the Free Library of Philadelphia. At public libraries that serve low-income populations, librarians can directly address social inequality through their daily work. In February 2005, in response to budget cuts, the City of Philadelphia eliminated librarian positions and experimented with neighborhood branches that were staffed only by nonprofessional library assistants. (Twyman "Libraries" B3) The public outcry by community members and city council members persuaded library administrators to reverse the decision by the end of the year. The library hired 80 new staff members including dozens of new Gen X librarians in late 2005 and throughout 2006. (Twyman "Library Branches" B1) Not only were these recently graduated staff particularly adept at the technological aspects of the job, many started new programs for the public even as they were still getting acquainted with their basic responsibilities. Upon being placed in the city's Parkway Central Library a fellow Gen Xer, Amy LeFager, and I discovered that years had passed since the city's main library offered computer training classes. In early 2006 we proposed an instructional program to the administration, designed classes, handouts, flyers, and a sign-up policy, and began teaching to full classrooms of eager job seekers, seniors, new immigrants, and other Philadelphians. The classes, now in their fourth year, are taught mostly by younger librarians who have volunteered to do their part in bridging the digital divide. While the Free Library reaches out to the technologically savvy with Facebook and Twitter accounts, podcasts, and social bookmarking, thanks to Gen X librarians, it has also not forgotten the many Philadelphians who still need to learn how to use a mouse or set up an email account.

Gen X librarians who work in the neighborhood branches also recognize needs in their communities. Aimee Thrasher-Hanson, a Gen X librarian at Philadelphia's McPherson Square branch, took the reins on a program that paired members of an honors sorority for education majors at St. Joseph's University with patrons in need of basic computer training for one-on-one tutorials. Sarah Stippich, a young librarian at the Blanche A. Nixon branch, had Philadelphia's underserved in mind even before she was hired. To fulfill a graduate school assignment, she researched the needs of an immigrant African community in the Paschalville neighborhood of Philadelphia and wrote and successfully submitted a grant for a Job Readiness Center that has helped hundreds of people create resumes and email accounts and apply for jobs. When the city announced it was closing eleven branches throughout the city in 2008, young librarians in West Philadelphia, including some who worked for local academic libraries, met to brainstorm ways to pressure the mayor to keep them open. Back at the Parkway Central Library, Karin Suni requested funding to buy video gaming equipment and initiated an after-school gaming program for area teens. In addition, Gen X librarians system-wide have joined committees to conceive ways to better serve specific populations, such as pre-kindergarteners and job seekers.

Examples of Gen X librarians who participate in social work beyond their regular responsibilities can be found all over the United States. Orquidia Contreras is a recent library school graduate who is a youth services librarian in San Diego County. When she discovered that teen parents were not bringing their toddlers to her story time sessions because they were in school and could not travel to the library, she took story time on the road. Twice a month she travels to the local high school campus so that the students' children do not miss out on gaining valuable reading and listening comprehension skills (Contreras). Carissa Purnell, a librarian in her twenties working at the Salinas Public Library in California, says that her youth is a blessing in disguise when working with young gang members that come to her public library. She runs an intervention program in coordination with a local nonprofit, Second Chance, to steer youth away from the gang lifestyle. In her spare time, she is an active member of REFORMA, a librarian association that promotes services to Spanish-speakers, and she has launched a website, www.latinalibrarian.com, as a forum for female, minority librarians to network and share ideas (Purnell). Angela Craig and Jason Hyatt, two young librarians at the Public Library of Charlotte & Mecklenburg County in North Carolina, used extra funds to develop a portable library branch to bring computer literacy services to senior communities, homebound patrons, teachers and care providers, and other groups that would otherwise have difficulty attending programs (Hyatt).

A good indicator of the social consciousness of younger librarians is the changing public image of librarians, away from the stereotype of being timid and bookish. The *New York Times* article, "A Hipper Crowd of Shushers," considered by the library community to be a mainstream "breakthrough" on young librarian culture, describes its subjects as activists and drawn to the profession because it is a "haven for left-wing social engagement" (Jesella). Indeed, many Gen X librarians not only counter social problems on the job, but are involved in political and social activism. The great majority of activist librarian blogs, organizations, and movements promote liberal causes, although there are a handful of conservative librarian blogs. Activist librarians say they are inspired by the actions and ideas of their seniors and predecessors, many of whom still contribute to causes and others whose articles and books have become critical reading. Interviews suggest that most librarians involved in activism were engaged in such work before becoming librarians but feel that their professional role has provided them with both inspiration and outlets to become more involved. Activist Gen X librarian John Beekman writes:

> From what I can observe, the field does tend to attract people who believe in liberty and an open society, who are dedicated to service and the promotion of independent thought. As is the case with me, the extent to which those principles are put into activist praxis, and the form that practice takes, seems to be consistent before and after library school.

Radical Reference was founded in 2004 by librarians who wanted to play a meaningful role in the protests against the Bush administration. While most of these librarians were already members of activist groups, they felt that, as librarians, they had a specific service to provide to the movement. Both on the Internet and on the streets of New York City during the Republican National Convention they promoted their group as an information service for the activist community, answering protesters' and passersby' legal and political questions, informing them of happenings, and giving directions. Radical Reference drew national attention through its website, www.radicalreference.info, and soon had chapters in various cities. The volunteer-run collective answers questions submitted on its website by activists and independent journalists, recognizing that these populations often do not have access to comprehensive information resources (Friedman 372). Reference guides and bibliographies on human and civil rights issues are created and made freely available on the website. Radical Reference also disseminates information through presentations, workshops, and leafleting at ALA conferences.

While Radical Reference members range in age from early twenties to Baby Boomers, the founding members were in their late thirties at the time and, according to a founder, the most active participants tend to be in their late twenties and early thirties (Freedman). As of January 2009, Radical Reference had over 300 registered members (Friedman 373). Members say that the group provides a means to organize around shared values and identify each other as librarians among the greater progressive activist community. Some members say that Radical Reference provides an outlet for their desires to promote social change that they do not find in their day jobs. According to co-founder Jenna Freedman, "[members'] librarianship is indeed integral to their activism and vice versa." Member Melissa Morrone says that as she became more politically aware she "saw the possibility of librarianship, particularly public librarianship, as a political act in addition to something to which I was constitutionally suited." Radical Reference also provides its members with a sense of community. Beekman, also a member, writes, "One of the great things about being involved in Radical Reference is to maintain and develop contacts with thoughtful, committed individuals, who inspire me and allow some little glimmer of hope to survive within my prevailing, overpowering pessimism about the future of human society.

Could Gen X Be More Socially Responsible?

So, many librarians are following the tradition of social responsibility. But could more feel called to take larger roles? Certainly, librarians need to have the time and energy to devote to extra responsibilities. Women are having children older which should mean that younger members of this female-dominated profession should have time to spend extra hours at their workplace or get involved in social causes. At the same time, salaries have stagnated, librarian jobs are scarcer, and libraries have to operate with reduced staff which means that librarians often have to work harder to make a living and contend with new sources of stress.

The second factor is whether young librarians feel compelled or even want to be burdened with social responsibility. A 2009 unscientific survey of members of the ALA New Members Round Table (who have been ALA members for ten years or less) showed that only 64 percent believe that ALA should be involved with social issues relating to libraries, such as benefits for same sex partners of library workers, and a mere 3 percent believe it should be involved with non-library social issues, such as American foreign policy (Emanuel). The survey does not further define what makes an issue "related to libraries" but it does suggest that many younger librarians fail to see their profession as an integrated part of society. A 1999 *American Libraries* survey of 391 librarians found that 107 chose their career based on a love for books and reading while 62 chose it for the public service aspect (Gordon 38). A similar 2006 survey of 96 graduate students at the University of Alabama's School of Library and Information Studies finds "love of books" as accounting for only 2 percent of student's reasons for choosing their course of study, but "job function" accounts for 40 percent, compared to 14 percent who chose it for the "clientele" they would serve. This suggests that a love for reading is being replaced, not by a desire to serve or create social change, but by enjoyment of other aspects of being a librarian (Ard 242).

Indeed, another impediment is that young people today are attracted to the evolving technological aspects of librarianship which can blind librarians to their social roles. University at Buffalo Professor Emeritus George Bobinski agrees with Varlejs, writing, "Too many librarians are being intoxicated with the power and abundance of technology" (154). Gen X librarians grew up with computers; many have used them daily since their early teens. Educated young people may choose to become librarians for the chance to apply their proficiency with computers and online environments. Being a librarian gives software enthusiasts a chance to build web pages and promote their institutions with the latest social media applications. But Stevenson and others point out that access to technology alone will not eliminate the digital divide or the conditions that create social inequality. They worry that libraries measure their effectiveness by the amount of access to technology they provide without considering whether the encounters are fulfilling the needs of the disenfranchised. If the librarian profession attracts the technologically savvy, then there is the potential of a divide between librarians' relationships with computers and that of the people they serve. Librarians risk becoming detached from the needs of their communities, much like they were when promoting literary classics during the Great Depression.

Larger trends in society contribute to a de-emphasis on social responsibility. Gen X librarians have embarked on their careers in an American culture that has become less communal and less encouraging of social activism. In his influential essay, "Bowling Alone: America's Declining Social Capital" (1995), political scientist Robert Putnam demonstrates that Americans have become more insular and less socially engaged. The percentage of Americans who vote, belong to unions, churches, and civic and fraternal organizations all dropped from 1960 to 1995, as Gen Xers were becoming adults and entering the workplace (Putnam 68–69). These trends were evident even before most Americans had computers with Internet connections to encourage them to stay inside. These social conditions make the ideals of librarianship harder to attain and librarians themselves are not immune to losing sight of the importance of social engagement. Family, friends, and media enforce the mindset that social responsibilities are only a concern until the end of the work day.

Keeping young librarians focused on their social responsibilities is the aegis of ALA and other professional organizations, graduate school instructors, and their senior colleagues. Among professional organizations there seems to be a lack of guidance on social responsibility. In fact, young activist librarians who belong to the Progressive Librarians Guild and Radical Reference pride themselves for being different from ALA, which they feel is too bureaucratic to realize social change (Friedman 387). It was not always this way. In the thirties when the ALA Junior Members Round Table was first active, one of its main objectives was to influence and improve American librarianship; it's mission statement read, in part, "to promote studies that will contribute to the advancement of librarianship" and "to cooperate with the ALA in fulfilling its aims and purposes" (Oldfather 618). Greg Landgraf points out that indeed most of the accomplishments of this group were to serve the field of librarianship as a whole. The current ALA committee for younger librarians, the New Members Round Table, in contrast, appears to be mostly self-serving; the four directives in its mission statement all relate to providing its members with experience and opportunities for professional advancement. Furthermore, while the New Members Round Table sponsors monthly online discussion forums on predetermined topics, they are mostly about furthering one's career as a librarian; since the forums started in 2005, few have discussed a librarian's social responsibility or how to best serve community members.

ALA's national magazine, *American Libraries*, also tends to steward young librarians toward career-building over fulfilling their professional mission and addressing the needs of the broader public sphere. Rarely is there a feature article on how librarians can improve an aspect of society. When an article written for Gen X librarians was featured on the front cover in May 2004 it exclusively concerned career advancement, summarizing a survey of library directors on what they look for in potential administrators. (To their credit, the directors chose "commitment to service" as a desirable managerial quality) (Hernon 34). Varlejs worries, "Even if today's aspiring librarians get their foot in the door, where are the leaders who can set an example for potential activists and help them to navigate an organization's structural and political mazes?" (25). Social activist Chip Ward points out that serving needy demographics such as the homeless and mentally ill is not covered in library science curriculums. Coursework focuses on learning specialized skills rather than working with the needs of specific populations. Varlejs writes, "[MLIS students] encounter, for the most part, professors whose academic personae project a dispassionate, neutral stance" (25). Librarian Jess Nevins argues that there are critical gaps in library school curriculums which fail to train future librarians in skills they will need regularly, including sensitivity training, teaching skills, outreach, and bridging the digital divide (46–47).

Conclusion

In the continued absence of high salaries and high regard, it remains that librarians choose their profession out of a desire to help. Just as in previous generations, there are many Gen X librarians who realize that their role is not just to fill a position, but to respond to the needs of their community. They allow librarianship to retain its relevance even as technological advancement has undermined many of librarians' traditional roles. The need for librarians to join the socially-engaged communities of volunteers and activists in advocating for democratic ideals and equal opportunities for the disenfranchised in the public sphere is just as urgent as it was in the thirties, seventies, and decades in between. Gen X faces new distractions and insecurities but the importance of librarians' time-tested social responsibilities must not be lost amidst the profession's evolution. Just as an underpaid teacher will work extra hours recognizing that the futures of their students are at stake, Gen X librarians must see their work as critical to the wellbeing of future generations and rise to the challenge.

NOTES

1. Articles in the ALA Bulletin from the 1930s corroborate this claim. At the 1935 ALA Conference, the Junior Members Round Table proposed a study of the effect of the Great Depression on American libraries (Stanford 495–96). In 1936, the South Carolina Junior Librarians' conference covered, among other subjects, "The Librarian's Responsibility to the Community" (Lent 898). At the Junior Members Round Table meeting at the 1938 ALA conference featured a discussion entitled "The Library as a Social Force." Essays were presented including one by William Tucker which read:

> Outright censorship of materials politically or economically repugnant to a particular librarian is still a too frequent occurrence. Often this censorship is unconscious, but nevertheless effective, which should cause us to realize the desirability of formulating more definite standards for the selection of material. This will call for a much greater knowledge of the contemporary world than the average librarian has today [883].

Dorothea Hyle argued in her essay that librarians ought to be a "true social force" and that they "cannot just sit back of the library desk and be a power for good" [886].

 2. See David Barstow, "Behind TV Analysts, Pentagon's Hidden Hand," *New York Times* April 20, 2008: n. p., Web. 24 February 2010. Renewal of the USA PATRIOT Act with only minor modifications has been passed in the House Judiciary Committee with the support of President Obama as of February 2010.

 3. See Frank Louis Rusciano, "Tabloid Ethics, News Reporting on the Iraq War & the Simulacrum of Objectivity," *Progressive Librarian* 25 (2005): 1–11.

WORKS CONSULTED

Ard, Allyson, Susan Clemmons, Nathan Morgan, et al. "Why Library and Information Science?" *Reference & User Services Quarterly* 45.3 (2006): 236–48.

Becker, Patti Clayton. *Books and Libraries in American Society During World War II: Weapons in the War of Ideas.* New York: Routledge, 2005.

Beekman, John. "Re: Radical Reference." Message to Peter Lehu. 26 Jan. 2010. Email.

Berry, John, III. "Americans Take a Stand Through Their Organizations." LibraryJournal.com. 15 April 2003. Web. 7 Feb. 2010.

Birdsall, William F. "A Progressive Librarianship for the Twenty-First Century." *Progressive Librarian* 28 (2007): 49–65.

Bobinski, George S. *Libraries and Librarianship: Sixty Years of Challenge and Change, 1945–2005.* Lanham, MD: Scarecrow Press, 2007.

Contreras, Orquidia. "Gen X Librarian." Message to Peter Lehu. 15 Dec. 2009. Email.

Durrani, Shiraz, and Elizabeth Smallwood. "The Professional is Political: Redefining the Social Role of Public Libraries." Ed. Alison Lewis. *Questioning Library Neutrality: Essays from Progressive Librarian.* Duluth: Library Juice Press, 2008. 119–137.

Emanuel, Jenny. "NMRT Survey on Council." ALA Council List. American Library Association, 12 Nov. 2009. Web. 14 Jan. 2010.

Freedman, Jenna. "Re: [other — from website] Radical Reference." Message to Peter Lehu. 19 Dec. 2009. Email.

Friedman, Lia, and Melissa Morrone. "Radical Reference: Socially Responsible Librarianship Collaborating with Community." *The Reference Librarian* 50.4 (2009): 371–396.

Gordon, Rachel Singer, and Sarah Nesbeitt. "Who We Are, Where We're Going: A Report from the Front." *American Libraries* 124.9 (1999): 36–39.

Hernon, Peter, Ronald Powell, and Arthur Young. "What Will Gen Next Need to Lead?" *American Libraries* 35.5 (2004): 33–35.

Huff-Hannon, Joseph. "Librarians at the Gates." *The Nation* 22 Aug. 2006. Web. 19 Dec. 2009.

Hyatt, Jason, and Angela Craig. "Adapt for Outreach: Taking Technology on the Road." *Computers in Libraries* 29.9 (2009): 35–39.

Hyle, Dorothea. "Miss Hyle's Paper." *Bulletin of the American Library Association* 32.11 (1938): 886–88.

Ireland, Norma Olin. "Juniors at Work in 29 States." *Bulletin of the American Library Association* 31:3 (1937): 156–58.

Iverson, Sandy. "Librarianship and Resistance." Alison Lewis, ed. *Questioning Library Neutrality: Essays from Progressive Librarian.* Duluth: Library Juice Press, 2008. 25–31.

Jesella, Kara. "A Hipper Crowd of Shushers." *New York Times* 8 July 2007: n. p. 21 Dec. 2009.

Joyce, Steven. "A Few Gates Redux: An Examination of the Social Responsibilities Debate in the Early 1970s and 1990s." Ed. Alison Lewis. *Questioning Library Neutrality: Essays from Progressive Librarian.* Duluth: Library Juice Press, 2008. 33–65.

Landgraf, Greg. "The Intergenerational Bicker-Off." *A CentenniAL Blog* American Library Association, 16 July 2007. Web. 12 Jan. 2010.

Lent, Edna Louise. "A Successful Junior Project." *Bulletin of the American Library Association* 30.9 (1936): 898.

McReynolds, Rosalee. "The Progressive Librarians Council and Its Founders." *Progressive Librarian* 2 (1990/91): n. p. 21 Dec. 2009.

Morrone, Melissa. "Re: [Fwd: FW: [srrtac-l] [plgnet-l] I need examples of librarian activism for an article (fwd)]]." Message to Peter Lehu. 5 January 2010. Email.

Nevins, Jess. "What Library Schools Still Aren't Teaching Us." *Revolting Librarians Redux*. Eds. Katia Roberto and Jessamyn West. Jefferson, NC: McFarland, 2003. 45–53.

Oldfather, Margaret. "Junior Members Round Table." *Bulletin of the American Library Association* 28:9 (1934): 618.

Purnell, Carissa. "Librarians and Social Responsibility." Message to Peter Lehu. 14 Dec. 2009. Email.

Putnam, Robert. "Bowling Alone: America's Declining Social Capital." *Journal of Democracy* 6:1 (1995): 65–78.

"Related Groups Activities." *ALA Social Responsibilities Round Table Newsletter* 3 (1969): n. p. Web. 1 Feb. 2010.

Samek, Toni. *Intellectual Freedom and Social Responsibility in American Librarianship, 1967–1974*. Jefferson, NC: McFarland, 2001.

Sparanese, Ann. "Activist Librarianship: Heritage or Heresy?" Ed. Alison Lewis. *Questioning Library Neutrality: Essays from Progressive Librarian*. Duluth: Library Juice Press, 2008. 67–82.

Stanford, Edward B. "Jottings for Juniors." *Bulletin of the American Library Association* 29.8 (1935): 495–96.

"Statement of Purpose." About PLG. *Progressive Librarians Guild*. n. d. Web. 4 Jan. 2010.

Stevenson, Siobhan. "Digital Divide: A Discursive Move Away from the Real Inequities." The Information Society 25 (2009): 1–22.

Tucker, William. "Mr. Tucker's Paper." *Bulletin of the American Library Association* 32:11 (1938): 883–84.

Twyman, Anthony S. "Libraries to begin half-day service..." *Philadelphia Inquirer* 20 Jan. 2005: B3+.
_____. "Library Branches to Regain Services." *Philadelphia Inquirer* 19 Oct 2005: B1+.

Varlejs, Jana. "Where Has All the Passion Gone? or, Time for Another Revolution?" Eds. Katia Roberto and Jessamyn West. *Revolting Librarians Redux*. Jefferson, NC: McFarland, 2003. 24–25.

Ward, Chip. "What They Didn't Teach Us in Library School: The Public Library as an Asylum for the Homeless." *Chip Ward Essays* 30 May 2009. Web. 5 Jan. 2010.

Skeptic/Activist: Gen Xers in Radical Reference

Melissa Morrone

We came of age in the 1970s and 80s. In the news were Watergate, Vietnam, AIDS, the Challenger explosion, the first Gulf War, the hole in the ozone layer. All of our parents got divorced. We were middle-class, but life was full of uncertainty. We never bothered voting. We knew we wouldn't be able to look forward to the stable careers of our parents' generation. Our cynicism shriveled our sensibilities. We did, however, have our culture and media to cling to, from childhood memories of *The Brady Bunch* to getting our minds blown by Nirvana. Here's a plain text tag cloud of the concepts by which mainstream writing on Generation X defined (and defines) us: materialistic, ignorant, apathetic, cynical, ironic, skeptical, pragmatic. This essay will discuss the work of Radical Reference, an independent progressive librarian project, in the context of perceptions of Generation X. As sweeping generational generalizations are dissatisfying at best, I will primarily use the voices of some individual Gen X members of Radical Reference to explain the appeal of the project and what they find meaningful and useful about it.

Radical Reference (RR) was started in the middle of 2004, a month before the Republican National Convention would descend upon New York City. A few librarians, some with backgrounds in independent media and infoshops, had the idea to bring together people from the library world to be part of the protesting communities. These leftist librarians and LIS students researched and compiled information about demonstrations, official RNC events, and NYC logistics; be in the streets (with distinctively marked ballcaps, like "the legal support activists!") to answer protesters' questions; and maintain a website that would allow people to submit reference questions before, during, and after the convention. Its mission stated: "Radical Reference is a collective of volunteer library workers who believe in social justice and equality. We support activist communities, progressive organizations, and independent journalists by providing professional research support, education and access to information. We work in a collaborative virtual setting and are dedicated to information activism to foster a more egalitarian society." (For more information about RR, see, for example, Yeo et al., and Friedman and Morrone.)

Response, both within librarianship and from activist communities in NYC, was positive, and for the last six years RR has been a functioning, evolving project. Street reference became much less of a focus, although there was radical librarian activity during the 2008 RNC in Minneapolis–St. Paul. Currently the national project (a large email list and the website) is quieting down, while local collectives are perhaps the future of RR.

Generation X and Activism

"I think that a certain level of pessimism and fatalism is a part of the Gen X mindset. Irony is a part of our natural language, tempering even committed gestures with an implied shrug," says RR member John Beekman, 46. Those of us on the left have a greater tendency towards pessimism and a stronger vision of uncertainty: "The libertarian dream of modeling all relationships on the basis of the market weighs heavily on people who have come of political age under Reagan, Bush [*père*], and Clinton. Conservative politics and everyday culture feed off one another" (Mattson 58).

But there is in fact a history of radical activism among Gen X. As RR member Dena Marger, 42, puts it, "Gen Xers were known as the slacker generation. They used to love to throw the word 'apathetic' around during the Reagan eighties, as though there was no anti-apartheid movement, no Central America movement, no radical feminism happening, etc. But the eighties saw far more activism on larger scales than the sixties ever did. And a lot of Gen Xers were young twentysomethings in the mid-eighties." Burns points out, "These campaigns continued well into the 90s, but the corporate media rarely reported on it. The tired cliché of Generation X as a lost generation with no purpose is a misconception that fits all too well with the interests of the power elites." (For more on campus activism in the 1980s and 90s, see also Vellela, Loeb and Featherstone.)

Of course, the "power elites" have also been setting the tone of much of the research and reporting about Gen X's failures. After presenting various statistics on voting patterns and media use in the early 1990s, Bennett and Rademacher conclude that "a variety of evidence seems to indicate that apathy and disengagement are even more pronounced among Xers than among young people in years past..." (38). But based on results from surveys conducted between 1992 and 1994, Owen (whose essay appears in the same book as the previous citation) reports that "70 percent or more of gen Xers say they (1) feel extremely good or very good when they see the flag flying; (2) have an extremely strong or very strong love for their country; and (3) approve or strongly approve of the basic constitutional structure of the U.S. government. [...] While they may currently find fault with institutions and individual leaders who are not dealing effectively with the issues that trouble them most, Xers are a long way from abandoning or actively rebelling against the system" (104).

So we are not, as a group, rebels — whether or not one thinks the idea of resistance is dangerous or inspiring. But that's hardly news, for any generation, for even the Boomers. When it was more broadly acceptable to go to anti-war marches and wear black armbands and so on, a lot of people did it, more than would in an era in which such behavior was seen as weird or trite or useless. And there were a lot of young people in the late 60s, so leftist movements were highly visible. The point is that, regardless of the specific socio-economic conditions in which we Xers grew up, and without discounting our history of campus activism, explicitly radical politics is always a draw for a small portion of society. Most people choose to live life in the status quo and don't assume a political element to most of society's dynamics. To us, RR's name automatically conveys a political identity, but as one Gen X colleague of a public librarian friend initially thought, the "radical" was meant to be taken in the 1980s slang sense of it — "You mean, like, really really good reference, right?"

Furthermore, the meaning of political engagement changes depending on the era and the community. Stefanie Sanford explores this question through the experiences of small groups of Gen Xers, including one type she calls "high-tech actors"— educated workers in Austin, TX, who may appear "disengaged" but who "use their creative impulses to stimulate a new civic life that is more consistent with *their values* and the changes that lie in the wake of technological and social advancement. These means of association are still very much in flux, consistently evolving as technologies and related enterprises advance" (170–1; emphasis in original). These people don't necessarily attend Rotary Club meetings or stump for local candidates or participate in civic life in the Robert Putnam (*Bowling Alone*) sense of it — but it doesn't mean that they're not looking for ways to be part of communities and improve their surroundings.

As an example, I attend the monthly meetings of a local civic association in a Brooklyn neighborhood as a representative of my library. The members are engaged in society in a way that would meet with approval from those who would criticize the traditionally apathetic "Gen X" outlook. But this type of civic activism — meetings that begin with the Pledge of Allegiance, end with a raffle to win a large American flag, feature community police officers and local elected officials, and are attended by homeowners who live in an almost entirely white, semi-suburban neighborhood — is relatively outside my experience of activism, municipal or otherwise. So while I enjoy the meetings and support people's involvement in their community, if I were to be judged by these standards of activism, I would certainly fall short.

Then we arrive at the mainstream idea of what Gen X activism is. If we're not being derided for being slackers, we are understood as "not starry-eyed idealists, but rather steely-eyed realists" (Chamberlain 5) who are cynical and outwardly apathetic because, "[h]aving grown up in the age of Watergate and Abscam, you look at it this way: When you vote, maybe you'll waste your time, or worse, later feel doublecrossed. If you pin too much hope on a candidate, you could end up feeling like a total sucker. On the other hand, when you give tangible help to your friends and neighbors, you're doing something that matters, if only on a small scale. So you like volunteering for little 'c' causes — like bringing food to the homeless, recycling trash, cleaning up beaches, or tutoring the disadvantaged. You express your civic virtue one on one, meal by meal, regardless whether anybody is paying attention. The president of MIT has likened your civic attitude to that of the Lone Ranger: Do a good deed, leave a silver bullet, and move on" (Howe and Strauss 129).

This kind of pragmatic activism is apparently so accepted as the current wisdom that the business writers have seized upon it: "Instead of a ropes course, send the management team to a Habitat for Humanity project, or paint a room at a local Day Care. [...] Go clean up a playground or volunteer your group at a soup kitchen. All of these projects will mean more to the Gen Xers and play to their unique needs and characteristics" (Muetzel 52). This attitude is also celebrated in Buck and Rembert and in the latter chapters of Gordinier.

However, is this type of activism the answer? According to Mattson, "[i]ndividual volunteerism and community service — as substitution for the collective world of political action — are the central linchpins of this new, allegedly postideological politics. Instead of protesting or getting involved in electoral or community-based politics, the critics argue, young people feed the homeless or tutor disadvantaged kids in school or clean up polluted rivers. All of this, of course, is somehow outside the realm of politics or ideology. [...] Generation X allegedly responds to this sort of message [of volunteerism] because we want immediate action and hands-on service — not the slow and conflictual world of political change." He further argues that the hope that a service mentality will evolve into a commitment to social change is deluded "in today's culture of narcissism."

Where does this situate a project like Radical Reference? For Beekman, "[t]he pragmatic, 'street level' activism of Radical Reference's presence at the RNC was attractive in seeming to combine the ethos of the Lower East Side anarcho-punk scene with the larger social agenda of the idea of librarianship as promoting liberation through information." Besides the tension between a service provider model and a mission of true social change, the self-consciousness of "activism" raises questions of efficacy. The terms "activist" and "activism" are used throughout this essay but should be taken with a grain of salt — people don't neatly divide between "activists" and ordinary folks. Everyone has the capacity to work towards radical change, whether or not they would consider being part of a vaguely subcultural project with the word "radical" in its name. Unfortunately, too many people reject this potential (this idea is discussed further below). Laura Crossett, 34, says, "I don't have a problem with [ALA's political stands]: I approve of it, in fact. And I don't think that my peers are totally apolitical — many of them care a lot about what I think of as library issues ripe for political activism, such as open access, intellectual property law, free and open source software, free law, etc. I wish I could figure out a way to draw more connections between those things and some of the other things I care about and think are important — poverty, inequality, war, etc."

Backgrounds and Motivations

As our own professional press asserts: "You are more than your job title. Further, librarianship is a career where anything we learn and anything we do comes in handy at some point" (Gordon 144). The Generation X RR members who responded to my questions have a range of work experience behind them — a selective list includes bookstore worker, paralegal, photographer, rhetoric and nonfiction teacher in Iowa, teacher of "missionary kids" in Albania, stage manager, theatre electrician, journalist, columnist, fact-checker, worker in a transitional living program for homeless youth, student radio operations manager, and one genuine punk rocker (John Beekman — bassist and singer for Fly Ashtray, 1983–98). (For more thoughts and discussion on this issue, see Freedman's post on "Jobs I Wouldn't Put on My Résumé that Make Me a Better Librarian.") Similarly, these librarians draw on their activist backgrounds to inform their work in the library.

- Marger, currently between jobs in Amherst, MA: "I was an activist before I was a librarian. [...] I'm very involved with the prison book project here, and I note that many Rad Reffers across the country are involved with those kinds of projects and that they are very radical projects."

- Jenna Freedman, 43, Research and Zine Librarian, Barnard College, New York City: "[My activism is] currently mostly the [Barnard College] zine collection [–] preserving young women's, feminist, activist, anarchist, angry, creative voices and making them accessible. Prior to this my activism was mostly focused through the arts — theater and poetry. In the early '90s I was involved in an abortion rights civil disobedience, and developed/directed a play on unplanned pregnancy and abortion. I was engaged in the anti-apartheid movement and other campaigns in college, and in high school got arrested at the Reagan White House."

- Jonathan H. Harwell, 38, Collection Development & Assessment Librarian at Georgia Southern University, Statesboro, GA: "I've learned a commitment to peace from the Quakers, and I led a faculty learning community on peace studies for its first two years here at Georgia Southern University. Our group has collaborated with the Georgia Peace & Justice Coalition in holding several events, including the State of Hope Tour.[...] Along with processing voter registrations at the courthouse, my wife and I volunteered a lot of time and effort to President Obama's 2008 campaign, working with the local Democratic Party where she served as secretary. [...] In a red county in a red state, where vandalism against Obama signs was widespread and where Tea Party rallies have been common on the courthouse lawn, this was kind of a radical set of activities. [...] As a librarian, I've been volunteering with the ALA-APA since 2003, advocating for the salaries and status of all library employees."

- Nicole Pagowsky, 28, Reference/instruction/collection development librarian for an urban community college, Dallas, TX: "Prior to library school, I ran a distro for a few years, promoting and selling alternative press items (and music), many of which included zines; and while earning my Bachelor's degree, I organized a sexual health fest with music and workshops, free to the public. During library school, through founding a chapter of Progressive Librarians Guild, our group helped a local infoshop organize their book and zine collection and also helped them get a circulation system in place. We also began a relationship with Read Between the Bars, a local books-to-prisoners group in Tucson, which I believe the current PLG chapter members continue to work with."

- Jonathan Cope, 31, Reference Librarian/Instructor, College of Staten Island, City University of New York: "I was an undergraduate during the rise of the 'global justice movement' and I spent a lot of time protesting the WTO, IMF and World Bank as a college student. [...] During that time a group of friends and I were involved in Food Not Bombs in Dayton, Ohio. For several years I volunteered at lefty bookstores in the cities I lived in (Portland, Oregon and NYC)[,] which I suppose eased my transfer into librarianship."

- Kate Adler, 31, currently between jobs and volunteering at the Museum of Modern Art Library, New York City: "Soup kitchen work with Catholic Worker, Food Not Bombs, Books Through Bars, zine and book collectives, political campaigns."

- Crossett, Branch Manager, Meeteetse (WY) Branch Library, and Virtual Branch Manager, Park County Library System: "I got started as an activist when I was 14 and attended the inaugural meeting of what became Operation U.S. Out, a coalition of university and community groups in Iowa City, Iowa opposed to U.S. military action in the Persian Gulf. Since then, I've also been active at various levels in assorted pro-choice, anti-war, anti-sweatshop, anti-poverty, labor, and justice in Palestine groups (and probably some other things I'm forgetting). In libraries, I've tried to advocate for the rights of the poor (lowering and eliminating fines, providing amnesty, etc.) and the homeless, as well as contributing to Rad Ref."

- Aliqae Geraci: "I'm heavily involved with a group called Urban Librarians Unite that includes a lot of Gen X librarians. ULU aims to serve as a network and organizing hub for NYC librarians in all sectors of librarianship, and has been recently prominent in the fight for public library funding. As a radical, I'm pretty skeptical about the long-term usefulness of politically-oriented campaigns, and have no desire to validate the current (flawed) library funding model in NYC. But I do believe in fighting hard to protect the immediate, everyday informational and educational needs of the public, and maintain the continued employment of NYC library workers. I'm also active in my union, which is a huge priority for me even though I'm a labor radical that questions the traditional union model. Ultimately, my priority is to work within my place of employment to build solidarity between my coworkers and to try and facilitate the same on a regional level."

Some of us are looking for communities of practice via RR, along with ways to simply connect with like-minded library workers.

- Beekman, Local History Librarian, Jersey City (NJ) Free Public Library: "During a period when much of the culture and media seemed complicit in the reactionary and militaristic mindset promoted by neoconservatives in power who built on the fear engendered by the 9-11-2001 attacks, librarians were among the very few professional groups sounding a cautionary note against the surrendering of civil liberties. This was very much what cemented my conviction that this was a profession I wished to be a part of."

- Pagowsky: "I found Radical Reference during library school when I was looking for more than just professional development opportunities from my program's student groups; learning how to gear a resume to library employers is no doubt essential, but I really wanted to go beyond that and make a difference during my time as a student (and beyond). I think I might have first ever heard of it from a *Punk Planet* article interviewing activist librarians before I started library school, but was referred to it specifically by Jessamyn West. [...] I really wanted a richer experience from library school, so I got involved to combine my interest with the profession with my desire to contribute to my community (local as well as the virtual activist community)."

- Geraci: "I felt immediate attraction to Rad Ref—I thought, those are my people, and that is what kind of librarian I want to be. I was heavily involved in various anarchist projects, and wanted a way to meet and organize with other anarchist/radical/ultraleft librarians in this new work world that I was entering."

- Crossett: "I was just starting library school at the time [2004], and I was really excited, because I was a long-time activist, and I was thrilled to learn that there were activist librarians out there doing things."

- Jeremy Brett, 35, Special Collections Project Archivist in the Special Collections and University Archives Department, University of Iowa, Iowa City: "Rad Ref's stated mission struck me immediately as important: a good way to provide people with the information they need while at the same time stressing the importance of social progressivism."

Some Gen X librarians were attracted to RR after experiences in other parts of the U.S. library left. As one RR member said, "I was simultaneously involved with [the] P[rogressive] L[ibrarians] G[uild] [while at library school], but quickly got disillusioned with them as I realized their politics are more old school and the group isn't very inviting to new/younger members." Others described similar impressions of disconnection, both with older and younger members of the profession.

- Emily Drabinski, 35, Electronic Resources and Instruction Librarian at Long Island University, Brooklyn, NY: "My personality is pretty split between politically engaged and professionally engaged. I was excited that there might be an organization that could blend both of those aspects of myself. I'd been to S[ocial] R[esponsibilities] R[ound] T[able] and PLG things at ALA events, but felt alienated and disconnected, in part because they seemed so dominated by an entrenched (white, male) old guard. [...] I was mostly looking for like minds, hoping to make friends and meet librarians who, like me, saw this as an automatically politically progressive/radical profession."

- Crossett: "When I first got involved in librarianship, I joined SRRT as a student member, because it seemed like the place to go as an activist librarian. This perception may be off, but it seemed as though most of the people involved were older than me. For a long time, I thought that was a reflection of the demographics of the profession overall, but since then, I've gotten to know a lot of other Gen X librarians via social networking, so it may be more a reflection of the nature of SRRT/ALA, or at least of my limited experience with them. I find myself drawn in a variety of directions. I'm not involved in ALA anymore, but not for the reason that a lot of my peers cite — ALA's involvement in taking political stands on 'non library issues.'"

- Freedman: "I didn't feel like I had a home in the NYC activist community, but I wanted to participate in a meaningful way in the protests against the RNC there in 2004. As it turned out, RR created that community I'd been longing for. Previously I had been very involved in PLG and SRRT. I believe I even pitched the idea for an RR-like service on the NYC-PLG list (that I'd created — I don't say that for ego, just to reinforce the fact that I was striving for a local activist librarian community and that I was deeply involved in PLG and SRRT), and it kind of went nowhere. [...] RR became both my local affinity group and my home in librarianship. My involvement in PLG and SRRT had already been waning. I had conflicts with some of the members, mostly men, mostly boomers, and didn't really like the atmosphere in those groups — which was mostly on discussion lists. [...] I don't mean to sound super critical of PLG and SRRT. I just don't think their tactics and goals were the same as mine."

- Adler: "Millennial types and X-cusp-ers seem to be into a hipster sort of librarian scene [...] that doesn't necessarily seem terribly political to me but rather more interested [in] art, technology, the aesthetics of librarianship [...] but the interest in tech and open source certainly has political potential. Among my peers I have not seen remarkable differences; the stereotypes around technology seem to break down to a large degree when folks consider themselves highly political, I think. I guess I see a small contingent of people interested in radical politics across the board (even among people who are politically very progressive) and those that are and are librarians certainly make a point to advocate for activist ideas and causes within the profession."

To reiterate, strong leftist ideologies and tendencies are always outside of the mainstream — there's nothing new about that. But perhaps would-be Gen X activists have an additional burden to bear, in the form of the 1960s. While the actual events of that era contain just as much complexity and obscure movements and struggles as does any swath of history, there is certainly an overarching narrative to contend with. "Xers bristle when they're told how to vote, how to behave, what to listen to, how to squander their time. They recoil at any hint of a presumption that *this is how things are done* or, even worse, *this is what you're supposed to think.* [...] Turn change into kitsch and you've inspired no one to change anything. You've told them that change has already happened—*it was beautiful, maaaan, you should've been there*—and you've frozen the very concept of transformation in a glob of museum-ready amber" (Gordinier 46–8).

As a Gen X librarian acquaintance of mine whom I was once telling about an upcoming anti-war demonstration said, "Oh, Melissa, you should have been around in the '60s!" This widely-held idea that there's a capital-a Activism that hasn't been relevant or acceptable since 50 years ago is applied to librarianship itself, too, as when Mathews writes in a piece about being a Gen X librarian, "While it is commendable that [ALA] routinely battles censorship, the Patriot Act, and the digital divide, it has always had a baby boomer, ultrapolitical, protest-remnant feel to me; I cannot identify with its Sixties-era spirit."

And the idea of "joining" a group or a movement makes people anxious, particularly us skeptical, individualistic Gen Xers. Scott Heiferman, cofounder of Meetup, explains: "It's such a scary word, to say 'join.' [...] By joining you're going to make your identity concrete, and that's scary. It's comfortable to stay on the sidelines, and more importantly, it's really fun to be able to make fun of everyone. I'm guilty of that. That is the comedic culture that we're in. If all of a sudden you've *joined* something, well, that means that you are one of the people to be made fun of" (quoted. in Gordinier 164–5; emphasis in original). So a project like RR struggles against a culture that looks with suspicion and condescension on engagement in a cause, a profession that continually debates where the line between political issues and "library issues" falls, and the idea that the time for activism has passed — along with some very real apathy.

Perceptions and Generational Differences

Gen X members of RR responded to questions about unbalanced perceptions, in and outside of the workplace, among themselves and their Boomer and Millennial peers. None cited any major differences based on broad generational generalizations, though some mentioned sometimes being taken less seriously simply because they look young, or being assumed to be more technologically adept. People did, however, make comparisons in terms of activist engagement in librarianship.

- Pagowsky: "I've noticed people of any age participating in activist librarian groups seem to be much more involved overall in the field than others who are not as interested or those who are even opposed. Clearly, many non-activist librarians contribute a great deal to librarianship, but it is truly impressive how many projects, presentations, and how much publishing Radical Reference librarians and other radical librarians do."

- Cope: "I have found no generational pattern in terms of the number of librarians with activist commitments. However, in those with activist commitments I do see a reflection of each cohorts generation in terms of their style of politics. By this I mean that activist librarian Boomers tend to reflect a political sensibility forged in the late '60s and early '70s, Gen Xers in the '80s and '90s, and Millennials in the '90s and '00s."

- Harwell: "It seems that some Boomers are more tied to institutions and organizations than the rest of us. I've long held the idea that Gen Xers tend to be loyal to ideals rather than institutions. If an institution abandons a set of valued ideals, I feel no qualms about abandoning that institution."

The uncertainty of job markets and our economic future also affects activist tendencies in our age group.

- Lacey Prpić Hedtke, 29, Grants Department at Planned Parenthood Minnesota, North Dakota, South Dakota; and photographer, Minneapolis, MN: "I feel there's not much crossover between activists and professionals. In the earlier generations we have people like Sandy Berman, who was an activist on and off the job. Now, people are afraid of losing their jobs and don't want a conflict of interest, so [they] give up activism for a job. I was one of the younger ones in library school, and was shocked to find how conservative my classmates were, comparatively. A lot of them were headed towards academia, or had never left it, and I definitely sensed from the few outspoken liberal staff there that students could be stirring it up a little more."

- Drabinski: "I always assume that everyone in this profession is an activist, that everybody will have progressive if not radical politics. But time and again I see people more concerned with their own careers than with anyone else. But that's probably always been true across time for most people."

- Cope: "At professional events there are times when some Millennials can seem like 'go-getters' but I suspect that has as much to do with the job market and the fact that library schools are churning out all of these graduates to fill fewer and fewer library jobs. I think that the precarious nature of the labor market in the last ten years is a really underexamined aspect of generational issues in librarianship that have been such a hot topic in recent years."

Technology is an obvious point around which generalizations about generational differences are drawn. RR members had thoughts on ways in which radical Gen Xers are using our skills and comfort level as part of our activism.

- Kate Kosturski, 32, currently between jobs in East Windsor, NJ: "I think the Gen X librarians are more 'plugged in,' and aware of the power of technology and social networking to advance causes and achieve goals. With this in mind, and our fluency in technology, we feel more comfortable expressing ourselves professionally and as activists/radicals."

- Harwell: "Regarding activism, it seems that some Boomers tend to value protest marches and other public displays of mass solidarity more than the rest of us. I'm seeing more opportunities for one-on-one change with the use of social software, as one example. So many of us are now using Facebook as a blogging platform, and our posts, action links, etc., can be read by everyone in our networks, whether we're politically in tune with one another or not. This is localizing politics in a new way, defined by relational lines rather than geographical. I've had challenging and meaningful conversations via Facebook with old friends and family members who saw something I posted and wanted to debate. I've also made a point of politely correcting misinformation through the use of Snopes and other sources, and people are often appreciative, even if we're politically opposed. Contrary to the attacks we often see in mass online discussions, a conversation in one's own social network seems to be more real, since it often relates the topic of discussion to a set of shared personal experiences. Of course this can be a challenge, because as we know from cognitive dissonance theory, people are actually more committed to deeply held beliefs after they are proven false."

- Beekman: "Gen X has come to be a mediating presence between the much more technologically defined generations before and after us. Not digital natives, we nonetheless grew up with the development of web communications during our early adult life and so have been able to integrate digital culture more fully and naturally in our lives that some of our Boomer predecessors, though not as immersively as some of our Millennial juniors. Being neither fish nor fowl in this way works in our favor in the workplace and wider profession as we can relate to the two generations on either side, who are mysteries to each other."

Visions for the Future

Like all volunteer projects, RR depends on the commitment levels of its individual members to keep it going, and people's ability to participate depends on many factors. Some of the respondents to the questions for this article are getting second master's degrees, while others have job responsibilities that preclude greater involvement in volunteer work. But the flexibility of a collective project like RR is also part of what keeps it going — as Geraci said, "I hope to continue plugging in and out based on my capabilities at the moment, and I really appreciate that Rad Ref folks don't guilt trip folks or have membership requirements!"

Some members have lessened or modified their involvement with RR due to specific aspects of the project.

- Crossett: "I was more active in some ways when I lived in the Chicago area and still went to national conferences. Now that I live in rural Wyoming, I am out of immediate, face-to-face connection with radical communities, and so in some ways I feel more distant, but I'm still committed to the cause, and I answer reference questions when I can (which is not that often, due more to a lack of skill and access on my part than to a lack of time)."
- Lana Thelen, 29, College Librarian, Oregon College of Oriental Medicine, Portland, OR: "Initially I was excited that such a group [RR] existed but was worried that it was reference focused. [...] I prefer face-to-face involvement versus virtual. I tend to spend less time monitoring the mailing lists or engaging with the group via email. I prefer doing direct action, be it talks, helping out with groups, etc. This is part of the reason why I helped get the Portland collective going and why I'm excited to move to NYC where there is already an active collective!"
- Drabinski: "I don't really answer questions on the site — that's actually the part of Rad Ref that interests me the least. I feel like I answer reference questions at my job all the time, and that doing that here is 'radical' enough, and always political. [...] To me, the reference part is just a standard aspect of my job, not something I'm interested in outside of the office."

The continued existence of RR in its current form is uncertain, but the spirit that led to its establishment and growth is still strong. The imagination essential to involvement in any social movement is clear when RR members express their visions of the future.

- Beekman: "I do like the way that Rad Ref seems to continue to be for others what it was for me early on — an approachable group of socially engaged librarians. [...] I would like to see us continue to be a presence as activists at the U.S. Social Forum, Anarchist Book Fairs and other gatherings of independent-minded people — where if nothing else we promote the idea of librarians as information activists who have a role in trying to steer culture towards greater liberation and respect for the rights of all."
- Pagowsky: "I think Radical Reference is a very important presence in librarianship to question the status quo, talk about alternative ideas, and open up new frameworks of thinking. Continuing to be a strong presence in librarianship and in the activist community, and merging the two, can improve the functioning of libraries for the public. An example of this could be the LCSH watching and blogging that has been done, alternative materials in libraries, and even just discussing relevant legislation (such as the Patriot Act)."
- Adler: "I think that advocating for the open and transparent flow of information, maintaining a robust and accurate historical record in this here digital age, edu-

cating people to be critical and savvy consumers and producers of information and culture are all among the most important issues of the day and I see Rad Ref having a role in all of that kind of work. I'm also interested in how libraries can help to support autodidactic unmediated learning and think that rad ref could do interesting work in this area (working with unschoolers and home schoolers, people doing independent unaffiliated research, taking time off from school, transitioning careers, getting GEDs, people who are in prison or in any way off the grid). [...] I think Rad Ref should also be an advocate for libraries and archives to acquire, maintain, make accessible radical, progressive, sub-cultural material."

- Hedtke: "I'd love for Rad Ref to become more well-known as a reference resource, among librarians and everyday researchers. It would be awesome if Rad Ref could have a physical space-whether that be a library, zine library, booth somewhere, traveling resource center or infoshop, I'm not sure."

- Harwell: "Along with continuing to support other activists and participating in events such as the Social Forums, I'm wondering whether we might want to consider creating an open-access repository sponsored by Rad Ref, through an open-source system. [...] We could provide a permanent open archive for infoshops, Rad Ref collectives, etc."

- Crossett: "I see Rad Ref as continuing both to be a central radical question answering site and as a sort of umbrella where related interested groups — like the local collectives — can find a home for projects they want to do. I've actually been inspired by the work of others in Rad Ref to try to start a books-to-prisoners project out here in the rural West. I think the mere existence of the group — amorphous and small and decentralized as it is — serves a function as a way of letting people know that there is radicalism in librarianship, and that the profession does have an activist streak, and activist roots."

- Geraci: "I view and utilize Rad Ref as a loose affinity group. It serves as a networking and informational hub that represents radical politics to the library world, and library/information issues to radical communities. It serves as a bridge between the two worlds, and is an important educational resource and activist presence in both. I see Gen X librarians as more likely to use the profession as a vehicle to promote their own ethical/social/political beliefs. I see that as a good thing. The profession has a habit of hiding behind the claim of 'objectivity' as an excuse to maintain the status quo in workplace practices, professional organizations, and relationships with vendors and politicians."

If the era in which we Gen Xers came of age led some of us to absorb attitudes of "cynicism" and "disengagement" and then channel them into critical thinking and questioning accepted civic and professional norms, so much the better. The word "radical" itself, of course, comes from the Latin for "root," as in getting to the root of things. And as for generation gaps and conflict between styles of work and activism, why not follow Freedman's "pragmatic" advice — "Can't we all just try to get along and get shit done?"

WORKS CITED

Adler, Kate. "Re: Gen X and Rad Ref." Email to the author. 16 July 2010.

Beekman, John. "Re: Gen X and Rad Ref." Email to the author. 23 July 2010.

Bennett, Stephen Earl, and Eric W. Rademacher. "The 'Age of Indifference' Revisited: Patterns of Political Interest, Media Exposure, and Knowledge Among Generation X." *After the Boom: The Politics of Generation X.* Ed. Stephen C. Craig and Stephen Earl Bennett. Lanham, MD: Rowman & Littlefield, 1997. 21–42.

Brett, Jeremy. "Re: Gen X and Rad Ref." Email to the author. 12 July 2010.

Buck, William R., and Tracey C. Rembert. "Just Doing It!" *E: The Environmental Magazine* 8.5 (1997): 28–35.

Burns, Andy. "Reclaiming Campus Power." *Clamor* 12 (Jan./Feb. 2002): 27.

Chamberlain, Lisa. *Slackonomics: Generation X in the Age of Creative Destruction.* Cambridge, MA: Da Capo Press, 2008.

Cope, Jonathan. "Re: Gen X and Rad Ref." Email to the author. 14 July 2010.

Crossett, Laura. "Re: Gen X and Rad Ref." Email to the author. 30 July 2010.

Drabinski, Emily. "Re: Gen X and Rad Ref." Email to the author. 14 July 2010.

Featherstone, Liza, and United Students Against Sweatshops. *Students Against Sweatshops.* London: Verso, 2002.

Freedman, Jenna. "Jobs I Wouldn't Put on My Résumé That Make Me a Better Librarian." *Lower East Side Librarian.* N. p., 13 Jun. 2008. Web. 29 Jun. 2010.

_____. "Re: Gen X and Rad Ref." Email to the author. 13 July 2010.

Friedman, Lia, and Melissa Morrone. "The Sidewalk Is Our Reference Desk: When Librarians Take to the Streets." *IFLA Journal* 35.1 (2009): 8–16.

Geraci, Aliqae. "Re: Gen X and Rad Ref." Email to the author. 19 July 2010.

Gordinier, Jeff. *X Saves the World: How Generation X Got the Shaft but Can Still Keep Everything from Sucking.* New York: Viking, 2008.

Gordon, Rachel Singer. *The NextGen Librarian's Survival Guide.* Medford, NJ: Information Today, 2006.

Harwell, Jonathan H. "Re: Gen X and Rad Ref." Email to the author. 20 July 2010.

Hedtke, Lacey Pripić. "Re: Gen X and Rad Ref." Email to the author. 19 July 2010.

Howe, Neil, and William Strauss. *13th Gen: Abort, Retry, Ignore, Fail?* New York: Vintage Books, 1993.

Kosturski, Kate. "Re: Gen X and Rad Ref." Email to the author. 17 July 2010.

Loeb, Paul Rogat. *Generation at the Crossroads: Apathy and Action on the American Campus.* New Brunswick, NJ: Rutgers University Press, 1994.

Marger, Dena. "Re: Gen X and Rad Ref." Email to the author. 8 July 2010.

Mathews, Brian S. "The Inevitable Gen X Coup." *Library Journal* 131.5 (15 Mar. 2006): 52.

Mattson, Kevin. "Talking About My Generation (and the Left)." *Dissent* 46.4 (Fall 1999): 58–63.

Muetzel, Michael R. *They're Not Aloof ... Just Generation X: Unlock the Mysteries of Today's Human Capital Management.* Shreveport: Steel Bay Pub., 2003.

Owen, Diana. "Mixed Signals: Generation X's Attitudes Toward the Political System." *After the Boom: The Politics of Generation X.* Ed. Stephen C. Craig and Stephen Earl Bennett. Lanham, MD: Rowman & Littlefield, 1997. 85–106.

Pagowsky, Nicole. "Re: Gen X and Rad Ref." Email to the author. 14 July 2010.

Putnam, Robert. *Bowling Alone: The Collapse and Revival of American Community.* New York: Simon & Schuster, 2000.

Sanford, Stefanie. *Civic Life in the Information Age.* New York: Palgrave Macmillan, 2007.

Thelen, Lana. "Re: Gen X and Rad Ref." Email to the author. 15 July 2010.

Vellela, Tony. *New Voices: Student Political Activism in the '80s and '90s.* Boston: South End Press, 1988.

Yeo, Shinjoung, et al. "Radical Reference: Taking Information to the Street." *Information Outlook* 9.6 (Jun. 2005): 55.

The Thin Red Line[1]: How Gen X Librarians Make It Thicker (Views from Bosnia and Herzegovina)

Mario Hibert and Saša Madacki

"If anyone in the United States, or anywhere else in this world, asks about the national differences between Serbs and Muslims, please tell them this kind of story. We are really mixed in a very special way. Like the books in my library. They have no ethical background, no cultural background, no racial or geographic backgrounds. They are simply one by one. Alphabetical, perhaps. The only differences are the size, the cover, and the things they say." — Kemal Bakaršić[2]

Fahrenheit 451 or Fahrenheit 45.1?

The ideas that led Agents of Fahrenheit 451[3] to destroy gateways of our identity and culture were of introducing long-term disorders to the society of dialogue. The intent to generate confusion, irritability, aggression, memory loss, and general withdrawal, such as that which deepens divides that proliferate in the silence which remains after books are burned, was launched from the hills above Sarajevo to prolong Bosnia's recovery and slow down democratization in the aftermath of war. Cultural Alzheimer's deforms societal identity. It is the Thin Red Line, the line between silence and sound, the line that differentiates Agents of 451 from Agents of 45.1, that needs to be mended so that the past can be preserved for the sake of a healthy future.

How can librarians — such an often neglected group of professionals — who fight Alzheimer's hopeless, degenerative, and terminal outcomes, prove that their work may be curative, regenerative, and life-prolonging? What should be the actions of Generation X professionals to improve life in post-war society? How shall they gather, preserve and disseminate information to actually prove that restoration of multidimensional collective memory is reachable? What is their share in a call of duty to reestablish the Thin Red Line?

The importance of memory for the construction of identity is enormous. Communities that do not remember are sentenced to disintegration. The phrase *cultural memory* marks a remembrance that mediates values and norms by which a community creates its identity.[4] Every community creates a past in which it will be able to dwell on its strategies of remembrance and oblivion; these are crucial for the collectives' identitary consciousness. It is through the process of building a collective memory, memories that society shares, expands, and customarily transforms, that a certain doctrine, idea or symbol is created from it. Reminiscences of burning the National and University Library of Bosnia and Herzegovina[5] and the Oriental Institute,[6] barbaric attacks on the City of Sarajevo (along with scenes of manuscripts, periodicals, and books on fire, and the inability to stop the destruction caused by the fire grenades being launched by Serbian artillery from surrounding hills) represent emblematic scenery of particular cultural genocide — culturicide impressed into memories of citizens of Bosnia and Herzegovina. The killing of memory has been confirmed as part of the strategy of aggression.[7] Therefore, embarking upon the future of libraries in the context of post-war librarianship demands not only for the preservation of the past; knowing that memories are never neutral, neither for patrons nor librarians, we need to refocus from mere service delivery to issues of responsibility and accountability that go along with situating truth in postwar society. In a society of denial and reconciliation, librarians' abilities to help patrons think more clearly is not an easy goal. Witnessing the destruction of institutions of our common cultural heritage while also experiencing two different socio-political systems (socialism and quasicapitalism, a.k.a., *transition*) emerge, Gen X librarians, the successors of tradition and the bearers of change, have to deal with a delicate post-war milieu while doing their jobs. Unfortunately, leaving few written traces of self-examination or critical reflections on postwar librarianship in Bosnia and Herzegovina, Gen X librarian survivors fail to elevate their awareness and instead end up in apathy. For that reason, breaking the silence seems to be indispensable. How will Gen X librarians cope with it? How will librarians in the aftermath of conflict cope with the objectiveness imperative of their profession and their human perception? What should be kept for the future and presented to their users?[8] When war ends how do we repair this inflicted damage? Can it be repaired at all? How does a library participate in a post-conflict process? What is its role? Can an imperative of *being objective* overcome the human perception and uphold tolerance and diversity as one of the *prime directives of librarians*?

Settling of Accounts?

These scenes of destruction, war crimes, and genocide have been differently deposited and valued by the three constitutive ethnic groups that have for centuries occupied and shared the common geographical space of Bosnia and Herzegovina, the "open house with four doors" (doors that symbolically represent influences of Islam, Christianity — both Catholic and Orthodox — and Sephardic Jewish traditions), a country where everything seemed possible as long as there was a consciousness that a nearest neighbor is different but somehow — ours.[9] Oppositely, when the benefits of sharing a common culture are abandoned, dangerous rationales for cross-cultural hatred are envisioned. The twentieth century phenomenon that saw bloody mass destruction, murder of civilians, genocide,[10] ethnocide,[11] culturicide,[12] and libricide[13] as a "method of problem-solving that is deliberate and systematic"[14] destroyed the multicultural utopia by which Bosnia and Herzegovina were envisioned as a place where a dialogical model of culture existed. When nationality and ethnic background become more important than humanity, and prejudices master judgment, interpersonal compassion fails. Therefore, each of us, individually, has to be faced with a settling of accounts with the heritage, with memory, settling of accounts with the past, which sometimes seems to us impassable.[15] Finding balance between memory and oblivion, called "remembrance" by Jan Assmann, is impossible without a foundation for the reconstruction of a cultural identity. Poetics of remembrance, reconstruction of lost contents, is an extremely important aspect of librarianship. Presumably, not all those who witnessed specific cultural genocide or "killing of the memory" will be faced with doubts about fact verifying propositions of truth as a sign of "cultural catastrophe in the heart of Europe."[16] On the other hand, problems of narration, storytelling, and "historical truth" are not easy to grasp when it comes to cultural memory formation because cultural memory formation is never democratic; in fact, every form of cultural memory is created by the process of assortment of the past covered by intellectual elites.[17] As shown by Aleida Assmann, cultural memory is formed in the process of canonization — functional cultural memory is oriented by a canon that is always connected to those in power: the purpose of functional memory is to legitimize rulers — origins and a continual past give legitimacy to functional cultural memory.[18] Characteristics of functional cultural memory are distinctions that serve for the selection of those elements of cultural reminiscences by which it is possible to create a specific cultural identity and its differentiation from "Others." That is how the framework for the creation of collective identity is formed. Cultural memory serves to direct orientation of an individual in the social present while questioning past as tradition (collectives' "stored" past, one that is no more reachable in direct communication). Oppositely, literature and art in general act subversively towards cultural memory and its techniques of forming "functional cultural memory" by becoming a possible source of diverse seeing, diverse history. While functional memory rests upon censorship as a precondition for the creation of collective identity through exclusion of unwanted traces of the past that could disturb artificial identity formation[19] libraries, archives, and museums are those kinds of institutions that strive upon neutrality or at least they should strive to (re)collect artifacts that testify about the past, even its unwanted traces. As impartial purveyors of information, liberal humanist enterprises grounded upon an ethos of social, democratic, and humanistic responsibility, libraries are fundaments of open, just, and free societies. Libraries should collect holocaust denial literature, not to promote it as a legitimate idea, but to document human wrongs. Libraries are not only temples of great human minds, but also warning points of civilization. Although perceived as defenders of such values, librarians often shy away from political confrontation in the name of cherished "impartiality." Keeping in mind the fact that totalitarian techniques of cultural memory formation may preclude cultural dynamics in general, the professional responsibilities of librarians emerge from a recognition of the temptation to intervene in the reservoir of the collectives' imaginarium. Whereas intellectual freedom and social responsibility are extremely important to the information profession, tendencies to support professional ethos should not be perceived as immune of political action: "the need for at least the perception of impartiality is in conflict with the desire for political action on the part of large number of librarians."[20] As libraries serve civic purposes, according to John Budd, the norms inherent in discourse ethics are necessary as an ideal framework of a profession that should foster politically pluralistic speech.[21] In building a genuine democratic public space, libraries should be the sites of critical assessment of not only multiple political perspectives, approaches, and claims but of social memories as well since formation of cultural identities rest on selection, censorship, and exclusion. Social memory is firstly a social product. If librarianship is to hold any values, the trust of our communities must be high among them; therefore, trust can be a necessary burden for us.[22] As proposed by Aleida and Jan Assmann, the concept of "communicative memory" (interactive practice located within the tension between individuals' and groups' recall of the recent past) arises from a differentiation of Maurice Halbwachs's concept of "collective" memory into a "cultural" and a "communicative" one.[23] Bound to the existence of living bearers of memory and to communication of their experience, contents of communicative memory can only be fixed through "cultural formation"—organized and ceremonialized communication about the past.[24] The dynamics of memory work bilaterally: symbolic codification is active and secures protonarrative potential, while traumatic codification is passive and prevents the ability of narration.[25] As a phenomenon that lies among individuals and groups, communicative memory is crucial for interrelation and dialogue. Assuredly, diverse communicative and cultural memories in Bosnia and Herzegovina, loosely united through the Dayton Peace Agreement[26] (which demarcates the Federation of Bosnia and Herzegovina and the Republic of Srpska), are either a platform for "continual cultural interaction"[27] or a continual division along ethno-national lines. Unfortunately, the imaginarium of national identity seems to be an insuperable obstacle for the former solution. The Dayton reality was shaped by the geopolitics of war, and the post–Dayton reality by the geopolitics of the peace process, the negation of democratic principles, and as the latent destruction of Bosnian state.[28] Neither war nor peace, but "un-war"— that is the true social status of artificial geopolitical structure, a State-in-waiting.[29] It's no wonder that Bosnia and Herzegovina operates two national libraries: National and University Library of Bosnia and Herzegovina (in the Federation of Bosnia and Herzegovina) and National and University Library of Republic of Srpska. Although widespread perception is of Bosnia and Herzegovina as a form of unity in difference, separation is visible in almost every aspect of today's existence: divided educational system,[30] language differences,[31] separated institutions, etc. Unfortunately, it is the dominant intellectual climate in which Bosnian citizens as well as librarians dwell. Shaping common goals and concerns towards reconciliation begin and end with settling memories, even though memories are unwanted guests in the battle over intellectual freedom disputes.

Un-War Trauma

Communicative memories are those shared with contemporaries. What is alive today, tomorrow will be mediated only if recorded. Gen X librarians in Bosnia are a generation of librarians that professionally experienced libricide or remember it as personal trauma. They are those who should encompass diversities by creating a forum for discussing those problems together. The objectiveness imperative, the recreation of library networks, and the navigation of the information wilderness in post-conflict society are great challenges for librarians in order to prove that libraries are "bastions of democracy." For such an awakening, or for reaching such an objective, Gen X librarians are asked to "go boldly where no one has gone before"—to help reconstruct a common cultural identity. Professional responsibility asks for nothing less. How do librarians respond to ideological discourses? Moreover, how will Gen X librarians in Bosnia and Herzegovina provide a forum for informed discussion, regain public trust, and act as enemy of ideology in a divided society?

Lacking a common institutional framework to lean on, communicative memory of Bosnians and Herzegovinians is more and more confined by separately organized cultural memory of each constitutive ethnic group: Bosniaks (Muslims), Croats, and Serbs. Such a rigid demarcation deepens the gap, making the meeting line thicker and resulting in further alienation instead of moving towards a point of convergence, uniting positions that could work together, or coming closer to a consensus over shared identity. Oblivion is therefore conditioned, yet going along with changes in context, and there is no doubt that the actual framework of Bosnian reality shows huge discrepancies among the past and the present.[32] If fostering intellectual freedom in serving civic purpose is a crucial task of librarians, then librarians' education in Bosnia and Herzegovina is certainly ripe for the application of discourse ethics, especially if we are to speak about Gen X librarians' responsibilities and the awareness needed to oppose the silencing of dialogue. In a transitional, postwar, yet consumerist environment, postmodern hybridization or hybrid resistance[33] of librarians as a tool for emancipatory struggle over grand narratives lacks not only an envisage of hegemonic master narrative of capitalism and liberal ideology but pacifies dangerous cultural conflicts preventing formation of a new type of trans-national political subject.[34] When the majority of information comes in the form of entertainment, it is far too optimistic to expect unregulated information markets to deliver civic education. Equating democracy with markets and citizens with consumers imposes values that, instead of civic education and rational deliberation upon the common good, favor discourse of corporate managerial class.[35] Globalization, as "symbolic imperialism"[36] introduces postmodern, consumer culture as a means for reaching universal political goals. The concept of transition suggests a new establishment of social contract of neoliberal globalization. And while we are drowned in recidivism, our libraries hardly even perceive dangers of culturalization as a means for depolitization; quite to the contrary, instead of "repolitization of culture as precondition for deconstruction of its ideological content"[37] we are engaged in processes of repolitization of identities as prerequisite for homogenizing separate cultural identities which are simultaneously lines of exclusion and subjugation.

Years in transition of librarianship in Bosnia and Herzegovina fails in epistemic reconciliation of the public forum as a place where people encounter ideas. Such status quo deepens cultural divisions and slowly but persistently erases (common) memories. Postwar Gen X librarians, in the midst of eroding public institutions, barely listen to its Other — users — while on the other side, users fail to ask themselves "what does it mean to be informed?" Consequently, such dialogical tension has no more common retrospective "framework of meaning" that could provide certain kinds of communication over place and identity. Discourse ethics within the context of postwar librarianship warns that answering the question "What does it mean to inform someone?" is where librarians win or lose. When considering the destruction of a referent framework or a position from which one could judge a crime as a crime we are immediately losing our ethical stance. It seems to be the core of evil for the present situation in Bosnia and Herzegovina.[38] Stigmatization through identification with an "ethnic" perspective automatically renders ones' judgments irrelevant or biased. Asim Mujkic explains how it perfectly fits the "orientalist" perceptions of this region (Balkans) as one of ancient hatreds. Thus, ethnically recontextualized crimes shall never be recognized, sanctioned and punished as crimes. If the library is a mirror of the community, then how do we put together pieces of a broken multicultural mirror without reflecting the community's guilt?[39] Gen X librarians have no easy task to accomplish — they should prove that manuscripts don't burn, after all. It is indispensable to articulate the past in not only in order to save memory, but the future as well.

Gen X (Librarianship) in Fraction

Halbawchs's theory of social frameworks contends that the individual and society are able to remember only what is possible to be reconstructed within the strongholds of present context. In other words, what is forgotten is that which does not have points of reference within the current framework. Recreating order in memory or fixing its reconstruction in cultural identity seems to be a constant failure, or a neglected responsibility of those allegedly willing to oppose the Hatred of Memory.[40] What is happening to our war memories? Are they irreversibly destroyed after the aggression on Bosnia and Herzegovina? Aren't postwar librarians liable to warn about the dangers of supporting publicide[41] that in post-conflict times emerge the consequences of "killing of memory"?

Modern societies transform and recreate its past by forcing out problematic spots of history. Here it is necessary to stress the essential operation of archiving cultural memory, that of storing, and keeping in mind the danger that not all created information is deposited in the archives, or is that information is being erased from archives. Those artifacts that are not deposited or erased occupy boundary areas of "imaginary archive." Sole remembrance cannot turn back the past, as it was or where it is. Yet, traces of war have a privileged place for the cultural memory in Bosnia and Herzegovina and at the same time they are the backbone of identitary differentiation: on the one side there are images of burned cultural institutions, destroyed relics of what one community wishes to remember, while on the other side those same evidences represent problematic spots in the memory of constitutive part of Bosnian society, since there are memories which would have rather been erased[42] without justification.[43] There is an interrelation of exe-cutioner and victim as a feedback memory mechanism: both enclose themselves in boundaries of their identities by interpreting its trauma by logic of its own community. In this framework, as humanist librarian Mark Rosenzweig emphasizes, memory should not be seen as the arbiter of "truth," but the facilitator of dialogue and interpretation, and of returning to dialogue and interpretation at a higher level.[44]

In its political incompleteness, Bosnian reality witnesses complexities and ambi-guity in dealing with the past. Therefore, by focusing on the dynamics of ongoing con-versation with the past, the work of librarians reminds us of the responsibility to engage in collective action for human betterment, reaching the goal of enabling human eman-cipation. Accordingly, cold dispassion masked in neutrality is neither a professional nor an ethical standard. In a world of increasing and destructive irrationality the cause of reason requires passion and engagement.[45]

Librarianship's irreplaceable contribution to postmodern questioning of the rep-resentation of history and cultural identities, plurality of interpretations, should be seen as vocational essence. Until today, we had four cornerstones of our profession: To collect. To store. To organize. To disseminate. The fifth element often remains neglected: To interpret.[46] Those are the noble tasks of librarians and archivists. One may say: "*So what?*" These are quite normal tasks that can be performed. It is quite simple to order a book, put it on the shelf and circulate it to the reader if s/he requests it! Maybe it is a routine task for skilled librarians in natural and applied sciences. There, we have one accepted and established truth; one scientific standpoint. Chemistry librarians purchase all publications of the latest research (if budget permits), and will certainly avoid alchemy books. Librarians will buy those only for a history of chemistry collection, but not rec-ommend it as laboratory protocol to transmute lead into gold. In pure science we have ultimate truths that we are dealing with. There is no danger of misinterpretation by young adults or minors. But how are librarians supposed to behave in fields where several truths are existing in parallel? A possible answer is found within the thoughts of Joseph Glanvill[47]: "*Truth is never alone; to know one will require the knowledge of many. They hang together in a chain of mutual dependence; you cannot draw one link without many others.*"

This means that social sciences and humanities librarians, public and reference librarians, and especially human rights librarians should be unbiased and open-minded, "providing materials and information presenting all points of view on current and historical issues"[48] and furthermore these materials "should not be excluded because of the origin, background, or views of those contributing to their creation."[49] Walter Benjamin's recognition of the non-neutrality of history[50] may warn us that social responsibilities of postmodern librarians are not only placed in preserving the idea of common heritage but seeing history as "what 'really' happened" (external to representation or mediation) versus history as a "narrative of what happened," a "mediated representation" with cultural/ideological interests. This asks from us, Gen X librarians, to be open towards "other forms of rationality," even more, to accept the schizoid nature of our profession knowing that the library "justifies its existence by both providing support for our heritage and providing material that exposes challenges and debunks the same supposed heritage."[51] In terms of postmodern understanding there is no doubt that having no consensus about history, identity, erosion or breakdown of national, linguistic, ethnic, and cultural identities undermines the collectives' capacity to retain its own past[52]; therefore, the thin red line of finitude and morality may be thicker only if we are to understand that multidimensional collective memory is reachable only through dialectical cultural history.[53] Similarly, it can be argued that the library profession uncritically accepts and adopts dominant discourses of information[54] it is also important to understand that our profession rarely critically analyzes dominant discourses on history. Thus, the perception of a library not as a container of knowledge but as a context for knowledge creation is crucial. The idea of neutrality, understood as not being involved in politics, should not be an excuse for not doing our job properly.

Unfortunately, the fear of losing our identity by not mirroring it through libraries, archives and museums is stronger than our fear of losing our patrons. It is traumatic to serve civil society goals in a country where traces of war bear the intent to kill others — memories of who we are, or, at least, were. If we cannot accept Otherness in terms of ethnic, religious or any other differences, how can we accept our natural antipode — User? Bosnia and Herzegovina is still a place of stringent separation, denial, and withdrawal. Common Bosnian and Herzegovinian identity does not exist. Having no consensus over how to recreate our common cultural heritage, strategies of making the thin red line thicker are also missing. Still, librarians' duties to direct Bosnia and Herzegovina towards a neutral goal of knowledge society[55] is challenging beside today's intellectual atmosphere that far from cherishes common heritage of (mis)understanding. Slavoj Žižek contends that different forms of traumatic experiences, irrespective to their specific nature (social, natural, biological, symbolic) all go to the same result — it is a new subject that grasps its own death.[56]

Identity of new subjects does not revolt from *tabula rasa*. Many traces that remind us of past existences survived, but totally reconstructed, extracted from past horizons and inserted into new context. Actually, in Bosnia and Herzegovina we have two kinds of posttraumatic subjects: those who lost continuity to its symbolic identity based on common cultural memory (Alzheimer's victims that lose bonds, basis, and framework in relation to their pasts) and a new, transitional, postwar subject unsuccessful in becoming a citizen but consumer at the moment of late, multinational capitalism.[57] Since the open market itself does not produce a civil society in which "institutionalism will replace emotionalism" but rather chaotic pragmatism[58] such that post-traumatic, autistic "citizens" are real evidence that the new subject or subject of death instinct[59] cannot identify itself with stories that tell about itself or with the narrative symbolic texture of its life.[60] Linage of memory and death could be found in the Legend of Simonides.[61] This basic myth on memory reminds how Simonides's mnemotechnic signifies that only in relation to death does it show its real importance, as the true identity of war librarians grasp their importance just in confrontation with the fact of "killing memory," even more with efforts in reconstruction of "irreplaceable originals."[62]

The barbaric verdict to coexistence in Bosnia and Herzegovina today shows its deformed face, the scar of division along ethnic lines of separation, the wound of aggression on Bosnia and Herzegovina which significantly damaged the beauty of its multicultural, multiethnic, multireligious face. Although traumatic memories destabilize identity, as much they promise the creation of a new identity from Gen X librarians who are expected to raise their voices in order to preserve their "common grounds," to recreate "common substance" of its wounded being. Therefore, cherishing a thin red line as a terminal spot of reentering the world of communication, not only rebuilding destroyed library collections but recollecting our moral responsibilities as information workers is crucial. Cornerstones of professionalism and the future of librarianship in Bosnia and Herzegovina depend on resisting current situations in which libraries contribute to speechlessness.

Instead of Indifference

In his curative book *Selfexamination* John M. Budd warns that if the public face of philosophy is vanishing from the collective image of library — librarians as intellectual freedom Gate-keepers or agents of social responsibility are lost. So far we do not have any research in which narratives of Gen X librarians in Bosnia and Herzegovina are presented nor examined at the crossroad of cultural memory and professional responsibilities. The librarian's identity is usually perceived as apolitical, neutral, and objective. Myths of librarians' neutrality connected to our profession generally confuse the task of providing unbiased access to information with indifference. Such approaches or generalizations almost detach librarians from social and political realities in which they work.

Information specialists, as it is common today to call librarians, are disengaged when it comes to taking firm standpoints in articulation of their opinions on changes in social and political systems. Such a choice to be "neutral" indicates "pretending that librarians do not have their own viewpoints, or that they do not count, which results in effective supporting of the actual power relations."[63] Obviously, librarians in our country have poorly reconceptualized the idea of objectivity under which hides positivistic heritage of thinking. After the war in Bosnia and Herzegovina there were very few articles in which librarianship was scrutinized in the postmodern context, or even articulated in reference to extremely complex communicative breakdown, as direct consequence of destruction of gateways of our identity and culture: libraries, archives, and museums as symbols of multiculturality. Abstraction of multiculturalism[64] is on democratic institutions to foster. Therefore, a civic discourse among librarians on the topic of libraries as public forums and democratic arenas should be part of their professional consciousness and ethics. Otherwise, libraries will not be seen as landmarks of democratic humanism or generators of critical pluralism. Rather, they would be seen as distant islands where memories are stored. Ideologues view libraries as problematic, their potential as instruments of indoctrination compromised by their humanistic and reactionary nature and ability to pose alternate realities or ideas.[65] For that reason, a critical self-reflection of social practices should be an essential part of modern institutions.

Unfortunately, our community cannot tolerate seeing itself in the mirror; the identification is too painful because the identification is innate.[66] Would a reflection that libraries, archives, and museums provide to its citizens be sufficient to prevent the past from becoming faceless? Librarians have a civic responsibility to collect, preserve, disseminate and interpret information essential to resist dehumanization of society. Public institutions therefore should be the strongest existing weapon to combat the kidnapping of belief systems and their misuse of negative narration that is still the dominant discourse of our reality. Otherwise, Bosnia and Herzegovina's society is going to capitulate no matter how hard librarians would try to make the thin red line thicker. In avoidance of collective responsibility to build healthy civic community, apolitical[67] librarians may be agents of latent function of ethnic cleansing. *Library cleansing* in this view will not be simple dusting, but removal of information, User, and public forum — it will be Library vanishing. Our professional and moral duty is to reconnect, reexamine, and reuse what was destroyed in order to prove wrong that "disintegration is the solution" or else to let win the ethno-nationalists mantra composed in Dayton: a fact of unbearable construct of political and cultural norm to the Bosnian reality. We cannot ask for less of librarians whose noble ethics asks not to remain silent or to pretend to be "neutral." Are we able to be guardians of such a red lines?

NOTES

1. Experience of loss, violence and humanity to which we refer naming our article after famous James Jones's novel and Terrence Malick's film *The Thin Red Line* stands for belief that even in the most devastating times of destruction there might also be the possibility of ethical transformation ... or to lend it from another source: "Where danger is, there salvation also grows" (F. Holderlin).

2. Kemal Bakaršić, *The Libraries of Sarajevo and the Book That Saved Our Lives* (New York: The New Combat, 1995). http://newcombat.net/article_thelibraries.html (12.10.2009.)

3. Farenheit 451 is the combustion point of paper. Fahrenheit 45.1 is a temperature for the preservation of paper. We use this comparison to differentiate barbarians from librarians. *Fahrenheit 451* is a dystopian novel by Ray Bradbury which was first published in 1953. The novel focuses on the historical role of book burning in suppressing dissenting ideas.

4. Jan Assmann, *Kulturno pamćenje* (Zenica: Vrijeme, 2005).

5. The number of cultural monuments of all religions destroyed or damaged during the war exceeds 1,500. A special feature of killing the cultural heritage was the deliberate destruction of libraries: the Oriental Institute in Sarajevo and the National and University Library of Bosnia and Herzegovina also located in Sarajevo. The City Hall — Vijecnica, built in 1892–1894 was the biggest and the most representative building from the Austro-Hungarian period in Sarajevo. In 1949 it was given to the National and University Library. Collections of the National and University Library of Bosnia and Herzegovina (approximately 1,200,000 books and 10,000 sets of periodicals) went up in flames on August 27, 1992. See more: Kemal Bakaršić, *Fragmenti kulturne historije Bosne i Hercegovine* (Sarajevo: Magistrat, 2005).

6. May 18, 1992, saw the deliberate destruction of the Oriental Institute manuscript collection (with 5,236 codices in Arabic, Turkish, and Persian, the oldest dating from 1023 AH (1614); 7,156 original handwritten documents dating from the 16th through the 19th centuries; and over 200,000 documents from the former Vilayet Archives (Regional archive) covering the last thirty years of Ottoman rule in Bosnia and Herzegovina. See more: Kemal Bakaršić, *Fragmenti kulturne historije Bosne i Hercegovine* (Sarajevo: Magistrat, 2005).

7. Kemal Bakaršić, *Fragmenti kulturne historije Bosne i Hercegovine* (Sarajevo: Magistrat, 2005), 264.

8. Feđa Kulenović, "Objective Librarian in Academic Sourounding," Nabil Alawi (Ed.), Conference Proceedings, *International Conference on Libraries from a Human Rights Perspective*, 31 March — 2 April 2008 (Ramallah: Center for Human Rights Studies, 2008).

9. *Ibid.*

10. The United Nations' 1948 convention narrowly defines genocide as actions involving bodily harm and physical circumstances committed with the intention to destroy, in whole or in part, a national, ethnic, racial, or religious group.

11. The term ethnocide was unofficially introduced to describe the organized commission of specific acts with intent to extinguish culture, utterly or in substantial part.

12. It was not only that traditional Bosnian multicultural society and "convivencia" that were rejected, but specifically that cultural genocide, or the "killing of memory," that turned the land into a cultural wasteland. Andras Riedlmayer, "Libraries Are Not for Burning: International Librarianship and the Recovery of the Destroyed Heritage of Bosnia and Herzegovina," *Art Libraries Journal* Vol. 21, No. 2 (1996), 19–23, www.fh-potsdam.de/~IFLA/INSPEL/61-riea.htm (15.12.2009).

13. Libricide refers to the "murder," or "killing," of a book, delineating patterns that occur within larger context of ethnocide. Politics and ideology form a theoretical framework in which to understand libricide. See: Rebbeca Knuth, *The Regime-Sponsored Destruction of Books and Libraries in the Twentieth Century* (Westport, CT: Praeger, 2003).

14. *Ibid.*

15. Predrag Matvejević, "National Culture and Globalisation," in *Best of Sarajevo Notebooks*, ed. Velimir Visković (Sarajevo: Mediacentar, 2008).

16. Council of Europe Parliamentary Assembly (Doc. 6756, 2 February 1993).

17. Jan Assmann, *Kulturno pamćenje* (Zenica: Vrijeme, 2005).

18. Aleida Assmann, "Tri stabilizatora pamćenja: Afekt — Simbol — Trauma," *Razlika/Différance* —

Časopis za kritiku i umjetnost teorije. God. 4, Br. 10/11 (Tuzla: Društvo za književna i kulturna istraživanja, 2005).

19. Vahidin Preljević, "Kulturno pamćenje, identitet i književnost." *Razlika/Differance—Časopis za kritiku i umjetnost teorije,* God. 4. Br. 10/11 (Tuzla: Društvo za književna i kulturna istraživanja, 2005).

20. Earl Lee, *Libraries in the Age of Mediocrity* (Jefferson, NC: McFarland, 1998), 69.

21. John Budd. *Self-Examination. The Present and Future of Librarianship* (Westport, CT: Libraries Unlimited, 2008).

22. Harald Welzer, *Communicative Memory. Cultural Memory Studies. An International and Interdisciplinary Handbook.* Eds. Astrid Erll, Ansgar Nünning, Sara B. Young (Berlin, New York: Walter de Gruyter, 2008).

23. *Ibid.*

24. Retrospective reconstruction of memories leads to its transformation to symbols as a process of identity stabilization, or its traumatic memories destabilize identity and prevent its coherence. Aleida Assmann, "Tri stabilizatora pamćenja: Afekt — Simbol — Trauma," *Razlika/Differance—Časopis za kritiku i umjetnost teorije,* God. 4, Br. 10/11 (Tuzla: Društvo za književna i kulturna istraživanja, 2005).

25. The General Framework Agreement for Peace in Bosnia and Herzegovina, also known as the Dayton Peace Agreement, is the peace agreement reached at Wright-Patterson Air Force Base near Dayton, Ohio, in November 1995, and formally signed in Paris on December 14, 1995.

26. Potential for permanent construction of identity in Bosnia and Herzegovina that Nirman Moranjak-Bamburac describes by terms of *interspace, non-place, nowhereness* in sense continual interaction without fixed base.

27. Democracy in Bosnia and Herzegovina is on an objective collision path with the peace process: from banal political trifles to issues of strategic importance for the Bosnian and Herzegovinian community. For a fuller treatment, see: Nerzuk Ćurak "(Post)Dayton Bosnia and Herzegovina. 21.11.1995 — 21.11.2006. / Eleven years of a divided society and an underdeveloped state," *Unity and Plurality in Europe, Part Two,* ed. Rusmir Mahmutćehajić, Forum Bosnae (39/2007) (Sarajevo: International Forum Bosnia, 2007).

28. *Ibid.*

29. The best example of highly politicized education in Bosnia and Herzegovina are schools in which pupils and teachers continually experience ethnic and religious segregation, intolerance and division. The Organization for Security and Cooperation in Europe (OSCE) Mission in Bosnia and Herzegovina devised the "Two Schools Under One Roof" plan in 2000 as a temporary measure to encourage people to return to their homes, and prevent ethnic violence. It was planned to be a transitional solution with administrative unification being a further step towards eventual integration, but classroom segregation and ethnic-based curricula are still present.

30. Identity of Bosnian language is continually at stake. The Bosnia and Herzegovina constitution does not name an official language for the country, so language is a still a tool for separating the three constituent people, Bosniaks, Serbs, and Croats.

31. Yet, this presents a moment to introduce the realization of the digital divide and the transition to a neoliberal, post-war, post-communist, ICT driven, contextualized framework which is not to be forgotten when speaking about identity deliberations. Having no intention to further expand threats for the current communicative situation in Bosnia and Herzegovina, there is no question that Gen X librarians should not neglect actual global political transactions of market fundamentalism and its consequences for function of places where knowledge is shared.

32. Hybridity can be grasped, first of all, as a factor of social harmonization. There, where cultural, racial and ethnic differences threaten to catapult society into a chaotic state of endless conflicts, hybridization promises to reinforce social cohesion. Invoking Ien Ang's skepticism over "liberal hybridism" Boris Buden explains that the harmonizing effect of hybridization lacks to prove itself as a progressive alternative since it oversimplifies the real situation, disguises power relations and thus leads to the dead-end street of depoliticization. Boris Buden, "The Art of Being Guilty Is the Politics of Resistance Depoliticizing Transgression and Emancipatory Hybridization," European Institute for Progressive Cultural Policies web journal (July 2002), http://www.republicart.net (11.11.2009).

33. Buden Boris, *Translation: The Mother Tongue of a Future Society?* (Maison de l'Europe de Paris, 12 October 2006).

34. Ed D' Angelo argues that "librarian work routines have been reengineered by eliminating their role as gatekeepers of the culture," hence the role of the critic is been lost. Ed D'Angelo, *Barbarians at the Gates of Public Libraries: How Postmodern Consumer Capitalism Threatens Democracy, Civil Education and the Public Good* (Duluth: Library Juice Press, 2006), 117.

35. Žarko Paić, *Politika identiteta: Kulutra kao nova ideologija* (Zagreb: Antibarbarus, 2005).

36. *Ibid.*

37. See: Asim Mujkić, "Articulating Evil / Lessons for Bosnia," *Unity and Plurality in Europe, Part Two*, ed. Rusmir Mahmutćehajić, Forum Bosnae (39/2007) (Sarajevo: International Forum Bosnia, 2007).

38. It was Richard Rorty who once said that pain is non-linguistic, and as long as it remains unarticulated, meaning the victim has not yet managed to deal with it, such pain remains his or her pressing and immediate frustration. Asim Mujkić, "Articulating evil / Lessons for Bosnia," *Unity and Plurality in Europe, Part Two*, ed. Rusmir Mahmutćehajić, Forum Bosnae (39/2007) (Sarajevo: International Forum Bosnia, 2007).

39. "Is it possible for anyone who identifies with Western civilization to remain calm in the face of the hatred that burned down the Vijecnica, that murdered the paintings, that burns private libraries and intimate memories? If permitted, that hatred would burn down the human world." Ivan Lovrenović, "Hatred of Memory," *The New York Times* (28 May 1994).

40. We see publicide as killing of public forum by librarians who do not engage themselves as Agoraic providers, but rather as passive keepers of the books without interest in civic librarianship.

41. Paul Ricoeur emphasizes that the thinnest line is that which divides amnesty from amnesia: every political body, in order to protect its identity, will choose amnesty over amnesia as a mechanism that protects its indivisibility. Amnesty is just a consequence of collective amnesia: if we are clever enough not to dig deeper into our own past, "everything will be all right,"; "we are all OK, and we are all together." Andrea Zlatar, "Protiv zaborava," *Gordogan, klturni magazin* God. 3 (2005), Br. 6 (Zagreb: Udruga za kulturu Gordogan, 2005).

42. Crimes against humanity as well as genocide are frequently denied mostly from political and public representatives of Republica Srpska. Moreover, some of their higest ranked officials as Milorad Dodik, the Prime Minister of Republika Srpska, frequently misuses his position by placing doubts on crimes against humanity commited by Serbs. Political leaders of Republic of Srpska still abstain from support for the Srebrenica Genocide Resolution adopted by European Parliament proclaiming the 11th of July a Day of Commemoration of the Srebrenica genocide — the bigest war crime in Europe since the end of the World War II throughout the European Union (EU).

43. Mark Rosenzweig, "The basis of a humanist librarianship in the ideal of human autonomy," *Progressive Librarian* No. 23 (Spring 2004). http://libr.org/pl/23_Rosenzweig.html (05.01.2010.)

44. *Ibid.*

45. Routine librarians' task of disseminating "objective" information may be easy only in natural and applied sciences, those scientific areas where all accepted truths result from firm scientific proofs. Librarians' task of disseminating "objective" information in social sciences is quite more complex since it asks for responsibility of offering to patrons thorough insight upon one subject for comprehension to be complete. See more: Saša Madacki.

46. "Pride and Prejudice: Role of Librarians and Archivists in Remembrance of War-Time Atrocities," *Balkan Yearbook of Human Rights* (2005): 70–76.

47. John Glanvill, *The Vanity of Dogmatizing*, 1661.

48. Library Bill of Rights, American Library Association. Adopted June 18, 1948. Amended February 2, 1961, and January 23, 1980, inclusion of "age" reaffirmed January 23, 1996, by the ALA Council.

49. *Ibid.*

50. The famous thought of Walter Benjamin warns that there is no document of culture that is not at the same time also a document of barbarism. It sees documents of culture as documents of barbarism. It appears in the context of a reflection on culture as the plunder of history's victors. Faced with the barbaric documents of culture and their transmission to the present, Benjamin rminds that it is the task of historical materialism to "rub history against the grain."

51. Earl Lee, *Libraries in the Age of Mediocrity* (Jefferson, NC: McFarland, 1998), 40.

52. Fredric Jameson, "Postmodernism and Consumer Society," *The Anti-Aesthetic: Essays on Postmodern Culture*, ed. Hal Foster (New York: The New Press, 1998), 143–4.

53. Historiography, for Walter Benjamin, is based not on absolute truth value of historicism — "just the facts"— but rather on the construction and deconstruction of rhetorical structures which produce historical significance and understanding. Benjamin identitifed fascism in politics, positivism in historiography, and orthodoxy in the Communist movement as the archenemies of the time. Rajeev S. Patke, "Benjamin's Thesis 'On the Concept of History,'" Andrew Benjamin, ed., *Walter Benjamin and History* (London and New York: Continuum, 2005). http://iph.fsu.edu/interculture/pdfs/patke%20rajeev.pdf (14.02.2010.)

54. Field of library and information science itself did not often negotiate with the model of knowledge developed by positivistic social sciences and its implications for epistemic foundation of librarianship in order and rationality. Ajit K. Pyati, "Critical Theory and Information Studies: A Marcusean Infusion," *Policy Futures in Education* Vol. 4, No. 1 (2006); Gary P. Radford, "Positivism, Foucault, and the Fantasia of the Library: Conceptions of Knowledge and the Modern Library Experience," *Library Quarterly*, 1992, 62[4], 408–424.

55. Kemal Bakaršić, "Bosna i Hercegovina na putu u društvo znanja: posljedice ratnog sukoba i rekonstrukcija nacionalnih zbirki," *Slobodan pristup informacijama*, 4, i 5, okrugli stol, Zbornik radova, Ed. Alemka Belan-Simić and Aleksandra Horvat (Zagreb: Hrvatsko knjižničarsko društvo, 2007).

56. Erasure, destruction, or killing of symbolic identity equals killing of "inner" nature. Subjective structure of such individuals is autistic; they are living deads, biologically alive, but emotionally indifferent, devoid of any engagement in reality. A new face of society makes post-traumatic disengaged subjects. Such a new form of subjectivity has a face of apathy, indifference, autism, and the death of instincts. See: Slavoj Žižek, "Neuronska trauma," *Zeničke sveske — Časopis za društvenu fenomenologiju i kulturnu dijalogiku*, June 2009 (Zenica: J.U. Bosanko narodno pozorište — Zenica, 2009).

57. It would be interesting to more deeply analyze how Gen X Bosnian librarians see (or oppose) tendencies of global market fundamentalism, prevent deepening of a digital divide, or perceive technomanagerialsm in its professional surrounding. Moreover, it seems to be a focal point of today's critical librarianship: standing against ideological pressure of economic globalization and its discontents.

58. Slovenian philosopher Rastko Močnik put forward the thesis that the practices of the institutions under the post–Yugoslavian condition have in fact a neoliberal character. Moreover, he argues that classical liberalism is in fact the ideology of this neoliberal practice. Instead of settling down in a stable regime of sovereignty, as promised by the teleology of transition, the institutions on the ground face the chaos of an uncontrolled globalization they are no longer able to escape. The conditions of their reproduction undergo a similar sort of precarization as the conditions of individual reproduction, of the reproduction of the globalized labor force, of migration, brutal competition on the market, etc. See: Boris Buden, "The post–Yugoslavian Condition of Institutional Critique: An Introduction on Critique as Countercultural Translation," *Transversal* (November 2007), eipcp — European Institute for Progressive Cultural Policies, http://transform.eipcp.net/transversal/0208/buden/en (22.02.2010).

59. In the seminar of 1954–5, Jacques Lacan argues that the *death drive* is simply the fundamental tendency of the symbolic order to produce repetition: "The death instinct is only the mask of the symbolic order." Jacques Lacan, *The Seminar. Book II. The Ego in Freud's Theory and in the Technique of Psychoanalysis, 1954–55*, trans. Sylvana Tomaselli (New York: Norton; Cambridge: Cambridge Unviersity Press, 1988), 326.

60. Slavoj Žižek. "Neuronska trauma," *Zeničke sveske — Časopis za društvenu fenomenologiju i kulturnu dijalogiku*. June 2009 (Zenica: J.U. Bosanko narodno pozorište — Zenica, 2009).

61. Cicero, *De Oratore II* (55. B.C.).

62. Kemal Bakaršić, *Fragmenti kulturne historije Bosne i Hercegovine* (Sarajevo: Magistrat, 2005).

63. Rory Litwin, "Neutrality, Objectivity, and Political Center," *Library Juice Concentrate*, ed. Rory Litwin (Duluth: Library Juice Press, 2006).

64. Multiculturalism understood as platform for competing view of history and tradition.

65. Rebecca Knuth, *The Regime-Sponsored Destruction of Books and Libraries in the Twentieth Century* (Westport, CT: Praeger, 2003).

66. Keith Doubt, *Understanding Evil: Lessons from Bosnia* (New York: Fordham University Press, 2006), 102.

67. Librarians, who consider their practice to be "neutral" and apolitical, might find Foucault's work both challenging and disconcerting and, perhaps, redemptive.

Works Cited

Assmann, Aleida. "Tri stabilizatora pamćenja: Afekt-Simbol-Trauma." *Razlika/Differance — Časopis za kritiku i umjetnost teorije*. God. 4. Br. 10/11. Tuzla: Društvo za književna i kulturna istraživanja, 2005.

Assmann, Jan. *Kulturno pamćenje*. Zenica: Vrijeme, 2005.

Bakaršić, Kemal. "Bosna i Hercegovina na putu u društvo znanja: posljedice ratnog sukoba i rekonstrukcija nacionalnih zbirki." *Slobodan pristup informacijama*. 4. i 5. okrugli stol. Zbornik radova. Ed. Alemka Belan-Simić and Aleksandra Horvat. Zagreb: Hrvatsko knjižničarsko društvo, 2007.

_____. *Fragmenti kulturne historije Bosne i Hercegovine*. Sarajevo: Magistrat, 2005.

_____. *The Libraries of Sarajevo and the Book That Saved Our Lives*. The New Combat. July 1994. New York: The New Combat, 1995. Web.

Budd, John. *Self-Examination: The Present and Future of Librarianship*. Westport, CT: Libraries Unlimited, 2008.

Buden, Boris. "The Art of Being Guilty Is the Politics of Resistance Depoliticizing Transgression and Emancipatory Hybridization." *European Institute for Progressive Cultural Policies* web journal (July 2002). Web. 11 Nov. 2009.

_____. "Translation: The Mother Tongue of a Future Society?" *Maison de l'Europe de Paris* 12 October 2006.

_____. "The Post-Yugoslavian Condition of Institutional Critique: An Introduction on Critique as Countercultural Translation." *Transversal* (November 2007). eipcp — European Institute for Progressive Cultural Policies. Web. 22 Feb. 2010.

Cicero. *De Oratore II* (55. B.C.).

Council of Europe Parliamentary Assembly. Doc. 6756. 2. February 1993.

Ćurak, Nerzuk. "(Post)Dayton Bosnia and Herzegovina. 21.11.1995 — 21.11.2006. / Eleven years of a divided society and an underdeveloped state." *Unity and Plurality in Europe. Part Two*. Ed. Rusmir Mahmutćehajić. Forum Bosnae (39/2007). Sarajevo: International Forum Bosnia, 2007.

D'Angelo, Ed. *Barbarians at the Gates of Public Libraries: How Postmodern Consumer Capitalism Threatens Democracy, Civil Education and the Public Good*. Duluth: Library Juice Press, 2006.

Doubt, Keith. *Understanding Evil: Lessons from Bosnia*. New York: Fordham University Press, 2006.

Jameson, Fredric. "Postmodernism and Consumer Society." *The Anti-Aesthetic: Essays on Postmodern Culture*. Ed. Hal Foster. New York: The New Press, 1998.

Knuth, Rebbeca. *The Regime-Sponsored Destruction of Books and Libraries in the Twentieth Century*. Westport, CT: Praeger, 2003.

Kulenović, Feđa. "Objective Librarian in Academic Surrounding." Nabil Alawi, ed. *Conference Proceedings. International Conference on Libraries from a Human Rights Perspective. (31 March–2 April 2008)*. Ramallah: Center for Human Rights Studies, 2008.

Lacan, Jacques. *The Seminar. Book II. The Ego in Freud's Theory and in the Technique of Psychoanalysis, 1954–55*. Trans. Sylvana Tomaselli. New York: Norton; Cambridge: Cambridge University Press, 1988.

Lee, Earl. *Libraries in the Age of Mediocrity*. Jefferson, NC: McFarland, 1998.

Library Bill of Rights, American Library Association. Adopted 18 June 1948. Amended 2 February 1961, and 23 January 1980, inclusion of "age" reaffirmed 23 January 1996, by the ALA Council.

Litwin, Rory. "Neutrality, Objectivity, and Political Center." *Library Juice Concentrate*. Ed. Rory Litwin. Duluth: Library Juice Press, 2006.

Lovrenović, Ivan. "Hatred of Memory." *The New York Times* (28 May 1994).

Madacki, Saša. "Pride and Prejudice: Role of Librarians and Archivists in Remembrance of War-Time Atrocities." *Balkan Yearbook of Human Rights* (2005): 70–76.

Matvejević, Predrag. "National Culture and Globalisation." *Best of Sarajevo Notebooks*. Ed. Velimir Visković. Sarajevo: Mediacentar, 2008.

Mujkić, Asim. "Articulating Evil/Lessons for Bosnia." *Unity and Plurality in Europe. Part Two*. Ed. Rusmir Mahmutćehajić. Forum Bosnae (39/2007). Sarajevo: International Forum Bosnia, 2007.

Paić, Žarko. *Politika identiteta: Kultra kao nova ideologija*. Zagreb: Antibarbarus, 2005.

Patke, Rajeev S. "Benjamin's Thesis 'On the Concept of History.'" Ed. Andrew Benjamin. *Walter Benjamin and History*. London and New York: Continuum, 2005.

Preljević , Vahidin. "Kulturno pamćenje, identitet i književnost." *Razlika/Differance—Časopis za kritiku i umjetnost teorije*, God. 4. Br. 10/11 (Tuzla: Društvo za književna i kulturna istraživanja, 2005).

Pyati, Ajit K. "Critical Theory and Information Studies: A Marcusean Infusion." *Policy Futures in Education* Vol. 4, No. 1 (2006).

Radford, Gary P. "Positivism, Foucault, and the Fantasia of the Library: Conceptions of Knowledge and the Modern Library Experience." *Library Quarterly*, 1992, 62[4], 408–424.

Riedlmayer, Andras. "Libraries Are Not for Burning: International Librarianship and the Recovery of the Destroyed Heritage of Bosnia and Herzegovina." *Art Libraries Journal* Vol. 21; No. 2 (1996).

Rosenzweig, Mark. "The Basis of a Humanist Librarianship in the Ideal of Human Autonomy." *Progressive Librarian* No. 23 (Spring 2004).

Welzer, Harald. "Communicative Memory." *Cultural Memory Studies. An International and Interdisciplinary Handbook*. Eds. Astrid Erll, Ansgar Nünning, Sara B. Young, Berlin, New York: Walter de Gruyter, 2008.

Žižek, Slavoj. "Neuronska trauma." *Zeničke sveske—Časopis za društvenu fenomenologiju i kulturnu dijalogiku*. June 2009. Zenica: J.U. Bosanko narodno pozorište-Zenica, 2009.

Zlatar, Andrea. "Protiv zaborava." *Gordogan. klturni magazin*. God. 3 (2005). Br. 6. Zagreb: Udruga za kulturu Gordogan, 2005.

About the Contributors

William Black is the administrative services librarian and a professor at the Walker Library at Middle Tennessee State University. He is the author of a number of articles on the human services component in libraries, one of the coauthors of the ACRL White Paper *Recruitment and Retention: A Professional Concern* (2002), and editor of *Libraries and Student Assistants: Critical Links* (Haworth Press, 1995).

Jessica Clemons is the science librarian at the College of Wooster. Born in the "gray" period between Gen X and Gen Y, she sees herself as an emerging leader. Her book reviews appear in *Choice*.

Jennifer Cromer is a library student at San Jose State University with a focus in young adult services. As a Generation X library paraprofessional, Jennifer has over eight years of public library experience in reference services and circulation.

Erik Sean Estep is the North Carolina reference librarian at East Carolina University. He holds degrees from Purdue University, Ball State University, and Indiana University. He has written reviews and articles in such diverse publications as *Library Hi Tech News*, *Digest of Middle East Studies*, *Portal*, *Progressive Librarian*, and *Three Percent: A Resource for International Literature at the University of Rochester*.

Rebecca Feind has been a reference librarian since 1993. She holds a B.A. in English from DePaul University and her M.L.S. is from the University of Missouri–Columbia. She is currently the librarian for art and design at San Jose State University.

Jenna Freedman is research and zine librarian at Barnard College and a member of Radical Reference, a collective of library workers that meets the research needs of activists and independent journalists. She has published articles and presented around the U.S. and in France on zine librarianship and other topics.

Christy Groves is the coordinator of user services and an assistant professor at the James E. Walker Library, Middle Tennessee State University. For nearly fifteen years she has been directly involved in recruitment, supervision, and development of library faculty and staff and has headed a number of service excellence initiatives.

Mario Hibert is a teaching assistant in the Department of Comparative Literature and Librarianship at the University of Sarajevo, Faculty of Philosophy. He is a Ph.D. candidate at the University of Zagreb, Faculty of Philosophy, Department of Information Science, studying issues in information ethics. He is the selector at the human rights film festival Pravo ljudski.

Lynda Kellam is the data services and government information librarian at the University of North Carolina at Greensboro. In addition to her regular duties she is the co-coordinator of

UNCG's Reference and Instructional Services Internship and Practicum Programs and a Gen X supervisor of primarily millennial graduate students.

Breanne Kirsch is the Evening Public Services Librarian at the University of South Carolina Upstate Library. She graduated from Bucknell University with a degree in animal behavior and anthropology and earned a master of library and information science degree from Dominican University. She is involved with educating students about plagiarism; another interest is using new technologies in library services.

Jonathan Kirsch served as Reference Librarian at North Park University, Brandel Library until 2010. He is currently a Reference and Instruction Librarian at Tri-County Technical College. He can be reached at: jon.kirsch@gmail.com.

Peter Lehu is a public librarian and social activist living in Philadelphia. In 2009, he coauthored a book on literary research, drawing on his studies in library science and American literature. He works in the Social Science and History Department and coordinates the Parkway Central Library's basic computer skills instruction program.

Dawn Lowe-Wincentsen is the Portland Operations Librarian at the Oregon Institute of Technology. She received an M.L.I.S. in 2003 from Louisiana State University and has worked in a variety of positions both before and after. She is the coauthor with Suzanne Byke of *A Leadership Primer for New Librarians* (2008).

Saša Madacki is the director of the Human Rights Centre at the University of Sarajevo, Bosnia and Herzegovina. Prior to that he was the head of the Information Research and Library Department at the Human Rights Centre. His research interests are human rights librarianship and information provision and delivery.

Leslie Porter Mathews is a reference and instructional services librarian at Fielding Graduate University in Santa Barbara, California. In addition to an M.S. in library and information science, she holds an M.A. in graphic and information design. She has written articles for such publications as *Library Hi Tech*, *Urban Library Journal*, and *Reference & User Services Quarterly*, and has won awards for innovative use of podcasts and video in education.

Lindsay McVey is a Gen X librarian working in a community college library as a specialist in reference serves and technology management. She received her M.L.I.S. from Kent State University in August 2006.

Rafia Mirza is a reference and instruction librarian at the University of Texas at Arlington whose work has appeared in *E-JASL: Electronic Journal of Academic and Special Librarianship*.

Melissa Morrone is a public librarian in Brooklyn, New York. She has been active with Books Through Bars–NYC, the NYC Anarchist Book Fair, and Radical Reference.

Sergio Rizzo is an assistant professor of English at Morehouse College, where he teaches classes in freshman writing, world literature and critical theory, and pursues interests in information literacy. He has published articles on poetry, film, and popular culture in journals such as *Journal of Modern Literature*, *Film Quarterly*, and *Convergence*.

Maura Seale is a research and instruction librarian and bibliographer at Georgetown University. Her work has appeared in *E-JASL:Electronic Journal of Academic and Special Librarianship* and is forthcoming in *Critical Pedagogy and Library Instruction: An Edited Collection*.

Kathy Shields is a graduate of the Library and Information Studies program at the University of North Carolina at Greensboro. Her primary areas of interest are information literacy and assessment of instruction techniques. As a graduate student (and a Millennial), she served as a reference intern at UNCG's Jackson Library.

Karen Sobel is a reference and instruction librarian at the University of Colorado, Denver. She holds an M.S.L.S. and an M.A. in English, both from the University of North Carolina at Chapel Hill. She belongs to ALA, ACRL, LIRT, and the Colorado Association of Libraries.

Emily Symonds is the metadata librarian at the University of Louisville where she works on digital collections. Previously she was involved with Wabash Valley Visions & Voices: A Digital Memory Project at Indiana State University. Emily received her M.L.S. from Indiana University. She also has an M.F.A. in creative writing.

Lisa Carlucci Thomas is the digital services librarian at Southern Connecticut State University and has held several positions at Yale working with library colleagues and patrons of all ages. She received her M.L.I.S. degree through the Syracuse University School of Information Studies. She is a 2009 American Library Association Emerging Leader.

Rebecca Tolley-Stokes is an associate professor and the faculty outreach librarian at East Tennessee State University. Her reviews appeared in *Library Journal, Choice*, and *Feminist Collections*. She is the co-editor with Carol Smallwood of *Librarians as Mentors in Librarianship for Adults and Students: Essays* (forthcoming from McFarland) and is the book review editor of *Tennessee Libraries*. She earned an M.L.I.S. from the University of North Carolina at Greensboro.

Martin K. Wallace, a Gen Xer, is a science and engineering librarian at the University of Maine, Orono, and the patents and trademarks depository representative for Maine. He is the editor of *Speaking of Information: The Library Juice Quotations Book* (Library Juice Press, 2009). He earned an M.L.I.S. from the University of North Texas in 2005.

Jessamyn West is a community technology librarian and a moderator of the blog MetaFilter.com. She lives in rural central Vermont where she teaches basic computer skills. She assists tiny libraries with technology planning and implementation, helping them with wi-fi, websites and making sense of their systems.

Wil Weston is the head of collection development and the engineering librarian at San Diego State University, Library and Information Access. He received an M.L.I.S. from Louisiana State University and a Ph.D. in higher education administration from the University of New Orleans.

Rachel Williams is a University of Pittsburgh library science student whose specialization is in academic library services in humanities and statistics. Rachel is a Generation Y student who has three years of library experience in circulation and public outreach.

Index